ANCESTRY OF NOYES P. GREENE

The Quest for the Connection Between Maternal Native American DNA and Genealogy

Shirley Holdridge Greene

HERITAGE BOOKS
2007

HERITAGE BOOKS
AN IMPRINT OF HERITAGE BOOKS, INC.

Books, CDs, and more—Worldwide

For our listing of thousands of titles see our website
at
www.HeritageBooks.com

Published 2007 by
HERITAGE BOOKS, INC.
Publishing Division
65 East Main Street
Westminster, Maryland 21157-5026

This book was originally published as
The Quest for the Connection Between
Maternal Native American DNA and Genealogy

International Standard Book Number: 978-0-7884-4252-X

TABLE OF CONTENTS

LIST OF ILLUSTRATIONS

MAPS

DNA RESULTS

PHOTOGRAPHS

PHOTOGRAPHS OF GRAVESTONES:

DEDICATION

This book is dedicated to my two children Corey and Kimberly and also my grandchildren Kelsey, Kayla and Tyler. Through them our ancestors will live on, long into the future.

I also would like to dedicate this book to Noyes' direct maternal ancestors who have passed on before us. These women are the foundation of Noyes' Native American DNA.

A very special dedication goes to Noyes's best friend, James L. Williams, Grand Chief Sachem of the Historic Eastern Pequots. He passed on to the Spirit World shortly after I finished writing this book. Once in a lifetime you may meet one true friend. For Noyes, James Williams was that man. James Williams may have left us, but his words and actions will always live on. He placed no value on material things. His friendship always came straight from his heart. Once he considered you a friend, you were a friend for life. He, also, thought in terms of what was best for his tribe. He based his decisions on the principles he was brought up with. He always thought in terms of how this decision would affect future generations of the tribe as well as the tribal members today. Some may not have agreed with him, but he never faltered on his principles. He made it possible for Noyes and I to meet many other Native Americans and learn some of their traditions. He was a very selfless and giving man. He was one of the reasons I wrote this book. He always told us to think of the grandchildren you will never meet. Think about the grandparents who have gone before you. You need to honor past, present and future generations. He was proud of his heritage, and he did not hesitate to talk about it. That is his legacy for future generations. Our legacy is to be able to also honor our Native American grandparents and to be able to pass down to our grandchildren and great grandchildren, their Native American heritage. We are proud that our granddaughters got a chance to get to know such a great man. James L. Williams left a lasting impression on anyone he met. His sincerity and kindness shows through, without him having to say a word. He will always have our deepest respect and he will never leave our hearts.

ACKNOWLEGEMENTS

This book was made possible with the help of many people and organizations. I have found that everyone I have dealt with, to be most cooperative and very helpful.

A special thank you is very deserving from the following people, without their help, this book would not have become reality for me:

James Avery for all the times he took me to the Connecticut State Library, Rhode Island State Library, and the National Archives in Washington, DC

Phebe Lewis for all her help at the Bill Library, Historical Room in Ledyard

Goldie Robbins for some of the pictures and information she remembered from her youth

Patricia Taylor for helping me edit this book

Vivian Williams for some of the pictures and information she has collected on local genealogy

I have always been treated with respect and I have always been given a great deal of help from the following places:

Groton Town Clerk office
Groton Land Records
Ledyard Town Clerk office
Ledyard Probate office
New London City Clerk office
New London Probate office
North Stonington Town Clerks office
Stonington Town Clerk office
Stonington Probate office
Bill Library Ledyard
Bill Library Groton
Connecticut Historical Society
Connecticut State Library
Indian Colonial Research Center

I have had double vision for about 1½ years. I decided to write this book now, while I still am able to do it. I recently had both eyes operated on and I am currently in the process of recovery. Thanks to Doctor Andrew Lavada, I know now I will be able to finish this book. A very special thank you to him.

INTRODUCTION

The task of doing this genealogy has been a bigger undertaking than I thought it would be. It has consumed most my life for the last six years. I have added to it each day, sometimes a little, sometimes a lot. It has meant a lot of research, including vital statistics, countless deeds and land records, Probate records and searching cemeteries. Noyes and I have read every book and manuscript we could get our hands on and usually came up empty. Some of this research was done on the Internet, but even if you find something there, it all has to be substantiated, so that means you must get out there and look to make sure it is correct. If you really are going to find your ancestors you need to realize that it can be costly and you need to be able to devote a lot of your time to it. It is a lot of work and it can be very exciting when you find anything, even just one small piece of information, on an individual.

At times, you can feel almost like you knew them personally through all the information you find on them. Noyes and I are at that point. We feel like we personally know each individual in this line. Who they were, where they lived, how they survived, how they interacted with their neighbors and sometimes even with the Western Pequot now known as Mashantucket Pequot. Through Census records we have been able to find what happened to their children. Some of these children moved to other areas of the country, while some stayed here locally and raised their families. You can very easily get caught up in piecing your past together.

There are times that you are ready to give up, especially when you haven't found anything in a long time. But suddenly you will find another piece of information and you are back researching again.

This is only one line of Noyes' genealogy. I feel this is an important line because of the breakthroughs in DNA research at this time. DNA and genealogy is still in the ground floor stages. In the next 20 to 30 years, there will be a lot of breakthroughs. Noyes and I may not be here for those breakthroughs, but our children, grandchildren and great grandchildren will be. I would like them to know as much as possible about these ancestors, so they will be able to continue on with my work and hopefully solve this particular line.

If Noyes and I can let other people know that this is an important legacy to leave our children, then writing this book will be worthwhile. Anything we can do now, while we are still living to find and record any information that is still available now, will help future generations understand their heritage, no matter whether it is Native American, Caucasian, Asian or African American.

This includes talking to Grandparents, aunts and uncles, friends or anyone who would have information about your history, it is well worth your time to do so. They may also have pictures of your ancestors or where they lived. It is amazing to see different generations of pictures to see where our children got their features from today. These people can be a fountain of information, if you only take the time to listen. They can tell stories of their childhood that can be passed down to future generations. They may be able to shed some light on the ancestor you are having trouble finding. One bit of information, can give you a new lead, but remember that it may not be exactly as they mentioned. If you use their information, as with any research you find, your ancestor's story can come to life.

Check with your historical societies as well, I have found that the volunteers in these societies are very knowledgeable about the locality that they serve. These are people who are interested in the history and genealogy of their town or areȧ. You can find out how these people interacted their local area as well as find quite a bit of local history. All of which can be very helpful in locating your ancestors.

These stories or information will be important to pass on to your children, so they can get a sense of how their family lived maybe 100 years ago. It is all part of who you are today and it will help make up future generations. I feel very strongly that it is important to know about your heritage, whether it is rich or poor, Caucasian or Native American or African American and <u>always be proud of where you came from</u> and honor every ancestor you have. Open up that closet that has been shut for so many years and see what is in there. That person needs to be recognized for who they were.

When Noyes did the DNA test and found that the direct maternal line was Native American, it opened a whole new line for us. I have been told other lines in Noyes ancestry were Native American, but this line seemed to be researched a great deal and I assumed it was English. Since the results have come back Native American, I believe this line is a very special line and needs special attention.

Noyes and I are both affected by this particular line because within this line we have a common ancestor.

Noyes's direct maternal line is as follows:

Noyes Palmer Greene
Sadie Avis Willcox
Grandmother: Mary Elvira Pierce
Great Grandmother: Mary Stanton Main
2nd Great Grandmother: Sarah Eliza Brown
3rd Great Grandmother: Annis Holdridge
4th Great Grandmother: Hannah Brown, who married Nathan Holdridge

My direct Holdridge line is as follows:

Shirley Ann Holdridge
Father: Joseph Fairfield Holdridge
Grandfather: William Leeds Holdridge
Great Grandfather: Joseph Enos Holdridge
2nd Great Grandfather: Randall Holdridge
3rd Great Grandfather: Nathan Holdridge, who married Hannah Brown

I will get into more details about Hannah Brown and Nathan Holdridge in Chapter 9. I found Noyes's direct maternal line very interesting for various reasons. One in particular was, as I was concentrating only on the women only, a pattern began to emerge. For at least six generations, all the women were born a very close distance to the Mashantucket Pequot Reservation in Ledyard, Ct. When they married, they lived within a few miles of the Mashantucket Pequot Reservation. Almost all his direct female ancestors are buried in the Brown, Peckham Main Cemetery on Iron Street in Ledyard, Ct., which is within a mile of the reservation. Hannah Brown and Nathan Holdridge are the exception to that. They are buried in the Holdridge Cemetery on Indian Town Road in Ledyard, which borders the Mashantucket Pequot Reservation.

Some of their husbands did work for the Mashantucket Pequots or the Eastern Pequots throughout quite a few generations, including Noyes's Grandfather, Ray Ernest Willcox. You will read more about that throughout this book.

I feel that because he has a rare DNA match and all the information I found where his female ancestors lived in the Ledyard area for so many generations, it would be a good topic for a book. We would like to see more people get their Mitochondrial DNA testing done, so we can contact others that match his Maternal DNA and see if there are any similarities in our genealogy.

Chapter One, I will discuss the DNA process Noyes went through and his results from those tests. I feel this needs a chapter by itself, because that is the reason for concentrating on this line exclusively.

In Chapter Two, I will discuss some of the Pequot History.

In Chapter Three, I will begin with Noyes and his childhood memories as well as recent history.

In Chapters Four through Nine, I will trace back each female ancestor with any information I have found on her, to show that she is Noyes' ancestor.

In Chapters Ten through Fourteen, I will discuss why Hannah Brown, who married Nathan Holdridge, may not be the child of Nathaniel Brown and Deborah Morgan. There is some evidence that she may belong to another family. I will present all the evidence in these chapters.

CHAPTER 1

NOYES MATERNAL DNA

Noyes and I had given up hope on finding any more genealogy, because there were so many dead ends. I knew that at this point it would be like looking for a needle in a haystack. So we decided to put the genealogy on hold for a while and talked about doing a DNA test. We have heard that you can now take a sample of your DNA and trace your Maternal line back thousands of years to, what Dr. Bryan Sykes calls, one of "The Seven Daughters of Eve". We realized that this type of DNA is in the beginning stages. We know as time goes on, there will be many breakthroughs in this type of DNA testing. Our thoughts are that at least we will be able to leave our grandchildren with a DNA certificate of their oldest female ancestor. I had heard about Oxford University through a woman I met during my travels in doing research. She had her maternal DNA done through Oxford University and Dr. Bryan Sykes a few years ago. So I checked the Internet and found Dr. Bryan Sykes and his book "The Seven Daughters of Eve". [1] I found out that he has been doing research on the Maternal DNA for many years and has been able to trace back from your DNA, your maternal line to one of "the Seven Daughters of Eve". Now the DNA testing is done through Oxford Ancestors.

Oxford DNA Test

Noyes and I decided to send for the test kits through Oxford Ancestors. We both decided to do our maternal lines. So we swabbed our cheeks with the swab they sent us and mailed it back the same day. It took a few months, but Noyes received his results back first. As you can see from his certificate, on page 11, his came back "Djigonasee". [2] She is not one of "the Seven Daughters of Eve".

In the letter we received from Oxford Ancestors with Noyes results, it stated:

> *"Yours is a DNA sequence which is very rare among native Europeans. It belongs to a clan which is found only occasionally within Europe and, because, it is so rare, is not among the seven clans which appear on our website."*
>
> *"You are a direct maternal descendant of Djigonasee. The name is taken from a heroine of the Ontario Hurons, Djigonasee was the mother of the peacebringer Deganiwada, founder of the Six Nations: Seneca, Cayuga, Onondaga, Oneida, Mohawk, and Tuscarora."*
>
> *"She is the founder of one of the four major clans which colonised both North and South America from Eastern Asia about twelve thousand years ago. Moving across the Bering Land Bridge, which joined what is now Alaska and Siberia, her descendants fought extreme conditions of cold and ice to reach the Great Plains. From there they spread out to reach all parts of North American and within a thousand years, all of Central and South American as well. Her evolutionary relationship to other clans from around the world is shown on your chart.*
>
> *"We think Djigonasee herself lived in North Eastern Asia but we are not yet sure exactly when or where."* [3]

Noyes was very excited after reading the above statement. Neither he nor myself thought that he related to a Native American ancestry through this particular female line. We knew this line went into the Brown Family, which is a very old New England name. I never took the time to research this line in depth. From the research I had already done, the Brown Family was one of the easier ones to find information on. I had never gotten a chance to concentrate on the female side of that family, but in many genealogy books they pretty much cover most everyone. Since Noyes received his results, I have spent all my time on this line, going over any document I can find.

Mine came back a few weeks later and I was one of "the Seven Daughters of Eve" called "Velda". I knew mine had to be one of the daughters, because my Grandmothers parents were born in Scotland and Ireland. It was very exciting to find a maternal grandmother that they can trace back that far. Velda lived about 14,000 years ago. I knew very little about my Grandmothers family and so I was very excited about these results. Both of these certificates, in my eyes are very valuable to leave our grandchildren.

With his certificate he also received the following explanation from Oxford Ancestors of interpreting your World Clans Certificate. In order to help you understand the DNA process, and how to interpret the certificate on page 12, I have included the following information with Oxford Ancestors approval:

Interpreting your Seven Daughters of Eve Certificate

"***<u>What is a DNA sequence?</u>***

Your mitochondrial DNA sequence was prepared from the cheek cell sample that you supplied ... As you can see, your DNA sequence consists of a long series of four different letters: A, C, G, and T. These letters are shorthand for the four different chemicals that are strung together to make the long chain we know as DNA. The exact order in which these letters occur is a code that tells our cells how to divide, how to grow into a human and how to perform the many different tasks required of them.

We have only read a small part of your DNA, four hundred letters to be exact. The total length of the DNA message is much, much longer; about 3,000 million letters longer, in fact, and these billions of letters are what make up your genome.

<u>Why do you read the mitochondrial DNA?</u>

DNA is passed on to the next generation in sperm and eggs. Mitochondrial DNA (mtDNA, for short) is special because it is only passed on through the egg. This means that everyone has inherited their mtDNA from their mother. She inherited it from her mother, who inherited from her mother, who inherited it from hers and so on back through time. Therefore, mtDNA provides a direct link to our maternal ancestors. We all inherit other genes from many other ancestors, but only mtDNA traces a direct maternal line.

<u>How do you compare my DNA sequence?</u>

Your mtDNA sequence, which is printed below your chart, is the DNA sequence that has been passed on to you with little or no change from your remote female ancestors. Think of it as a very long word with four hundred letters. To compare the distinct spellings that we find in different people, we use what we call a reference sequence, actually the most frequent sequence found in Europe. Where your sequence differs from the reference "spelling", we have picked-out the letters in red. If there are no red letters, then your mtDNA sequence is identical to the reference sequence.

<u>Why do DNA change over time?</u>

When cells divide, the DNA that they contain has to be copied. Fortunately, this is an extremely accurate process and mistakes occur only very rarely. When they do, however, they are called mutations. If they happen in a gene responsible for an important cell function, they can give rise to severe inherited diseases, like cystic fibrosis or muscular dystrophy. However, the great majority of mutations occur without having any obvious effect at all. Mutations in the section of mtDNA that we sequenced are of no consequence to your health, but they are extremely useful for studying our ancestry. This is because, on average, one mutation occurs in mtDNA every twenty thousand years!

<u>How do I interpret my DNA chart?</u>

The chart that you have received is made up of interconnecting circles. Each of these circles represents a DNA sequence and their colours indicate the geographical distribution of the modern day descendants of the clan. The details of the chart have been worked out in Oxford using over 13,000 sequences from people living all over the world.

The lines connecting the circles trace the evolutionary pathways of our ancestors. Each line connects two circles whose sequences differ by one or more change (mutations) and most of them represent only a single change out of the 400 DNA letters that we read.

The grey star, or node, near the bottom-left of the chart represents the sequence of the ancestral mother through whom we are all related, the woman known as "Mitochondrial Eve". It is through her that we are related to the other, now extinct, species of human, Homo erectus and Homo neanderthalensis, shown on the chart as a dashed line. The other grey nodes on the chart represent DNA sequences that we have not yet found in any person living today, but we know from our reconstruction's that it must have existed.

How does my DNA fit into the chart?

The star shows the chart position of your own sequence. It belongs to one of the 36 groups or clans that have been identified to date, each of which is shown by a coloured circle. The members of each clan are all descended from a single female ancestor through the direct maternal line traced on the chart. We call these women clan mothers and from your DNA sequence we are able to tell to which clan you belong and which of these 36 women is your maternal ancestor.

Who were our clan mothers?

It is an entirely logical, yet still awe inspiring fact, that we are all related to each other through our mothers. Over the past ten years, research by Professor Bryan Sykes at Oxford University has identified just 36 women, who lived thousands of years ago, from whom almost everyone on Earth is directly descended through the maternal line. Professor Sykes has named these women and determined upon which continent they lived. The so-called "Seven Daughters of Eve" sub-group are the seven clan mothers from whom almost all native Europeans are descended.

There was actually nothing remarkable about any of these clan mothers when they were alive. We know that each one of them must have survived long enough to have children and that each had at least two daughters, starting off lines of descent that reach right down to all of us living today. These were real people, real women who brought up families, but who lived in very different circumstances to those that we enjoy today. These really were our true ancestors.

The World Clans

The 36 clusters (or clans) that have so far been identified vary in frequency across locations, but there is no specific association between genetic clans and tribal structures. This is a reflection of the great antiquity of our genetic roots, which predate our modern notions of race, tribe or other ethnic classification system by more than a hundred thousand years.

The vast majority of native Europeans are descendants of 12 clans, which includes the Seven Daughters of Eve. Of these dozen clans, descendants of Helena make up over 45% of the European population.

The descendants of four clans, Chochmingwu, Djigonasee, Aiyana and Ina, dominate the Native Americans. Also, about 1% of Native Americans are found to belong to the clan of Xenia, which had its origins on the borders of Europe and Asia. The clans of Chochmingwu, Djigonasee and Aiyana can all be found in modern inhabitants of Siberia and Alaska, but this is not the case for Ina. Her descendants are found in South and Central America, but only as far north as Vancouver Island on the northwest Pacific coast. Intriguingly, this same clan is also the one that is closely associated with the colonisations of the Polynesian islands from Southeast Asia.

The natives of the Far East are predominantly descended

from Djigonasee, but there is considerable representation from the "native American" clans of Ina and Aiyana and from six further clans Fufei, Yumi, Nene, Malaxshmi, Emiko and Gaia.

Africa lays claim to 13 of the maternal clans. Although these are easily the most ancient clans in the world, a reflection of Africa's status as the cradle of humankind, it is still possible to construct the genetic relationship between them. By doing this it is possible to show there is one maternal ancestor for all of Africa, and therefore for the rest of the world. She is referred to as "Mitochondrial Eve", and is shown on your certificate.

Obviously, she would not have been the only woman alive at the time, but it is only her maternal lineage that has survived unbroken to the present day. She in turn would have had an ancestral mother, and this line reaches back millions of years to the very beginning of our species.

Although modern humans had their origins in Africa, only the descendants of one of these clans, Lara, have so far been found in the peoples of the rest of the world. She probably lived in what we now know as Kenya or Ethiopia." [4]

From the information we received, I believe that "Djigonasee" descendants came across the Bering Land Bridge and down to North America and settled in the Midwest of what is now the United States of America. Of course, this took many generations. I also believe that from there, Noyes's Ancestral Grandmother, migrated to where the present day upstate New York and Canada is. That is the area the Tribes of the Six Nations are from, which include the Mohawk Tribe. From local legend the Pequots migrated from the Mohawk tribe in New York to Connecticut. The exact date the Pequot's came to Connecticut varies anywhere from 500 years to 1000 years ago.

I feel the following quote helps explain the trek these ancient people had to take to make their way across the United States to the State of New York. From the book, "Iroquois Culture &

Commentary" by Doug George-Kanentiio Page 19, 21-22:

"How accurate are the legends? I contacted my friend Dr. Dean Snow, an archaeologist at the State University of New York at Albany who has spent many years collecting material from various Mohawk settlements in central New York.

I asked Dr. Snow specific questions as to where he thought we came from, based solely on the evidence he had collected. His conclusions largely substantiate what I had been told by the elders of the Mohawk Nation, namely that we were originally a people from the desert area of the American Southwest who had gradually moved into this region over a period of many generations.

"Our elders tell us we first grew to become a distinct people in the Southwest, in the land where the Hopi live. Indeed, to this day the Iroquois refer to the Hopi as our cousins, relatives whom we remember even after passing of thousands of years.

"For some reason, the Iroquois began to wander away from the Southwest and eventually settled at the eastern edge of the Great Plains, where the Missouri and Mississippi River, meet, near current day St. Louis. It is said we were close allies with the Wolf Nation, now called Pawnee.

After many generations, the Iroquois again moved, this time toward the northeast following the Ohio River. During the course of this journey several small bands split off to venture north, where, over time, they grew into the Tobacco, Neutral, Huron, Petun, Wenro, and Erie nations. Another group went to the southeast and became the Cherokees, while a large number settled in central Pennsylvania and were known as the Susquehannas or Conestoga Nation.

Undeterred by these divisions, the main Iroquois party continued on, paddling their canoes along the shores of the Great Lakes and down the St. Lawrence River until they stopped at a place near Three Rivers, Quebec, by the

Algonquins. It is said the Iroquois were enslaved by the Algonquins and spent many years laboring for a people we called the Adirondacks, or "bark eaters", because they had the habit of flavoring their food with shredded bark.

After many years had passed, the Iroquois managed to escape. They retraced their steps along the St. Lawrence and into Lake Ontario. As they were about to land near the mouth of the Oswego River, they spotted the Adirondacks coming fast in an effort to recapture them. In a scene reminiscent of the "Divine Wind", or kamikaze, said to have protected the Japanese against invasion, a great storm came from the west and upset the canoes of the Adirondacks, drowning many of their men an driving the rest far into the lake.

Having landed safely, the Iroquois liked what they saw. Within a few years their population had grown so quickly that it was necessary to expand further into that territory. One group decided to set up their villages along the Mohawk River and became known as the People of the Flint because of the flint quarries in this eastern area. In the Iroquois language, they are the Kaiienkehaka, but are also called the Mohawks.

To west of the Mohawks were the Oneidas, followed by the Onondagas, the swamp dwelling Cayugas, and along the Genessee River, the People of the Great Hill or Senecas. Another group went far to the south to what is now North Carolina, but eventually retraced their steps to this region in the early 1700s. They are called the "shirt wearers' or Tuscaroras.

This is a very abbreviated summary of the Iroquois story of our beginnings, of how we came to be in New York State." [5]

By using the DNA and other information we have found, I only need to cover the last 400 years, if Noyes is through the Pequot line. I believe the genealogy that we have done points in that direction. I can prove from the present back to about 250 years ago (which would be between 1740 and 1750), through genealogy.

The Pilgrims landed in Plymouth, Massachusetts in 1620 and there were only a few other white visitors to this area previous to that. The Vikings visited often, but never settled here. That would only leave about 150 years to complete the link between the DNA and genealogy.

Noyes did his direct Maternal line, so this is the line that we are discussing in the following pages. We talked to Noyes's, Aunt Goldie Robbins, about Noyes's DNA results. Goldie Robbins is Sadie Willcox's sister. We asked her if she would consider doing a DNA test through Oxford Ancestors. We wanted to see if her results matched Noyes. She did the test and when her results came back, she was also "Djigonasee".[6] Noyes and his Aunt Goldie Robbins both had two mutations of their DNA.

Noyes believes he is Native American and this DNA test, in our opinion helps prove it. I am trying to locate the Grandmother who married into the white world. As of May 2003, when I checked Oxford Ancestors website, Oxford Ancestors will let us contact others from the "Djigonasee Clan". There are only 3 other people at the present time that wish to be contacted. These three have more mutations than Noyes does, so they are not exact matches. The ones that Noyes matches exactly are mostly from Japan and a few from the USA. But none of those wish to be contacted at this time.

Since we have been working on this direct maternal line, we have found that between 7 to 9 generations of females have all either been born or lived in Groton/Ledyard within a 1½ mile radius of the Mashantucket Pequot Reservation. This takes us back to about 250 years ago.

Family Tree Maternal Native American DNA

We talked about getting a second Native American Maternal DNA test done on Noyes, to see if it could confirm Oxford Ancestors results. Again, I searched the Internet and found that Family Tree does DNA testing. Family Tree test for more markers than Oxford Ancestors. We also felt that Family Tree is in this country and could possibly be able to help us find this ancestor through their database. I have used Family Tree Maker for my database since I have been doing genealogy. Family Tree has been in business for many years and they seem very reputable, that is also one of the reasons we chose them. The test we had Noyes do was for Maternal Native American. Again, his results showed that he was from Haplotype D group, which is from one of the five groups of Native American groups to settle in the Americas. A copy of Noyes's Maternal Native American DNA results from Family Tree DNA is on the page 13. [7]

They told him he is definitely from one of the five Native American Tribes. Noyes had 3 mutations with Family Tree. They also told me, in the telephone conservation I had with them, that it is extremely rare for someone to get these results without previously knowing that line would be Native American. Most people who have this type of test done, already know which ancestor was Native American and has the history on that line.

At the moment, which is October 2003, there are no matches for his DNA through Family Tree. The gentleman I talked to, said they are hoping within the next year more people will be doing DNA testing and that should help our chances of matching someone else who also is in Haplotype Group D.

Now with two different companies giving us the same results, I feel strongly that this direct maternal line is Native American. According to what I have seen on Oxford Ancestors web site, there are a total of 35 people whose results came back "Djigonesee".

OXFORD ANCESTORS DNA CERTIFICATE FOR NOYES P. GREENE

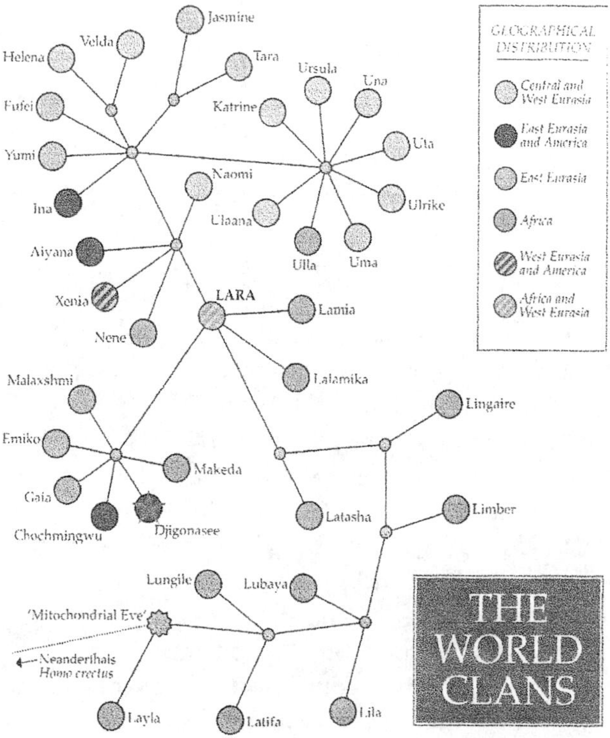

DNA sequence for *Noyes P Greene* of the clan DJIGONASEE

ATTCTAATTT AAACTATTCT CTGTTCTTTC ATGGGGAAGC AGATTTGGGT ACCACCCAAG TATTGACTCA CCCATCAACA ACCGCTATGT ATTTCGTACA
TTACTGCCAG CCACCATGAA TATTGTACGG TACCATAAAT ACTTGACCAC CTGTAGTACA TAAAAACCCA ATCCACATCA AAACCCCCTC CCCATGCTTA
CAAGCAAGTA CAGCAATCAA CCTTCAACTA TCACACATCA ACTGCAACTC CAAAGCCACC CCTCACCCAC TAGGATACCA ACAAACCTAC CCACCCTTAA
CAGTACATAG TACATAAAGC CATTTACCGT ACATAGCACA TTACAGTCAA ATCCCTTCTC GTCCCCATGG ATGACCCCCC TCAGATAGGG GTCCCTTGAC

No M4866

Certification Bryan Sykes MA PhD DSc
Professor of Human Genetics, University of Oxford, England

Oxford Ancestors

FAMILY TREE DNA CERTIFICATE
FOR NOYES P. GREENE

FamilyTreeDNA

Native American Ancestry - Female

Certificate

Report of HVS-I Sequencing of mtDNA from Client # [redacted] Noyes P. Greene

<u>**Test Protocol**</u>: We amplified a region of your mtDNA that encompasses the first hypervariable segment (HVS-I). This rapidly evolving region provides considerable information about the sequence diversity of a human mtDNA, including the maternal lineage to which it belongs. We next used specific primers to decode the precise nucleotide base composition of your HVS-I sequence, that is, the exact order of A's, C's, G's and T's that is present in this region. The sequenced HVS-I was subsequently read by a DNA Sequencer, and then checked against the human Cambridge Reference Sequence (CRS) to find all of the mutations, or polymorphisms, that differentiate your mtDNA sequence from it.

Results:

The five Haplogroups present in modern Native Americans are the A, B, C, D and X included in the table below. Based on the results of our genetic analysis, we can say that your mtDNA *does belong* to one of those five Haplogroups. In the following table, you will see the consensus HVS-I sequences of each of these five mtDNA lineages. The numbers in the top row indicate the position at which a polymorphism is present in one or more of these haplogroups. Each number should have a "16" in front of it, so that "111" would read "16111" (position 16111 out of 16569 nucleotides in the whole mtDNA genome), but the "16" has been left off in this shorthand form.

16223T, 16362C, 16519C **Your Haplogroup: D**

Cambridge Reference Sequence match

Haplogroup	111	189	213	217	223	278	290	298	319	327	362
A	T	T	G	T	T	C	A	T	A	C	C
B	C	T	G	C	C	C	G	T	G	C	T
C	C	T	G	T	T	C	G	C	G	T	T
D	C	T	G	T	T	C	G	T	G	C	C
X	C	C	A	T	T	T	G	T	G	C	T

<u>**Native American Geographic Maps**</u>: We have included several images loaned to us by Dr. Theodore Schurr, Ph.D. One shows the migration out of Africa, another shows the areas in Asia that have major population bases similar to that of peoples known as American Natives. Lastly, we have included a map of the Western Hemisphere that gives a location of various major tribes, and a general breakdown of the Haplogroups found within each region of North and South America.

David E. Rothschild, M.D.
David E. Rothschild, M.D.

3/6/2003
Date

CHAPTER 2

AN OVERVIEW OF THE PEQUOT HISTORY

This will be an overview of the Pequot History as I have read and learned about during my research.

One account that I found on the Pequot Indians was from "The History of Stonington", by Richard Anson Wheeler, this is some of the Pequot history that he included in his book:

..."The Pequots were doubtless a branch of the great Mohegan natives, whose principal seat or central place of residence was on the east bank of the Hudson River nearly opposite Fort Orange, now the city of Albany, New York. In their efforts to enlarge their dominions they crossed the Hudson River and attempted to invade the tribal land of the Mohawk Indians, which resulted in war, and after an exhaustive struggle they were driven back across the Hudson and away from their tribal homes and lands in a southeasterly direction, until they reached the territory now known as the State of Connecticut. During their war with the Mohawks, a powerful sachem by the name of Pequoat greatly distinguished himself, and his followers assumed for him the name of Pequot, and in their eastern progress they gave him the name of Wopigwooit, alias, Wapyquart, signifying a powerful leader.

After the defeat and dispersion of the Mohegan tribe by the Mohawks, they emigrated easterly and became divided into small tribes, under, and sometimes hostile, chiefs. The Pequots were the most powerful clan of the great Mohegan tribe and lorded it over the smaller clans with a high hand, and in their progress they crossed the Connecticut River and invaded the tribal lands of the Niantic Indians, which bordered on the seashore between the Narragansett and Connecticut Rivers.

The Pequots succeeded in dividing the Niantic tribe into two clans, leaving one clan to occupy Niantic in Rhode Island and the other clan to occupy Niantic in Connecticut, taking possession of and holding all the lands between the divided clans of the Niantic Indians.

After establishing their authority over the central tribal lands of the Niantic Indians, they commenced and built for themselves two wigwam villages, one on each side of the River Thames, now known as the city of New London and Groton Bank, which the Pequots occupied when Governor John Endicott, in 1636, came with ninety men to chastise them for murdering Capt. John Oldham and others...

...So they built two forts to protect themselves from any invasion of the eastern Niantics and Narragansetts, on or near what is now known as Fort Hill in the town of Groton, and the other farther east on Mystic Hill in said town, which they regarded as an all sufficient defense against their eastern enemies.

Thus protected, they felt able to extend their dominions to the north and west and after arming themselves with their rude munitions of war, they invaded the tribal lands of the Sequeen Indians, which lay on both sides of the Connecticut River in the present county of Hartford, Conn., which was doubtless one of the clans of the original Mohegan tribe, and after three hand to hand conflicts with them compelled the Sequeens to acknowledge their power and authority and became tributary to them.

According to the Dutch account the successful invasion of the tribal lands of the Sequeens by the Pequots was after the discovery of our seacoast by the Dutch in 1614, but no exact date of the time has been preserved..."[8]

Another account of the very early Pequot, comes from "The History of the Town of Ledyard" by Rev. John Avery:

..."Two hundred and sixty years ago all the south-eastern portion of New London County was occupied by a powerful tribe of Aborigines known as the Pequot Indians. Their dominions extended from the Niantic river on the west to the Pawcatuck River on the east, and from Long Island Sound on the south up a dozen or more miles into the interior; and included the territory now covered by the towns of New London, Waterford, Groton, Ledyard, Stonington and North Stonington. The territory to the east of them was occupied by the Narragansetts; that to the west by the Nehantics; that to the north and north-west by the Mohegans. The Mohegans were originally Pequots, and had revolted and set up for themselves, under the leadership of Uncas, who subsequently acted a very important part as the friend of the early English settlers in their conflicts with the hostile Indian tribes. The Pequots were altogether the most powerful native tribe in Connecticut, and one of the most powerful in New England. Hence, as soon as they became unfriendly, they presented one of the most formidable obstacles to the peaceful settlement of the English in this portion of the country. They numbered altogether about four thousand souls. Sassacus their chief, had twenty-six sachems under him, and some seven hundred warriors..."[9]

As you can see, these two accounts differ in the origins of the Pequots and their native lands. But what happens during and after the Pequot War of 1637, both sources agree.

In 1637, the English sent Captain John Mason to destroy the Pequot Tribe. In local history, it was known as the Pequot War. The Pequot chief or leader at this time was called Sassacus. He was a very powerful leader. Much has been written on it locally, but the outcome remains the same. A Pequot fort on Mystic Hill in Mystic, Connecticut was burned and many Pequot's died. The distribution of the remaining Pequots was as follows:

"...After the close of the Pequot War, Uncas, Miantonomo and Ninigret, with the remaining captive Pequots, on the 21st day of Sept. 1637, met the magistrates of Connecticut at Hartford and after mutual friendly intercourse, a treaty was entered into between the colony of Connecticut and the Mohegan, Narragansett and Niantic Indians, which by its terms established perpetual peace between the colony of Connecticut and the Mohegan, Narragansett and Niantic Indians and then with imposing ceremonies the magistrates divided the remnant of the Pequots among the Mohegan, Narragansett and Niantic Indians as follows:

They gave eighty to Uncas, to Miantonomo they gave eighty and to Ninigret they gave twenty, upon condition that the Pequots were no longer to be known by their tribal name..."[10]

Some Pequot's were given to the Colonists to be their servants and some were sent off on boats to far off lands, never to return. There were also bounties put on their heads by the English. The Colonists wanted all Pequot's destroyed. After the War, it was decided that the Pequots could no longer practice their customs. Even the word, Pequot, was not allowed to be spoken. From the Pequot Indians an Historical Sketch:

"...They were to be called Pequots no more, but Mohegan and Narragansett; nor were they ever to dwell again in their old haunts, or occupy their planting or hunting grounds..."[11]

Some Pequot's were sold off as slaves and others were made to live among other Native American tribes, the Mohegans, Narragansetts and Nehantics. From the Indian Colonial Research Center, this quote tells of what happened to other Pequot Indian survivors in 1637:

"...The Indians had at least two names for this swamp—one was Ohmouwauke, or as it has been translated, the "owl's

nest", and Cuppacommock, "the hiding place".

"The hiding place" it was in 1637 when the remnants of the starved and frightened Pequots fled from Groton to seek shelter in it vastness'. They thought no one could penetrate its secrets and search them out but a Pequot who had lived with the Narragansetts remembered the trails and led the pursing white men. The Pequots were surrounded and soon starved out and captured just as the "golden hearted rhododendrons" were in bloom. The life of the old chief Puttaquaponk was spared in the hope that he would reveal the hiding place of the grand chief sachem Sassacus. The thirty or more men who were captured were taken out in the Sound and slain and the women and children were sold as slaves, some being sent to the Barbadoes and others were placed in the homes of their captors...".[12]

The Pequot's who were sent to live with the different tribes rebelled and would not stay with those tribes. This band of Pequot would later become known as the Groton Pequots, the Western Pequots and the Mashantucket Pequots. From The History of Stonington, Richard Wheeler tells of what became of the 80 Pequots given to Uncas:

"...The eighty Pequots who were assigned to Uncas by said magistrates would not live with him and his tribal clan at Mohegan, now Montville, Conn. To offset his enforced obedience to Sassacus, he lorded it over them with a high hand, which caused them to leave him and pitch their wigwam tents in the present town of Groton, where they continued to live until a reservation was provided for them by the Connecticut Colony of Mashantuxet, in the present town of Ledyard, Conn., which they reluctantly consented to accept in lieu of their Noank homes, reserving the right of fishing in Mystic River, Conn..."[13]

The other Pequots that were given to Miantonomo and Ninigret also were not content living with their assigned tribes. This band of Pequots would later become known as the Eastern Pequots and the Paucatuck Eastern Pequots and today the Historic Eastern Pequot Tribe:

> "*...for as soon as those assigned to Miantonomo reached Rhode Island, they left him and were afterward joined by those who were assigned to Ninigret, and in disobedience of the terms of the treaty with the Connecticut magistrates, they located themselves at a place called Massatuxet in Westerly, RI, about three and one half miles north of Watch Hill, where they built a wigwam village and planted adjoining lands with Indian maze or corn...*
>
> *...These Pequots remained at Massatuxet until 1660, when they were driven from their homes where they had lived for over twenty years (long enough to have acquired to title thereto by possession in any civilized community) over Pawcatuck River into Stonington, Conn., and occupied land at Causet point, on the north side of Pawcatuck or Little Narragansett Bay, for a few years. Subsequently, they occupied land at Taugwonk and Cosatuc Hill, then in Stonington, and finally on a reservation, now in North Stonington, provided for them by the Connecticut Colony in 1868, and there the remnants of the Miantonomo and Ninigret and Pequots resided, until nearly all of them found homes elsewhere or departed this life, subject to more or less annoyance by some of the surrounding English settlers and yielding a passive obedience to their overseer, appointed by the Connecticut General Court at first, and later by the Superior Court of Connecticut...*"[14]

The Pequot's fought with the white Colonists in King Phillip's War, French and Indian Wars as well as the Revolutionary War.

After the Revolutionary War, there were very few full blood Pequot's left. On the Groton Reservation in 1839, there were only two full blood Pequot, the rest were mixed with the Black and White races. The Pequot's who were a proud people 200 years ago in 1839 were reduced to just a handful. They had to adjust to the white man's ways and even though they lived on the reservation, still had to be accepted in the white man's world.

Much of the Western Pequot reservation land was sold off. The original reservation may have been around 2500 acres of land. By 1720's, the Natives of the Western Pequot tribe, probably had about 2000 acres left. By the early 1800's, it was down to about 1500 acres. I found on the Ledyard Tax List in 1854 the Western Pequots had 1500 acres of land. In 1855 they had 500 acres of land. Each time the best land was taken from them for the white colonists. By the mid 1900's they were only left the 275 acres of land, which was mostly ledge and rocks and a hill.

There has been many archeology digs that has been done here in the Ledyard area over the years. These digs are still ongoing today by the Mashantucket Pequot Museum and Research Center. They have found evidence of Native People living here in the Ledyard area up to 2,000 years ago. Whether they were the Pequot's or another band of Native people is not certain. But the artifacts speak for themselves; there have been people here in southeastern Connecticut for many thousands of years.

The three tribes that remain today in eastern Connecticut are the Mashantucket Pequot Tribe, the Historic Eastern Pequot Tribe, the Mohegan Tribe.

The Mashantucket Pequot Tribe and the Mohegan Tribe are federally recognized tribes as of today. Their tribal rolls are presently **closed** to new members. The Mashantucket Pequot membership requirements were that your direct ancestor had to be listed on the Indian Population Census of 1900 and 1910 Federal Census Rolls. The Mohegan Tribes requirements for membership were that your ancestor had to be on one of the membership rolls of the Mohegan tribe in the 1860's. The Historic Eastern Pequot Tribe is in the process of trying to get federal recognition.

If you are looking for more extensive Pequot History, the

Mashantucket Pequot Museum and Research Center, which is located on the Mashantucket Pequot Reservation and is opened to the general public, has a very helpful staff. Their library is devoted to all Native American subjects, from their history to politics to their many crafts, plus much, much more. The library staff is also very helpful with trying to find answers to your questions. The books are not allowed to be checked out, but you can read them there. I have used their library to find out how to make a flute and also find quite a bit of local history on whites as well as Native Americans. In their research department, they are always working on many archaeological digs and are always adding to the history of the local Native Americans.

If you are looking for the genealogy of the Pequots, you must check at the local town halls for births, deaths and marriages. There is no one place where you will find all the genealogy on either the Mashantucket or Historic Eastern Pequot tribes. The Indian Colonial Research Center in Old Mystic, Ct. does have a little of their genealogy. They would be a good place to write to see if they have any information on an ancestor you are looking for. The Connecticut State Library has extensive Probate records for Stonington, New London and Norwich, as well as church records, Census records, cemetery records and newspaper articles. They also have a tremendous State Archives there as well. They are a great place to start on your search to find any ancestor including Native American.

We know some of our ancestors were neighbors with the Pequots for almost the last 300 years or more. Some of the Pequots probably worked for some of our ancestors. In other cases, our ancestors worked for them, plowing their gardens, selling them cloth, sawing wood for their houses, delivering wood for heat in the winter months and digging graves for their burials.

CHAPTER 3

NOYES PALMER GREENE

Generation 1

Noyes Palmer Greene, was born May 19, 1945[15] in New London, Ct. He was the son of **George Frances Greene, Jr.** and **Sadie Avis Willcox**. He married **Shirley Ann Holdridge** on August 28, 1970[16] in Pawcatuck, Ct.

Shirley Ann Holdridge was born July 05, 1950[17] in Westerly, RI. She was the daughter of **Joseph Fairfield Holdridge** and **Priscilla June Tift.**

Noyes Palmer Greene

Shirley Holdridge

Children of Noyes Greene and Shirley Holdridge are:

1. **Corey Adam Greene**, he has one daughter, **Kelsey M. Greene**
2. **Kimberly Lynn Greene**, married Marc Pendleton.

They have two children, **Kayla A. Pendleton** and **Tyler J. Pendleton**.

The following pages only include Noyes' direct maternal line. This line will follow Noyes' DNA, which must be a straight maternal line. I have included both spouses for information purposes only, except in the case where both spouses are affected by the DNA results. When both spouses are affected, you will find information on both families.

On page 24 and 25, I have included a portion of a Map of the Town of Ledyard[19] (this map was made in the late 1800's, Ledyard Historical Society has the entire original map), because it will help show where the maternal grandmothers were born, raised, married, died and are buried. As you can see from the Map, all his maternal grandmothers back to Hannah Brown, lived their entire lives around the Western Pequot Reservation, usually within a few miles of it. Is this a coincidence or does it have something to do with their DNA Native American roots? His direct female ancestors starting with Sadie Willcox and going back to Hannah Brown who married Nathan Holdridge stayed in that area for about 220 years, if not longer.

The map will also show where their spouses bought or inherited property and made their homes. The map shows where the other connecting families lived as well, such as, Thomas and Lois Main, Robert and Deborah Willcox and Nathaniel and Charlotte Brown.

Hopefully, this will help give you a better understanding of the area of Ledyard that will be discussed in this book and how closely each generation lived to the previous one. It will also help you locate cemeteries, routes, houses, schools, mills etc. as they are talked about throughout this book.

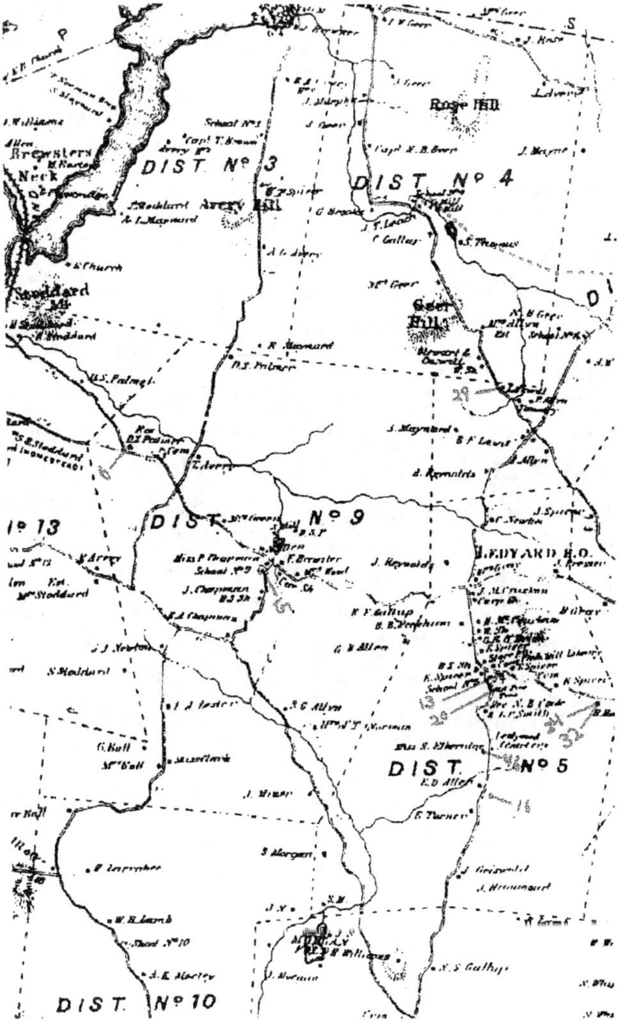
DIST. No 3
DIST. No 4
DIST. No 9
DIST. No 5
DIST. No 10
No 13
Rose Hill
Avery Hill
Brewsters Neck
Stoddard Hill
Geer Hill
LEDYARD P.O.

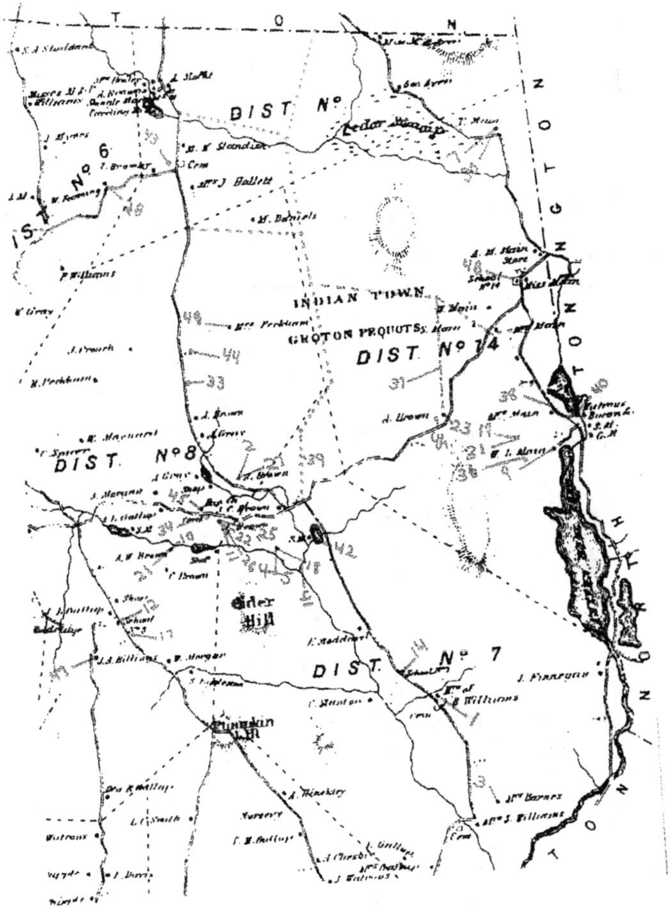
T O N
DIST No
Cedar Swamp
DIST No 6
INDIAN TOWN
GROTON PEQUOTS
DIST No 14
DIST No 8
DIST No 7
Cider Hill
N O T G N I N O T S
H I L L
N O T O N
P Williams
J. Crouch
M. Daniels
J. Brown
A. Brown
W. Maynard
A. Gray
J. Finnegan
R. Williams
A. Hinckley
Mrs Barnes
Mrs S. Williams

Map of Ledyard

Key to Map on pages 19 and 20

#	Person/Place	Location
Births:		
1	Sadie Louise Greene	Shewville Road
2	Sadie A. Wilcox	Shewville Road
3	Mary Elvira Pierce	Shewville Road
4	Ray Ernest Willcox[20]	Iron Street
5	Raymond Willcox[21]	Iron Street
6	Mary Stanton Main[22]	Stoddards Wharf Road
7	George Park Main[23]	Route 2
8	Timothy Main[24]	Homestead Road
9	Williams Leeds Main[25]	Homestead Road
10	Sarah E. Brown[26]	Iron Street
11	Avery Wilbur Brown[27]	Iron Street

Schools (all schools are shown on the 1868 Map of Ledyard by District Number):

12	Sadie A. Wilcox	Gallup Hill Road
13	Mary Elvira Pierce	Ledyard Center
14	Ray Ernest Wilcox	Shewville Road
15	Mary Stanton Main	Stoddards Wharf Road

Houses:

16	George F. Greene	Center Groton Road
17	Ray Ernest Wilcox[28]	Home on Gallup Hill Road. Also, land on the corner of Iron St. and Shewville Road
18	Willcox Homestead[29]	Iron Street
19	Robert Wilcox, Sr.[30]	Homestead Road
20	Chester Pierce[31]	Center Groton Road
21	Avery Wilbur Brown[32]	Iron Street
22	Albert Brown[33]	Iron Street
23	Phinehas Holdridge[34]	Indiantown Road
24	Nathan Holdridge[35]	Colonel Ledyard Highway
25	Nathaniel & Charlotte Brown[36]	Iron Street
26	Nathaniel & Deborah Brown[37]	Iron Street
27	Aaron Brown[38]	Shewville Road
28	Nathaniel & Mary Brown[39]	Fanning Road
29	Nathaniel & Anna Brown[40]	off Colonel Ledyard Hwy

30 Timothy Main[41]	Route 2
31 Thomas Main[42]	Homestead Road
32 Randall Holdridge[43]	Colonel Ledyard Hwy
33 Flower Cottage[44]	Shewville Road

Cemeteries (All cemeteries are shown on 1868 Map of Ledyard):

34 Brown Peckham Main Cemetery	Iron Street
35 Holdridge Cemetery	Indian Town Road
36 Thomas Main Cemetery	Homestead Road

Routes and Roads:

37 Route that Nathan Holdridge could have taken to Punderson Store[45]

38 Route that Dan Toby could have taken to Punderson Store for Phinehas Holdridge[46]

39 Kate Swamp Road[47]

Mills:

40 Phinehas Holdridge Mill[48]	Lantern Hill Road
41 Robert Willcox Grist Mill[49]	Iron Street
42 Robert Willcox Saw Mill[50]	Iron Street

Miscellaneous:

43 Toby Orchid[51]	Shewville Road
44 Mary Pierce, Wish Mountain	Shewville Road
45 Second Baptist Church[52]	Iron Street
46 James Etheridge property[53]	Center Groton Road
47 Stephen Billings property[54]	Colonel Ledyard Hwy
48 School House #14[55]	Lantern Hill Road and Indian Town Road
49 Mrs. Almira Peckham[56]	off Shewville Road

To help you understand this area of New London County, you should know that Ledyard was part of the Town of Groton before 1836. It was known as North Groton, Second Society and the North Society. I have come across all these names in researching land transactions, Vital records, Probate records and in many manuscripts. When researching vital, land or probate records you must go back to either the Town of Ledyard or Groton or Stonington or New London, depending on the time frame you are looking for. The following tells which Town you can find vital records, land records and probate records for the Town of Ledyard and the years that each applies:

1666-1705	New London City Hall Vital, Probate and Land Transactions
1705-1836	Groton Town Hall Vital and Land Transactions
1766-1837	Stonington Town Hall Probate Records
1836 to present	Ledyard Town Hall, Town Clerk office Vital and land transactions
1837 to present,	Ledyard Town Hall, Probate Office Probate Records

Also, Connecticut State Library[18] has many Probate Records from Stonington and New London on microfilm.

NATIVE FEELINGS

As I look back over the years we have spent together, there were many incidents that have lead us to believe that Noyes had Native American in his background.

Noyes has lived almost his entire life in Ledyard. For a short time, we lived in Stonington and North Stonington. He also left the area for 2 years when he was in the U.S. Army in 1965 to 1967. As you will see from the next generations, all the direct females were also born in Ledyard as far back as we can take them.

In the 33 years we have been together I have known that Noyes has an acute sense of his surroundings. We have taken many walks in the woods, such as Bluff Point, Lantern Hill, Haley Farm, Billings Lake, and of course through the woods in our own neighborhood. No matter where we are, he always knows which direction to take and has never been lost. He notices even small details in his surroundings that I don't see. He has a keen sense of smell and can identify animals, people, and plants by their smell. He has always wondered why all these things were important to him.

Noyes and I have always had an interest in history of all forms, whether it was Town, State or just family history. When we first met, we would talk for hours about our family history. How both of our backgrounds and ancestry was so close in many aspects. We both came from large families. Our Dads both worked at Lantern Hill Silica Mine in North Stonington, Ct. Both of our Dads died at a very young age. We were related several generations ago through Nathan and Hannah Holdridge I was through their son Randall and Noyes through their daughter Annis. We were also related through Thomas and Lois Main. I was through their son, William Leeds Main and Noyes through another son Timothy Main.

The home we have lived in for 30 years is located in between my Holdridge ancestors and Noyes' Pierce ancestors. We have many common ancestors. Some of our families have lived and worked side by side in Ledyard for many generations. We have always talked about moving out of Connecticut, but we feel that is why it has been so hard for either of us to leave this area. Our roots have been here for so many generations, that it is extremely hard to leave them behind.

We have always respected our ancestors. Most of our ancestors have been here in the Ledyard/Groton area since the late 1600 to early 1700. They were not the rich and famous from this area, but the farmers, laborers and tanners. They had to work very hard at survival on a daily basis, to be able to keep producing future generations. Some of our ancestors owned grist mills, saw mills and even a cloth mill. These were our white ancestors. I was able to find quite a bit on these ancestors through some of the following sources: manuscripts, account books, historical books, biographical book, genealogy books, Church records, military records, tax lists or in Family Bibles just to name a few.

We have searched almost every Town Hall in New London County, as well as some in Windham County. We have been to numerous Historical Societies in Connecticut and Rhode Island. We have searched the National Archives in Washington, DC (such as Military Records and the Kansas Claims), the Connecticut Historical Society, the Connecticut State Library, Godfrey Library along with various local libraries.

We heard very little about the Native American background, except a few stories that were passed down by word of mouth. As we began our search for our ancestors, we have been told that Noyes has Native American in the Pierce family line. It has been a hard road of trying to find that ancestor or ancestors through any written record. Many papers from Stonington and Groton were burned or destroyed during the Revolutionary War and the War of 1812. Also, over the years, many personal records which would include personal letters, diaries and possibly accounts books, were either lost or just thrown away. It could take years of searching to try to find even one small link to these ancestors.

We would like to honor our Native American ancestors in what we feel is the real sense of the recognition they deserve. They are very special to us because we know that they are the true founders of this country. They had been here for many, many generations before the white Colonists came to this country. Once the Colonists were here, there were many conflicts between the Colonists and the Natives.

I believe that Noyes' maternal grandmother was born during the early Colonial times of this country, as a Native American. If she could marry into the white world and be accepted, that would guarantee her survival. Of course, she would not be able to mention her background to anyone including her children.

I can prove from the present, which would be Sadie A. Willcox, back, through genealogy, to Noyes's maternal grandmother Hannah Brown who was born in 1779. But beyond that, I do not feel comfortable with what has been written. I assume Hannah Brown's mother could have been anywhere from the age of 15 years and up when Hannah was born. This would make her born about 1755 to 1764. There were still full blood Pequots at this time in Ledyard but very little information about them is available.

We have tried to educate ourselves in many ways of the Native American way of life and cultures. Through places like the Mashantucket Pequot Museum and Research Center (located on the reservation) and attending as many Native American functions as we can.

We have both discussed that we would like to learn more about the customs and ways of our Native American ancestors. To us, it makes more sense to live as a Native American than a white person. We have spent all of our years living in the white man's world and there is a lot of waste, pollution (that we did to ourselves), and stress. It makes sense to us that we must take care of this earth and honor our ancestors who came before us. This is a culture we would both like to be a part of. Noyes has always felt there was something missing in his life, but never knew what it was. He now knows that it is the Native American culture that is missing in his life. He would truly like to be able to learn and practice the Pequot culture.

We have joined the Mashantucket Pequot Museum and Research Center and have tried to get involved with as much as we can. We did a day seminar on clay pipes and firearms. We got so involved that we were truly reluctant to leave. We decided to take Kelsey with us on a tour of the Fort at Mashantucket on the reservation as well. The Fort is an archaeological site they have been exploring for a while. Noyes and I also went on one of their archaeological digs at Randall's Ordinary in North Stonington, Ct. It was a very educational day for us as well as an exciting day. Our site, was filled with various pieces of ceramic, glass, pottery, metal fragments and bone pieces just to name a few of the things we found in the ground that day.

Kim (my daughter) and I went to the American Indian Archaeological Institute in Washington, Ct. This was a group trip, that was offered through the Mashantucket Pequot Museum. That was truly a very gratifying day. We were allowed to tour the Museum and had a lecture on The Medicine Wheel garden. Kim and I both enjoyed it thoroughly.

I have taken seminars on making clay pottery, preserving your family heirlooms, and Native American genealogy. I always come away with a sense of belonging, as well as more knowledgeable on each topic. It also helps me to understand some of the Native American culture.

The Museum is a place where Noyes and I love to go to do research in their library. The atmosphere there is tranquil. The Library has large windows that give you a beautiful view of the surrounding woods, while you can sit on very comfortable chairs and couches. It is a place that we feel right at home in. It is the best place we have found for doing research compared to all the other places we have been. The Museum itself takes you back in time. Their exhibits are informative and help you understand the Native American history of this area. It draws you into the day to day life of a Native American and how they had to survive. It makes you feel like you are part of that history. It helps clear your mind and lets you get away from the troubles of the real world for a few minutes. I used to work at the Mystic Seaport Museum as well. It also takes you back into time. I really loved walking the grounds of the Museum, but I knew they concentrated on living on the seashore rather than inland. Whereas, the Pequot Museum makes me feel more comfortable, because it is more woodland orientated and that is where my roots are.

We give the Mashantucket Pequot Museum and Research

Center a lot of credit for all the work they have done and are currently doing in preserving our past. They have taken the Native American back 2000 years and more. We need more people who are willing to dig into the real past of our ancestors and see how they really lived. They also work on local history as well, with their archeological digs. It helps to put the history of this area back together again, whether it is Native American or White. They show you how the Natives had to live, along with the Colonists role in their lives. It has helped us to piece together some of our past as well.

We have been going to Schemitzun for the last four years. We love to go through the booths and talk with other Natives from around the country. They have always accepted Noyes and myself as one of them and we have discussed some of their customs with them.

Noyes has made many walking sticks, canes and hatchets. He feels honored that he could give his walking sticks to many Native American people. He has talked to other Native Americans about how they make many of their crafts. The Native Americans he has met, has always been eager to talk about their crafts. They feel that the traditional way these items are made are important to pass down to future generations. Many traditions have been lost, so it is important to pass down anything whether it is a flute, walking stick or ceremonial dance.

Many years ago, Noyes and I went to a Mohegan Powwow at the KOA Campground in Old Mystic, Ct. That was the first time we had ever been to one. We had always wanted to go to one but never had the opportunity to do so. We wandered around looking at the crafts, when we finally came to the Sacred Circle. As we watched and listened to the drummers and dancers, we both had a feeling of belonging and peace. We really felt that they truly understood the meaning of life. It is not just for the taking, it is for the giving back as well. It was a very moving experience for both of us. We left there feeling an inner peace we had never known before and it was truly an inspirational experience.

That same year, I was working on Route 49 in North Stonington. Noyes came to have lunch with me. On his way, he noticed that the Pawcatuck Eastern Pequots were setting up for their Annual Powwow. He said he wanted to stop and see if they needed a hand setting up and I told him to stop and see. He has volunteered every year since then doing various jobs for them before, during and after the Pow Wow. That friendship has grown over the years between Noyes and the Grand Chief Sachem, James L. Williams.[57]

I have volunteered in the Groton office, during their recognition process. Over the course of the last six years, while I was doing my own research, if I found anything that pertained to Native American, I would take it to the Paucatuck Pequot office. Noyes and I have met many other Natives, historians and genealogists through the Paucatucks.

At the Ninth Annual Paucatuck Powwow, Noyes and Kim got a chance to dance in the dance called "the Friendship Dance". That is where a Native American can ask anyone to dance inside the circle. Noyes and Kim were both asked to dance. They both accepted and entered the circle. It is a great honor to be asked. After the Native Americans have made their choices, the announcer says that anyone who would like to dance may join in. Noyes and Kim agreed that it was a truly moving experience for them.

Noyes and Kim's memories from October 1999: [58]

> "*I was going to the Paucatuck PowWow to volunteer as I normally do. Only this year I brought Kayla, my granddaughter, with me today so Kim could go to work. I always did various duties, such as trash, help with the food, help with the set up of the Sacred Circle and cook tents and their craft booth, or anything else that needed to be done to get ready for the opening.*
>
> *When I could get a break, I would watch their opening ceremonies and any of the other ceremonies that I could get a*

chance to see. I really enjoyed watching the ceremonies that are performed in the Sacred Circle.

When I had a free moment, I would go through some of the booths to see all the Native American crafts that was on display. This was when I would get a chance to talk to some of the Native Crafters about their items on how they are made.

It was late afternoon. I was expecting my daughter, Kim, to come and get Kayla. When she got there, she was in a pretty bad mood. She had a bad day at work, everything had gone wrong for her all day. I was in a good frame of mind. So, I just listened. Kayla had gotten involved with some of our Paucatuck Pequot friends granddaughters. The girls were going around looking at the booths. Then they were playing in the teepee that had been set up. They were really having a great time.

While we were keeping an eye on the kids, Kim and I were standing at the entrance to the Sacred Circle where the Closing Ceremonies were taking place. We tried to watch the Closing Ceremonies inside the Sacred Circle as well as watch the girls. Kim was still grumping about what a bad day she had. Telling me about everything that went wrong. The Closing Ceremonies got over and they were about to start the Friendship Dance in the Circle. Kim and I were talking to a few of the Paucatuck Pequots as they came out of the Sacred Circle.

The Friendship Dance is a dance of friendship between the Native American and their guests. This is one dance that anyone is allowed to come into the Sacred Circle and dance. A Native American can ask a guest of their choice if they want to come into the Circle and dance. Of course, we've heard that if you refuse to dance it brings bad luck. I was ***not*** *going to refuse if I was asked.*

They announced that The Friendship Dance was going to start and all of the sudden an elderly Native women came out and asked me if I would dance with her. It totally shocked me.

I never expected anyone to ask me. She extended her arm and I accepted. I looked over at Kim and gave her a look of joy as we headed into the Sacred Circle. As we were going into the circle I was telling her that I really don't know a lot of the steps. She said, "don't even worry about it. I will take you by the hand and lead you through the whole thing." That gave me a little confidence. The elderly Native American woman and I entered the circle.

I was watching for Kim trying to pinpoint her in the crowd. At the same time, I was trying to listen to the elderly woman who asked me to dance. Then all of the sudden, I looked across the circle and here is Kim. As soon as I saw who she was with, I was even more excited. The Male Head Dancer of the Powwow had asked her to dance. I knew she did not realize who he was. I was so happy for her. Even though she did not realize who she was dancing with, she had a grin ear to ear. She looked so happy. Kim looked up and saw me at the same moment. When our eyes met, you could see the excitement in each of us. Then everyone was waiting for the drums to begin.

During some of the earlier ceremonies, the announcer was saying they did not want pictures taken of the Dancers while they were in the Sacred Circle during the ceremonies. The purpose of the Sacred Circle is for the Spirits of your Ancestors to feel that they are welcomed to come down and dance with you. If cameras are taking pictures the Spirits will leave.

If you follow the beat of the drums during the Friendship Dance, it consumes you and helps you follow your partner easier. As the woman had told me, she led me through all the steps. It came pretty easy once we got started. After we were into the dance itself, I was thinking about what the announcer had said earlier. I said, "Wow, I wonder if the Spirits from my Elders are here dancing. It feels like they are ***really*** *here with me." If my Ancestors Spirits were there that very moment, I hope they felt what I was feeling.*

Once I started to dance, it felt like nothing was beyond this

Sacred Circle. Everything outside that Circle was blurred as if you lost some of your vision. The only thing you were aware of, was what was taking place inside that Circle. All I felt was tranquillity, but still excited at the same time. It has been very hard to explain the feeling you get while you are dancing. I have never felt anything like this in my life. I was hoping that Friendship Dance would never end. I wanted it to go on forever and ever.

When the drums stopped we exited. I was anxious to talk to Kim about this experience. When Kim came out, she looked extremely excited. I was pretty darn excited myself. We had a lot to discuss about our feelings. I was trying to ask her how she felt when she was dancing. I wanted to see if she had the same reaction I did to this experience. I asked, "Did you feel like nothing mattered outside the circle while you were dancing." She said, "Yes, Dad I did. It did feel like that to me. My body was there but my mind wasn't. It took me into a different dimension, whether it was spiritual or not, I do not know. The sound of the beating drum drew me deep into the moment. The constant beat of the drums keeps your mind in the center of the ring. Your whole focus is on what you are doing and not your surroundings. It seemed like everything on earth was taken place in that circle at that time."

I asked Kim, "Do you realize who you were dancing with?" She said, "No, who was he?" I replied that, "he was the Chief of the Lakota Sioux Tribe and the Male Head Dancer at the Powwow." She was shocked that a Chief had asked her. She felt very honored that he had chosen her.

It was amazing to see Kim, go from such a bad mood, to walking on clouds. Kim was still excited when she stopped back at our house, later that day. Shirley had gotten home from work and could not believe the change in her. The last time Shirley had seen Kim, Kim was really grumpy. Both Kim and myself had that tranquil feeling for a long time after the dance was over.

Kim said that she wishes she could go and dance a couple times a week never mind maybe once in her lifetime. I feel the same way. This is something that both Kim and I feel should be done much more often than it is done. It gives you a whole different feeling than what you are used to experiencing. It was so exciting to be able to participate in such a moving tradition. You felt like you were among a lot of friends when you were dancing. I still believe to this day, that there should be more events like this, so we could be more involved with dancing in the Sacred Circle and all the other traditions that go along with it. Kim and I have both talked often about how amazing it was after we danced that day."

Over the last few years, Noyes wanted to teach our granddaughters about some of the Native American customs he has learned about. He had read about how Native Americans honor the earth and everything it provides for us. Also, that we should give back to Mother Earth for anything we take from her. If you give back to Mother Earth, she will provide for you.

Noyes thought the following two journeys may be a good way to introduce Kayla and Kelsey, our two granddaughters, into some of the customs of the Native American.

One winter day, when both Kayla and Kelsey were visiting at our house, Noyes decided to take them for a walk in our woods next to our house, to see if they could find some deer tracks. The girls were probably about four or five years old at that time:

"I knew that the snow would make it much easier for the girls to follow any tracks we found. Not far from our house, I spotted the first set of deer tracks. We had a good discussion on how to determine which way the animal you are tracking was heading and where they had come from. I showed the girls what type of tracks the deer made and how to identify them. I told them, that it would be their job to follow the tracks in the snow and see where it leads us. Both girls were excited

that they were going to lead the way and follow the tracks. They did not care where it took us. Along the way, we saw many different types of tracks, from squirrels to birds along with the deer tracks we were following.

Suddenly they came upon some deer feces. They did not know what it was, so I explained that it was deer "poop". They later came across some rabbit poop, which, again, the girls spotted first. That was my chance to show them the difference between the two feces, as well as, show them how to identify rabbit tracks. The rabbit feces is a lot smaller, where as the deer feces was much larger.

When we were following the deer tracks, we came upon a spot where a raccoon had fought for his life. There was fur all over the snow and tracks of many in this spot. But you could see another set of tracks which was not the raccoons tracks. After I studied them for a while, they looked like they were from a coyote. Which would make sense, after witnessing the remains of the raccoon. I told the girls this raccoon must have been sick or old, because he would of never been caught out in the open like this.

By this time, the girls were cold and wanted to go back home. To this day Kelsey still brings up that day and how we tracked the deer in the woods."

Noyes decided to take them on a hike to Lantern Hill in North Stonington, Ct. He has taken Kelsey up the hill three times and he has taken Kayla up the hill twice. The last time they went was in late autumn of 2003.

Lantern Hill is the highest point in our area. When you reach the top, you can see Long Island Sound on a clear day. It is a special place for Noyes and myself for various reasons. The Silica Mine was located next to Lantern Hill. Both of our fathers worked there before they died. Noyes spent some of his childhood visiting relatives who lived on Wintechog Hill Road, which borders the backside of Lantern Hill. If you want to walk to the top of the hill, you have to start from Wintechog Hill Road on the pathway there. The following would be a typical day at the top of Lantern Hill with Kayla and Kelsey:

"I have told my granddaughters, Kayla and Kelsey. that once you are at the top of the hill and make a sacred circle, you can make a wish and someday it may come true. Of course the girls are anxious to go. I try to make it an adventure, but also to relate some Native American traditions to them, while we journey up and back. Along the way, I point out different animal tracks and show them how to identify the tracks. I also show them how to identify some of the fauna of the area. Sometimes, we can see the hawks flying below us. We stood silent and watched them fly. I remind them to keep their eyes and ears open for different sights and sounds. There is a lot of activity in nature that we all take for granted. Most human beings can walk through this habitat and not even notice it. You have to take the time to be aware of your surroundings.

We have a ritual we do each time. I will have them find a stone or small rock and tell them to set the rock on the ground and roll it down the hill. They need to listen very closely and count the number of times the rock makes contact with the earth, before it finishes its journey to the bottom of the hill. On the average, people think you just throw a rock down a hill and listen for its final impact. The stone has its own story to tell from the beginning of the roll until the final impact. You can tell what the rock saw on the way down, by the different sounds it makes when it comes in contact with different objects.

When we reach the crest of the hill, we decide to have our snacks and drinks we carried up with us. After we are finished with our little break, Kayla and Kelsey wanted to make the Sacred Circle. Kayla and Kelsey knew when it was done they could make their wishes. We gathered up stones and we also found some moss and made a circle from them. We sat in the circle in total silence. I explain to them, that before you make your wish, you give thanks to the four-corners of the earth (North, South, East, and West). Then you can make your wish. I also, told them, that your wishes could come true anytime during your life, it may not happen right away. Kayla and Kelsey are eight years old, they assume everything happens within a short span of time. Once you have made your wishes, then you must give back something to the earth. On our way up the hill, I had them collect different items. Kayla had a stick that she had used when we were climbing the hill as her walking stick. She wanted to give this walking stick back to the earth. Kelsey had collected many rocks and stones along the way up. She had trouble deciding which stone, she was going to give. She finally made her decision which stone it would be. They sat their gifts down in the Sacred Circle and we had a few moments of silence, before we made our journey back down the hill. The last time we made this journey, Kayla said on our way back down the hill, "Gramps, one of my wishes has already come true." I never questioned her on her wish, but I could tell that she was very happy that one of her wishes came true."

CHILDHOOD EVENTS

This is one of the memories Noyes has from his childhood, when he, his brothers and sister and parents would visit Harold and Goldie Willcox Robbins[59] and their family. Noyes's mother and father had six children at this time. Harold and Goldie lived on Wintechog Hill Road in North Stonington at this particular time. They were renting from Fred Wright, who owned about 80 acres of land next to the Eastern Pequot Reservation.

"I can remember back to one event, when we were visiting my Aunt Goldie in North Stonington, it was a day like today July 1st, it is hot, hazy and humid. The older boys and myself

were discussing how hot it was. We would do anything to cool off. We decided we wanted to go swimming, so we kept pestering our parents to let us go. We had an aunt who lived on Lantern Hill Road by the dam on Bush Pond. We knew that is where we wanted to go. We knew if we would run across the Eastern Reservation to get to our aunts house, we could be there very quickly.

So we decided to make a bet with our parents that we could beat them over to our Aunts house. We had already planned it out. We would go over across Fred Wrights property to the Eastern Pequot Reservation and then down to Lantern Hill Road by foot. It was a straight route, by the way the crow flies. We knew if you went by automobile, you would have to go all the way down Wintechog Hill Road to Route 2 and pick up Lantern Hill Road and then down to Bush Pond. But if you went the way the crow flies, like the way we were going, across the Eastern Pequot Reservation, you could get there much quicker.

Our parents did go along with it. We, boys, were ready to go. We were discussing between ourselves, "They think they are going to beat us to Bush Pond, we will see."

Once we got going, it was like a running race, wanting to see which one of us was going to get there first and who could run the fastest. It would be a game we would play in hopes that we would beat the parents to Lantern Hill. Looking back today, I bet there wasn't an animal left in the woods within a mile, with all the noise we were making.

So we would start out running from my Aunts house, across Fred Wrights property to where it comes to Mr. Roberts house. Right beside Mr. Roberts was the entrance going down on to the Eastern Pequot Reservation. This entrance was more like a Pentway. You could drive down quite easily. It was perfectly fine, no rocks, no stumps, there were a few pieces of brush that grew up through it over the years. Then we would come down to an abandoned house and just past this house you would reach a brook. We followed the brook down the pentway, which led down to Lantern Hill Road. It only took minutes at a fast pace to reach there. We would be dodging tree limbs and running as fast as we could down through the path. We came out at Lantern Hill Road just to the right of the brook, at the other entrance to the Eastern Pequot Reservation. Then we would turn left on Lantern Hill Road and we'd race down to the bridge. The bridge is where the water from Long Pond and Bush Pond connects. We would hang out there for a short time. Then we would continue on our way down the street to our aunts. You know what, we always seemed to beat our parents over there because they had to get the younger kids of the family ready and get them all in the cars.

Looking back on those times now, those were exciting times for us as kids. While running through the woods, it was like being a part of nature. This was just one of the many instances that I experienced as a child. I spent more time in the woods than I did in our own yard."

See the map on the next page, this will help show you the route the boys took.

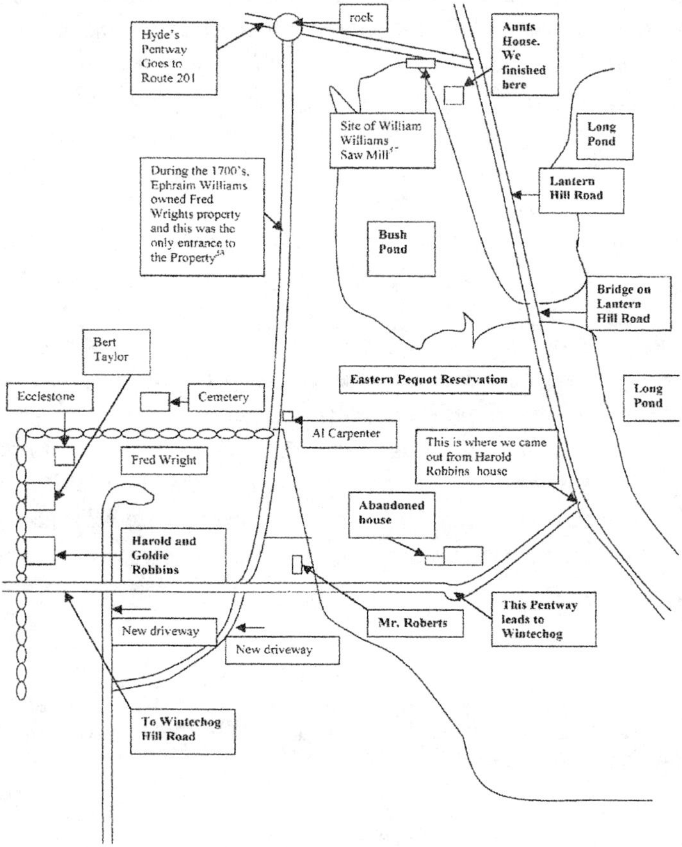

The above map was drawn by Shirley Greene with the help of Noyes Greene

To help you see the footnote numbers better, they are the following numbers:

[60] During the 1700's Ephraim Williams owned Fred Wright's property…

[61] Site of William Williams Saw Mill

The next event is about one Indian man, named Al Carpenter, Noyes knew when he was growing up. Al and his wife lived on the Eastern Pequot Reservation off of Wintechog Hill Road in North Stonington.

"When you have six children to feed, it could get very costly feeding everyone. So my Dad would raise pigs and chickens (for meat and eggs) for food. There was this one pig, a male pig, he was about two years old. This pig got so huge to the point where we used to ride him when we were kids. Sometimes two of us would ride him at one time.

It was during the winter months, when it came to a point that Dad knew the time had come to butcher the pig. He was hesitant about telling us kids, but he knew he had to. We looked at this pig as a pet, not as food. We knew that the pig was raised for food and not as a pet, but you become attached to animals just the same. Dad told us, "We are going to butcher this pig to eat. It is way over due."

My Dad and my Uncle Harold Robbins and Al Carpenter butchered together on occasion. My Dad asked my uncle and Al to help him with this pig. Al Carpenter had been a butcher most of his life, so he knew how to make the cuts of pork. They did it at our house on Center Groton Road in Ledyard.

After much effort, they got the pig down where they were going to butcher him. After they finished, they hung him up in a tree. Down the hill from our house it was stony, there was a good tree with an arch in it where they could hang the pig on a tackle block. They got him butchered and got him cut in half. My Dad, my Uncle Harold and Al decided to lower half the pig down. Let's face it, this was a big pig. Half of this pig weighed a lot dressed out. They let him down on a big wheelbarrow we had.

My uncle and my Dad decided they were going to push the wheelbarrow up around the rocks. One was pushing the wheelbarrow and the other one was on the front of the wheelbarrow pulling, trying to guide it and keep it so it didn't tip over. They had to guide it up and around the rocks.

Al called to them and said "Hey, I'll tell you what you guys, stop right there and take a break and come on back here. Lower this other half down on my shoulder and I will carry him." They bickered back and forth, "Al you can't do that. That half is too heavy, it is going to drop you to your knees," said my Dad and Uncle. "I am telling you, put this thing on my shoulder. I am taking him up the hill," said Al Carpenter.

They decided to put that half of the pig on Al's shoulder. Al bent his back and shoulders forward and let that pig lay right down across the side of his head on his shoulder. And as soon as they let the pig off the hook, Al headed for the house. That was probably a good 150 feet he had to go up a hill. But he had to walk around the rocks and through brush.

As a child, I could hardly believe my eyes. I did not think anyone could have been strong enough to put that pig on his shoulder and carry it as well. What Al Carpenter reminds me of, is the song Big Bad John, he was in a mine and he held the mine shaft up while the other people got out of the mine

He was a huge man to me as a kid. He was a man of very few words. But when he spoke, what few words he did speak, you had to listen, because that was all you were going to get.

He had this pig on his shoulder and up over the hill he went. He was bent forward because he was going up a hill and he was reaching forward with his hands pulling at brush or small trees, helping himself up and over the hill. And after he reached the driveway where it was level he leveled himself up and went up to where Mom was waiting.

Dad had laid out tables with plywood on it so they could section out the different cuts of meat. Mom saw Al coming across the driveway and she didn't expect anyone to come up that quick with the pig. She said, "Gee wait a minute Al, I got to lay this wax paper down first." So Al stood there, patient as all can be, with the half of pig laying across his shoulder. Mom said, "all right you can lay it down here." He laid that pig down just as soft as can be on that plywood. Mom tried to help a little bit, but all she could do was get out the way to be truthful.

And then he went down to see how my Dad and uncle were doing. He was just standing there shaking his head, with a smile on his face. He was watching them come up with the wheelbarrow pushing and pulling trying to avoid the rocks. They did look comical trying to maneuver that wheelbarrow with the other half of the pig in it. When they got up by the driveway Al helped them pull it across to the other side and put the other half up on the tables.

Years later as I think about Al Carpenter, he was what I, as a child, thought of as a Pequot Indian. He was a very tall man and was as strong as an ox, which could be very intimidating to most people. But there was another side to him that you did not expect from a man of his size. He had a friendly and helpful way about himself and was very soft spoken. But Al would not hesitate to help others in need. If you told him to meet you at 7 am, you could set your clock by him."

CHAPTER 4

SADIE AVIS WILLCOX GREENE

Generation No. 2

Sadie Avis Willcox was born June 05, 1924 in Ledyard, Ct. [62] She died April 16, 1992 at the L&M Hospital, New London, Ct. [63] She was the daughter of **Ray Ernest Willcox** and **Mary Elvira Pierce**.

George Frances Greene, Jr. was born September 05, 1919 in East Lyme, Ct. [64] He died October 06, 1960 in Uncas on the Thames Hospital, Norwich, Ct. [65] He was the son of **Claude George Frances Greene** and **Henrietta Rowley**. He married **Sadie Avis Willcox** on July 18, 1942 in Groton, Ct. [66]

George F. Greene

Sadie A. Willcox

Children of George Greene and Sadie Willcox are:

1. Private
2. **Noyes Palmer Greene**
3. Private
4. Private
5. **Sadie Louise Greene**[67]
6. Private

Sadie also had two more children after the death of George Greene.

1. Private
2. Private

SADIE WILLCOX'S CHILDHOOD

Sadie was always proud of the fact that she was born and raised in Ledyard. She was born in the Burns house on Shewville Road in Ledyard, Ct. (see #2 on the map on page 25). The Burns house burned sometime after Sadie was born. The Mashantucket Pequots bought that property back years later. She always told of her other Grandmothers who were born on Iron Street and other areas of Town, but she felt proud that three generations in a row were born on Shewville Road. Most all of her children were born in a hospital, except her daughter, Sadie Louise Greene[68], who was born in the Williams house (Paul Massey owned it at the time George and Sadie lived there) on Shewville Road, Ledyard (see #1 on page 25). Her mother, Mary Elvira Pierce was born on Hoot Owl Hill, which is on the Morgan Farm, (see #3 on page 25).

Sadie was raised on Gallup Hill Road behind where the current Ledyard High School is today. Sadie went to school at the Gallup Hill School (see #12 on page 25). Sadie always talked about helping her father with the chores and the animals. Even as a child she liked being outside and helping the man of the house. She felt more comfortable with a shovel in her hands than being in a dress doing housework.

When Noyes was a child, Sadie would take her children to help her father when he would have to hay. One of Noyes's memories of what they had to do:

> *"My grandfather Willcox had a lot that he used to hay in West Mystic. My grandfather had an old flatbed truck, which he used for hauling the hay. After the hay was cut, it had to be tethered (or turned) which my mother liked to do. My*

grandfather had a horse drawn tether he used, but because of rocks in the fields, some had to be done by hand. When it was dry enough, he would bring the truck up. Someone needed to be on the truck to position the hay, so the hay stayed on the truck on the trip home. Everyone else was on the ground pitching the hay onto the truck. My mother would be right along with everyone else pitching the hay. You could tell she had done this many times previous to this, because she could tell you what the next step was and how to do it. During the haying season, this became a ritual for our family."

She also helped her Grandmother Mary Main Pierce with canning and housework. Her Grandmother, at that time, lived near Ledyard Center. I believe Sadie could have learned some of her home remedies from Mary Pierce.

SADIE WILLCOX MARRIED LIFE

After she married George Greene, they lived in various places. They lived in the Williams house on Shewville Road for the early years of Noyes's childhood. These are Noyes's memories of living on Shewville Road:

"While we lived there, I can remember one of the times my mother decided to take us for a walk. We almost never took walks on the road, even though in those days there were very few cars on the road. She always liked to take us into the woods for nature walks. This particular day, we were walking up a path. We didn't make it very far away from the house before we came upon a huge snake hanging from the trees. It was draped from one tree to another tree across the path we needed to take. As soon as she saw the size of this snake, she turned us around and went back to the house. She kept saying she had never seen such a huge snake like this one in her life. This is one snake she could not identify because of the coloring

and length and width. Sadie had never feared snakes up to this point. She felt it was better to leave the area then try to confront this snake.

She also told us that, you should not kill a black snake because they keep your property free of rodents.

She also told her children many times, while in the woods, if you smell the scent of cucumbers, get out of there quickly because there is a red snake or copper head in the close vicinity. Red snakes or copperheads are in the Lantern Hill area of Ledyard. They can be found as far away as Shewville Road and also along Indiantown Road."

George and Sadie bought property from her Uncle Chester Z. Pierce on Center Groton Road in Ledyard, Ct. in 1953.[69] (See #16 on page 24) Sadie spent the majority of her adult life on this property. Sadie and George lived a simple life. They started out with no running water or electricity. Sadie lived most of her life without the modern comforts that other people had. She never complained. She did have her gas range and an inside bathroom (after George died) and she was happy with that. She loved washing up in her little pond in the summer months. She always had a kettle of water on the stove heated for various uses, cooking, coffee, and for doing dishes. Living without electricity was second nature for her. She could still do all her daily chores whether there was electricity and running water or not. People today think that it was a hard life to live like that, but their family was happy.

During Thanksgiving, she would pluck turkeys at Charles Lamphere's farm (which is where Randall Holdridge lived), for extra money. During May and June, she picked strawberries for Holdridge Farm Nursery here in Ledyard.

Sadie was right at home being outdoors most of the time. She loved her gardens and spent hours in her gardens, both vegetable and flower. As you can see from Noyes memories about butchering the pig and haying with her father, Sadie was involved with what women considered at the time as mans work.

She also spent many years doing genealogy on the Main family. She knew a lot of information on the Main line. When I worked at the Town Hall, Town Clerks office, in Stonington in 1968, Sadie came in for information on the Maine line. When Noyes introduced me to her when we first met, that was the first thing she said to me. That she still had the receipt that I made out for the vital records she needed that day in Stonington. She was the first to tell me that Noyes and I were related through the Holdridge line. She told me it goes back many generations. She said "that her ancestral grandmother Annis Holdridge and my ancestral grandfather Randall Holdridge were brother and sister."

She also took the time to find the many cemeteries where her ancestors and George Greene's ancestors were buried. When we first started doing our research, the cemeteries are one of the first places we looked. The cemeteries in Ledyard, we already knew about, but Sadie had shown us cemeteries in Lebanon as well. Lebanon was our starting point for the Greene genealogy. Noyes also remembered going to Cedar Grove Cemetery as a child, which lead us deeper into the Greene side of his family.

Sadie had a keen sense of things around her. She knew when someone was at her home by the tire tracks in the driveway or if someone had touched her door on her house a certain way. She was always aware of things going on around her, whether she was present or not. For instance, one night she was in bed and said she could smell a cigar burning outside the windows of the house. She got out of bed and took the shotgun outside. She shot a few rounds into the air and said, "that will take care of that".

Noyes told me that his Mom was really fun to be around when she was outside showing off her plants or garden. No matter what question you asked her about plant life, she always had the right answer. She could come as close as anybody he knew, as far as naming just about any plant on the face of this earth. I don't care if it was vegetable, fruit, weed or tree. She also knew if it had any uses for medicinal purposes. She knew what could be eaten and what could not be eaten. She knew which things could be turned into jams, jellies, wines, or syrup, which could be eaten in salads or used as spices.

Noyes is allergic to bee stings. When we were building our house here, he got stung one day. I went to Sadies house (because we built our house next to her house) and asked, her if she knew of anything we could use to stop the swelling. She took me on a small hill near our house and showed me what she called the medicine plant. She picked a few branches off the little bush and told me to boil them in water for a few minutes. Then take the liquid and put it on the bee sting. We tried it and it worked. We have used that remedy ever since. In fact, our son still uses that remedy today whenever he gets a bee sting.

Sadie took over the Brown, Peckham, Main Cemetery Association, after her mother passed away. Sadie was responsible for the mowing and upkeep of the cemetery. As well as the contact person for anyone who wanted to be buried there. She had to make arrangements for the graves to be dug. She took pride in the cemetery and she was responsible for identifying some of the graves that never had any gravestones put on them. She grew concerned that the cemetery was becoming full. There was not going to be enough space for future generation to be buried there. She tried to get more land for expansion for the cemetery. So, she petitioned to the Town of Ledyard for more land to be turned over to the Cemetery Association, but the Town of Ledyard did not agree. The cemetery borders land owned by the Town of Ledyard. The Up and Down Sawmill is directly behind the cemetery.

There was also a Family Reunion that Mary Wilcox planned every year called the Main Brown Reunion. After Mary passed away, Sadie also took on that responsibility. From what I have been told and the newspaper articles I have read, this Main Brown Reunion started with descendants of George Park Main and Sarah Eliza Brown. The people that attended were always offspring from these two people. This was an occasion when everyone could get together and go over genealogy and discuss the Brown Peckham Main Cemetery and all other business. Officers were elected the day of the Reunion. They would hold the position they were elected for until the next Reunion.

The Ledyard Grange, which Sadie belonged to, had a booth set up each year at the Ledyard Fair to sell chowder. For many years, Sadie helped make the well-known, New England clam chowder, which was sold there. The chowder was clear broth, which many people from this area think of as **real** Clam Chowder. Many people made a special trip to the fair just to get a "bowl of chowder". Sadie also made this same chowder for the Main Brown Reunion along with her wonderful baked beans that everyone enjoyed.

George and Sadie are buried in the Brown Peckham Main Cemetery on Iron Street in Ledyard, Ct (see #34 on page 25).

CHAPTER 5

MARY ELVIRA PIERCE/WILLCOX

Generation No. 3

Mary Elvira Pierce was born September 18, 1900 in Ledyard, Ct. [70] She died on May 17, 1974 in Putnam, Ct. [71] She was the daughter of **Chester Latham Pierce** and **Mary Stanton Main**.

Ray Ernest Willcox was born June 29, 1893 in Ledyard, Ct. [72] He died January 09, 1951 in New London, Ct. [73] He was the son of **Raymond Willcox** and **Phebe E. Waite**. He married **Mary Elvira Pierce** on September 30, 1916 in Ledyard, Ct. [74]

Ray Ernest Willcox Mary Elvira Pierce
Courtesy of Goldie Ada Willcox Collins Robbins[75]

Children of Ray Willcox and Mary Pierce are:

1. Private
2. Private

3. Sadie Avis Willcox was born June 05, 1924 in Ledyard, Ct. She died April 16, 1992 in L&M Hospital, New London, Ct. She married George Frances Greene, Jr. on July 18, 1942 in Groton, Ct. They are buried in the Brown, Peckham Main Cemetery, Ledyard, Ct.

4. Goldie Ada Willcox married (1) Noyes Talcott Collins December 6, 1941 in Ledyard, Ct by Rev. Chase, married (2)

Harold Avery Robbins August 3, 1945, Old Mystic Village Green, Groton, Ct[76]

5. **Infant Son Willcox** was born November 01, 1927[77] and he died in 1927.[78] He is buried in the Brown, Peckham Main Cemetery, Ledyard, Ct

6. Private

7. Private

8. **Jerry Edmund Willcox** was born May 12, 1932[79] and he died in 1932.[80] He is buried in the Brown Peckham Main Cemetery, Ledyard, Ct

9. Private

MARY ELVIRA PIERCE

Mary Elvira Pierce was born on Hoot Owl Hill in Ledyard (see #3 on page 25), which is now part of the Morgan Farm. Stephen Caswell owned the property when she was born[81]. Shortly after she was born, her parents moved to Center Groton Road in Ledyard Center. So she grew up there. She went to school at the Ledyard Center School (see #13 on page 24)

She and Ray Ernest Willcox lived on Gallup Hill Road across from the High School (see #17 on page 25). Mary knew just about everyone in Ledyard. She was well liked by everyone. Mary, also known as Vi, always had people at her house. She loved to sit and chat and talk about everything from genealogy to what was going on in Town.

She was known as a midwife in her early years. Sadie told me when Mary and Ray lived in Old Mystic, my Grandmother Holdridge helped Mary with the delivery of Sadies sister. Mary repaid her by helping my Grandmother deliver some of her children as well. Mary also helped her daughter, Sadie, with the delivery of Sadie Louise Greene, when she was born on Shewville Road in Ledyard.

Mary and Ray started out without any running water and electricity. As time went on, he wired the house for electricity and installed inside plumbing. Up to that point, they were using an outhouse or privy. Once the plumbing was done, the privy was still used, up until the time when Mary died.

Mary and Ray had an old kitchen wood stove right up until the time she died. She always kept flat irons on the top of the stove for ironing. If you kept the irons warm on top of the stove, you could iron any time and you would not have do it all in one day. In those days, washing clothes and ironing them could and usually did take a whole day to do each process. Most women used scrub boards to wash their clothes and would rinse them in a different sink. After which, they would hang them on a clothesline to dry.

Mary was the typical farmers' wife. She loved going down to the barn and helping with the chores. She had a vegetable garden and they also had fruit trees. She knew how to can fruits and vegetables. She could make her own butter, cheese, whipped cream, cottage cheese and ice cream from milk. She always had hams hanging in her cellar to cure. She made her own lard. She passed many of these traditions down to her daughters.

She also helped Ray when it was haying season. Once the hay was on the truck and you were back at the barn, you would fill the loft in the barn. The excess hay would go outside on boards that were laid on the ground. Once the haystack got too high on the boards, you would need someone on top of the haystack with a pitchfork to take the hay off the pitchfork from the person below. Ray made a wooden ladder so you could get to the top of the haystack. You would set the ladder up against the haystack and climb to the top. Mary used this ladder often. When she reached the top of the pile, she would take the hay from the person below passing it up with a pitchfork. She would arrange the hay uniformly around the top of the stack so it would not tip over. Once you had finished, a canvas was placed over the stack to keep the weather from molding the hay.

Mary Pierce Willcox

Ray E. Willcox

Courtesy of Goldie Ada Willcox Collins Robbins[82]

In Mary's later years, she worked for Dew Drop Inn in North Stonington. She made their pies for them as well as cooked their dinners. She was well known for her pies. She always used lard not shortening for her crust. The crust would melt in your mouth. To this day, Noyes still has people approach him and tell him how much they loved her pies she made when she was working at Dew Drop.

Mary kept a black Doctors satchel with all of her important papers, such as personal letters, genealogy papers, newspaper clippings and family pictures in it. Often she would be having a conversation with someone that was visiting her. They could be discussing any topic, such as where someone lived, or when a particular person died. If they did not agree on it, she would go into the satchel and pull out the right paperwork to prove who was right. Somctimcs when she was asked a specific question about someone and she wasn't sure about it, she would search her satchel, until she found the answer she was looking for. She was the only one who could put her hands in that bag. When Noyes was a child, there were a few times he had tried to get something from inside that bag and she would hit his hands hard. All the children learned very early that this bag was something that no one touched but Mary. The old Doctors satchel (especially the big ones) would fold out on the top to either side. You were able to see everything in the top compartments as well as down to the bottom of the bag. The top two sides had smaller compartments for bandages, needles, swabs, pills, etc. The bottom of the satchel was for the bigger items such as stethoscopes, etc.

Mary had to have learned some of her remedies from her mother Mary Main Pierce. Many of these remedies were passed down to each generation. Some of her remedies that Noyes can remember are:

> *"I had a lot of earaches when I was young. Mary told my mother to use urine in my ear for the earache. The warmth from the urine soothes the ear and helps fight the infection. But I never let my mom use this remedy.*
>
> *I also had acme as a teenager. Again, Mary told my mother to have me eat a cake of yeast once a day.*
>
> *I am also allergic to bee stings. I swell very badly in a short span of time once I am bitten. Mary told my mother to use the medicine plant. It helps relieve the sting and stops the swelling. This really works.*
>
> *In the spring and summer, my mother used dandelions in salads or just boiled them like spinach and that would be part of our dinner.*
>
> *Also, dandelions were used for dandelion wine, which was rank by the grownups only. It was considered a good spring tonic to help clean your system of bad toxins that accumulated over the winter months.*
>
> *If you had warts, Mary's remedy was to take a* <u>*dried*</u> *kidney bean, split it in half, rub on wart and throw over your shoulder. You were not supposed to see where the kidney bean landed. This was supposed to make the wart go away and from what I was told it worked.*
>
> *Use a mixture of tar and kerosene and apply to bald spot on your head. One of my brothers had a good-sized bald spot*

on his head when he was very young. My mother called Mary and she told mom to use the above remedy and it would go away. It really worked, within a short period of time probably a month or two, the hair had grown completely back."

Mary never drove a car in her entire life. She had to rely on other people, particularly her children to drive her where she needed to go. If you were in the car with her, you would always get a history lesson on the area you were passing by. She knew where people lived and where they were born, just by seeing the property. As a child, you would look out the window of the car to see what she was talking about and there was nothing there. You may see an old cellar hole, or an old field that had grown back in.

Noyes remembers one time when his mother, Sadie Greene, took her mother Mary Willcox and Sadies kids for a ride:

"As we were driving down Shewville Road heading to Route 2, my Grandmother said, "We called that Wish Mountain when I was a child. That is where Indian couples would go when they decided to make a commitment to each other." (see #44 on page 25)

If you go down Shewville Road on the right was the Flower Cottage[83] (see # 33 on page 25), go past the Cottage and over the bumps in the road. Looking to your right there is a tall hill there. It is before you get to Pequot Trail and Silas Deane Road. It is very rocky.

I believe Mary heard this story from either her parents or her Grandparents or Jane Durfee or Martha Langevin. Her parents, Chester and Mary Pierce, lived next to Martha and Napoleon Langevin according to the 1920 Census for Ledyard, Ct. Chester and Mary lived on Center Groton Road in Ledyard Center (see page 84).

"Jane Wheeler married John Noyes Hoxie and Frederick B. Durfee. Jane had only one child Martha Ann Hoxie. Martha Hoxie married Cyrus George and Napolean Langevin.[84]"

Martha Langevin was listed as a Pequot Indian on the 1900 and 1910 Census for Ledyard.[85] Mary's Grandparents, George and Sarah E. Main, lived next to Fred and Jane Durfee on the same Census, but they lived on Shewville Road at that time.[86] Jane was also listed on the 1900 and 1910 Census as being a Pequot Indian.[87]

If Mary heard this story from her Grandmother, Sarah E. Main, could it be that Sarahs Grandmother, Hannah Brown, and Grandfather, Nathan Holdridge, went there when they made the commitment to each other? Nathan lived on the eastern border of the Mashantucket Reservation at that time with his father Phinehas Holdridge. Or is it possible Sarah's parents, Avery W. Brown took Annis Holdridge there to ask her to marry him? We will never know for sure.

Another way Mary could have heard this story, possibly through Jane Durfee. Jane could have told this story to either Sarah or Mary when Jane and Fred lived next door to George P. and Sarah Main. Fred and Jane Durfee had to be living in the Flower Cottage at this time. If you are at the Flower Cottage, you can see Wish Mountain very easily. Or did Mary hear this story from her mother, Mary Pierce who heard this from Martha Langevin, when Martha and Napolean lived next door to Chester and Mary Pierce on Center Groton Road in 1920.

Mary always enjoyed going to the Main Brown Reunion. The Main Brown Reunion is more than just a reunion of family members. They have yearly meetings along with elections for officers, such as president, vice president, secretary and treasurer. Anyone who attends the Reunion is allowed to cast a ballot. In her later years, Mary was elected President of the Reunion.

Mary also oversaw the Brown, Peckham Main Cemetery Association. She was responsible for any new burials and the mowing of the cemetery. After her death, her daughter Sadie took over this position.

Mary and Ray Ernest are buried in the Brown, Peckham Main Cemetery on Iron Street in Ledyard, Ct (see #34 on page 25).

RAY WILLCOX

Ray Ernest Willcox was born and raised and Ledyard just off Iron Street at the Willcox Homestead (see #4 on page 25). He was the youngest son of Raymond and Phebe Willcox. He probably went to school at the Shewville Road Schoolhouse (see #14 on page 25)

After he married and was able to buy his own property, Ray raised cows and chickens. He also had horses but they were for working purposes only. Ray used a half acre of land to plant corn at a nearby neighbors, for food for the animals.

Ray Ernest, it is told, did work and visited the Mashantucket Reservation when he was alive. He was friendly with Elizabeth Plouff who lived on the reservation at that time.

Ray could do just about anything he needed to do to make money to support his family. He was a carpenter by trade, but he also did anything he could to make money. He sold birch and witch hazel to the mills. He dug graves and septic systems. He also sold firewood. He built and ran a blacksmith shop on his property on Gallup Hill Road as well.

He bought 1 acre and ¼ acre of land in the Cedar Swamp from Lurie Main in 1949[88]. He would have to go to the cedar swamp in the wintertime because of the quick sand. He would sell the tall cedars for masts for ships. He would cut the birch for the Birch Mill in Preston. I have traced this property back. Lurie inherited it from her father Horace Main[89]. Horace inherited it from his father William Leeds Main[90]. William Leeds Main bought it either during or just after the State of Connecticut sold off 1000 acres of Mashantucket Reservation land in 1855. This property is now surrounded by the Mashantucket Reservation. It is only a small piece, about 1½ acres of land.

He also bought 14 acres on the corner of Indian Town Road and Shewville Road[91] (see #17 on page 25). From this piece, he would get firewood, witch hazel and birch. I believe back in the early 1700's this was a piece of the original Mashantucket Reservation.

On the 1930 Census for Ledyard[92], Ray and Mary lived between James Holdridge and Fred Burton. Mr. Holdridge lived on the corner of Spicer Hill Extension and Gallup Hill Road and Mr. Burton lived in the big house on Gallup Hill just down the street from the High School.

The following story is a story that Noyes was told by one of his uncles about Ray Ernest Willcox. Ray never owned a tractor. He always used horses to pull the logs out of the woods. There are many legends told that the Cedar Swamp had quick sand in it. Many horses supposedly were caught in that quicksand and never got out. Ray knew the dangers of the Cedar Swamp, so he came up with the following idea, which he never lived long enough to see happen:

> *"If you laid logs side by side and end to end into the Cedar Swamp, it would make two tracks, similar to railroad tracks. Ray made up a flat wagon to go on top of the logs, with no tires, just rims. The logs would have to be the same size as the tire rims. Once the wagon is on the tracks, you have a tackle block attached to a tree back into the swamp. The rope from the tackle block is run out of the swamp to where the horses are. The horses will pull the wagon into the swamp, while they are still moving further outside the swamp. When the wagon comes to the tackle block it stops. Then you could put the cedar logs on to the wagon. You would then attach a rope to one end of the wagon and tie the other end to the team of horses. You would have the horses pull the wagon out of the swamp along the tracks.*

This way the horses never enter the Cedar Swamp at all. It would be like a railroad train running on its tracks."

THE "WILLCOX" ANCESTORS

Besides the direct maternal line, this will be the first line I will be discussing that links back to Nathaniel Brown and Deborah Morgan. This line goes back through the males until it comes to Robert Willcox and Deborah Brown. Deborah Brown was the daughter of Nathaniel and Deborah Brown. I will explain more on this relationship in a later chapter. This section will give you some background information on this line.

RAYMOND AND PHEBE WAITE WILLCOX

Raymond Willcox was the son of **Robert Willcox 3rd**, who married **Mary Ann Reed**. Raymond was born in 1844[93] in Ledyard off Iron Street on the Willcox Homestead (see #5 & #18 on page 25). He was brought up strict Baptist. Raymond had a brother named Robert N. Willcox. He left Connecticut during the Gold Rush years and went to California. He finally settled in Ohio. From the book entitled "Reminiscences"[94] in the section "The California Life, by Robert N. Wilcox", he stated that he was brought up with strict religious beliefs. They were raised as Baptists, but Robert N. Wilcox always questioned the validity of this religion. He turned to Spiritualism once he left Connecticut.

Raymond and **Phebe Elizabeth Waite** were married March 15, 1868[95] in Groton, Ct. Phebe was the daughter of **George Reynolds Waite** and **Hannah P. Brown**. Phebe was born on August 23, 1850[96] in West Greenwich, RI. Her mother died on the same day Phebe was born.[97] Her father, George left West Greenwich, RI and came to Groton and settled at Burnetts Corners.[98] George was a millwright by trade.[99] I believe that Raymond met Phebe at her fathers millwright shop. Raymonds' father may have needed some mill work done on his grist mill and sent him to George Waites shop. When Raymond and Phebe Waite were first married, they lived with Robert and Mary Ann Wilcox at the Wilcox Homestead in Ledyard, Ct.

Phebe Elizabeth Waite

George Reynolds Waite

Courtesy of the Indian Colonial Research Center, Old Mystic, Ct [100]

All of Raymond and Phebes' children were born and raised on the Willcox homestead.

Children of Raymond and Phebe Wilcox were:

1. **George R. Willcox** was born in 1868[101] and died 1886.[102] He is buried in the Brown, Peckham, Main Cemetery
2. **Julia A. Willcox** was born in 1871[103] and died 1904.[104] She is buried in the Union Cemetery, North Stonington, Ct
3. **Jeremiah Willcox** was born in 1872[105] and died 1890.[106] He is buried in the Brown, Peckham, Main Cemetery
4. **Bernice Willcox** was born in 1873[107] and died 1926[108]. She married George G. Miner.[109] They are buried in the Jewett City Cemetery, Griswold, Ct
5. **Charity A. Willcox** was born in 1875.[110]
6. **Arthur Willcox** was born in 1877[111] and died 1890.[112] He is buried in the Brown, Peckham, Main Cemetery
7. **Mary Ann Willcox** was born in 1879.[113]
8. **Benjamin Franklin Willcox** was born in 1881[114] and died 1939.[115] He is buried in the Jewett City Cemetery, Griswold, Ct
9. **Frances Willcox** was born in 1883.[116]

10. **Grover C. Willcox** was born in 1885[117]

11. **Betsey Willcox** was born in 1887[118] and she died in 1900.[119] She is buried at the Brown, Peckham, Main Cemetery

12. **Fairy Willcox** was born in 1890[120] and she died 1890.[121] She is buried at the Brown Peckham, Main Cemetery

13. **Charles Willcox** was born in 1891.[122]

14. **Ray Ernest Willcox** was born in 1893 and he died in 1951. He married Mary Elvira Pierce. They are buried at the Brown, Peckham Main Cemetery

On the 1870 Census for Ledyard, Raymond and Phebe lived next door to Robert and Mary Willcox. There were no other children living with Robert and Mary Wilcox at this time. The entry states: [123]

229 239	**Wilcox, Raymond**	age 26	farmer	born Ct
	Phebe	age 20		born RI
	Geo. R.	age 1		born Ct
230 240	**Wilcox, Robt**	age 67	farmer	born Ct
	Mary	age 70		born Ct

On the 1880 Census for Ledyard, Raymond and his wife, Phebe, still lived with Robert, who was widowed at the time. This is the entry: [124]

273 297	**Willcox, Robert**	age 74	farmer	born Ct
	Raymond son	age 35	carpenter	born Ct
	Phebe E. wife	age 29		born Ct
	George R. son	age 11		
	Julia A. daughter	age 9		
	Jeremiah son	age 8		
	Bernice daughter	age 6		
	Charity A. daughter	age 3		
	Mary A. daughter	age 1		

In 1871 Raymond had 8 acres of land according to the Ledyard Tax List.[125] In a deed, from Robert Wilcox to Raymond Wilcox, dated February 27, 1869, Robert sold Raymond 8 acres of land with a saw mill and shop there standing.[126]

Raymond inherited part of his Fathers estate, when his father Robert Willcox died in 1885.[127] Raymond's brothers, Robert N. and Martin Wilcox inherited the other half of the property. Raymond bought from his brother Robert N. Willcox, Robert's ¼ part of the real estate of their father Robert Willcox, deceased, on February 10, 1885.[128] Robert N. Willcox was from Milane, Erie County, Ohio, at the time of the sale. Raymond also bought from his brother Martin Willcox, Martin's ¼ part of his inheritance from his Father, Robert Willcox, on March 18, 1885.[129] Martin Willcox was from Lehigh, Jasper County, Missouri. Raymond now owned 140 acres of his Fathers estate.

Raymond ran a saw mill on the property. I found that he was appointed Elector in 1867[130] and a Pound keeper in the same year[131]. He died in Groton, on March 23, 1904[132]. Phebe sold the 140 acres in 1913.[133] Phebe died October 17, 1935[134] at Lawrence and Memorial Hospital in New London, Ct. She was residing at the Spicer Home, in Noank, Conn., before she was admitted in Lawrence and Memorial Hospital. Phebes' death certificate also listed her parents as Geo. R Waite, birthplace unknown and Hannah P Brown, birthplace unknown.

Raymond and Phebe are buried in the Brown Peckham Main Cemetery on Iron Street in Ledyard in the Willcox plot (see #34 on page 25).

Raymond and Phebe Waite Willcox Gravestone
Picture is of front and back of their stone
Brown Peckham Main Cemetery, Iron Street, Ledyard, Ct.

ROBERT AND MARY ANN REED WILLCOX

In the next three generations, all three males were named Robert Wilcox. Anywhere that a Robert Wilcox is mentioned I will try to distinguish them by using the following:

Birth Year	**Will be written as**	**Married to**
born 1753	Robert Wilcox 1st	Sarah Wilbur
born 1783	Robert Wilcox Jr. or 2nd	Deborah Brown
born in 1803	Robert Wilcox 3rd	Mary Ann Reed

Hopefully, this is help you follow which one I am discussing.

Robert Wilcox 3rd was born in Lyme, Ct on January 11, 1803.[135] He was the son of **Robert Willcox 2nd** and **Deborah Brown**. After Robert the 2^{nds} death in 1811[136], Robert the 3rd, mother, Deborah Wilcox was appointed as his guardian.[137] He married **Mary Ann Reed** in Groton on April 4, 1824.[138] She was the daughter of **James Reed** and **Dorothy Allyn**. Mary Ann was born August 11, 1799.[139]

Children of Robert and Mary Ann Wilcox:

1. **Robert Wilcox** was born in 1825[140] and he died in 1825.[141] He is buried in the Brown, Peckham, Main Cemetery

2. **Mary Ann Wilcox** married Mr. Chapman[142]

3. **Frances Wilcox**, she was born July 27, 1827[143] and she died May 10, 1884.[14\4] She married Charles H. Palmer.[145] Frances and Charles Palmer are buried in the Brown, Peckham, Main Cemetery

4. **Betsey Wilcox** married Mr. Turner[146]

5. **Amos Wilcox** was born in 1830[147] and he died in 1832.[148] He is buried in the Brown, Peckham, Main Cemetery

6. **Robert Nelson Wilcox** was born in 1831[149]

7. **Robertson Wilcox** was born in 1834[150] and he died in 1863.[151] He is buried in the Brown, Peckham, Main Cemetery

8. **Martin Wilcox** was born in 1836.[152]

9. **Chauncey Wilcox** was born in 1842.[153] He died in the Civil War in 1863.[154] He is buried in the Brown, Peckham, Main Cemetery

10. **Raymond Wilcox** was born in 1844 and he died in 1904. He married Phebe E. Waite. They are buried in the Brown, Peckham, Main Cemetery

11. **Reuben Wilcox** was born in 1848[155] and he died in 1848.[156] He is buried in the Brown, Peckham, Main Cemetery

When Robert Wilcox 3rd became of age, he inherited his section of property from his Fathers estate.[157] Robert Wilcox 3rd also bought two tracts of land from his brother Nathaniel Wilcox. The first tract had 37 acres. The second tract had 35 acres and was the dower for my mother Deborah Wilcox. The deed was dated May 16, 1827.[158] Robert also bought 51 acres from his sister, Deborah Crandall, and her husband Joseph. This was all her right in her father Robert Wilcox Jr. Estate. This deed was dated November 25, 1828.[159] Robert also bought from his brother Robertson Wilcox, 21 acres and 31 rods, which was Robertson's right to the Robert Wilcox estate. This deed was dated December

16, 1832.[160] He had bought back the entire 120 acres that his father once owned. He also bought more acreage as the years went by, which help add more value to his property. He built a grain or grist mill (see #41 on page 25) on the property and later built a saw mill (see #42 on page 25).

From the Ledyard Tax records at the Bill Library in Ledyard, Ct:[161]

Year	*Property Owner*	*House*	*Acres*	*Mill*
1836	*Robert Wilcox*	*1*	*98*	
1839	*Robert Wilcox*	*1*	*106*	
1850	*Robert Wilcox*	*1*		
1851	*Robert Wilcox*	*1*		
1858	*Robert Wilcox*			*Grain*
1859	*Robert Wilcox*			*Grain*
1860	*Robert Wilcox*	*1*	*130*	*Grain*
1871	*Robert Wilcox*	*1*	*128*	*Grain*

Robert Wilcox 3rd was listed on the 1850, 1860, 1870 and 1880 Census in Ledyard. The 1870 and 1880 Census are mentioned in Raymond Willcox section.
On the 1850 Census for Ledyard, some of his neighbors were Albert Brown and family, Avery W. Brown and family and Elizabeth Brown.
The entry states: [162]

119 138 **Robart Wilcox**	age 48 farmer	born Ct
Mary A.	age 51	born Ct
Robart L.	age 19 carpenter	born Ct
Martin	age 13	born Ct
Chaney	age 8	born Ct
Raymond	age 6	born Ct

On the 1860 Census for Ledyard, some of his neighbors were Albert Brown and family, Jeffery Brown and family, Aaron Brown and family, Asa Gray and family, and Stephen Peckham and family. The entry states: [163]

224 241 **Robert Wilcox**	age 57 farmer
Mary A.	age 60
Robert N.	age 28 Carpenter
Raymond	age 15
242 Wilcox, Martin	age 24 Farmer
Melinda	age 24
Andrew J.	age 4

When I was going through the Town Meetings, records at the Bill Library in Ledyard, Ct, and I found that Robert was also a surveyor of roads and highways in the Town of Ledyard, in the following years: [164]

1837, 1838, 1846, 1865, 1867, 1868 and 1873

At the Indian Colonial Research Center in Old Mystic, Ct., under the Wilcox notes under Robert Wilcox 3rd: [165]

> *"...Robert Wilcox Born in Connecticut Jan. 7, 1803. He married Mary A. Reed. They lived in Mystic and Ledyard, Conn. In 1849, he had a very fine large house built. It took 18 months to build. He owned a Grist Mill near Mystic and his son Robert N. Wilcox said "The old farm I found under fine cultivation producing bountifully in all kinds of farm crops..."*

Robert and Mary Ann were members of the Groton Baptist Church on Cold Spring Road in Groton, Ct. Robert was received and baptized in Sept.1831. He was dismissed March 28, 1843. He became a member of the Ledyard Branch Oct. 15, 1842. He was also Received at 3rd Church of Groton December 16, 1843 and

December 24, 1843.[166] His wife Mary Reed was received and baptized in April 1820 at the same church.[167] Robert signed a petition on March 2, 1843, for the formation of the Second Baptist Church (see #45 on page 25), which was going to be located on Iron Street across from the Brown, Peckham, Main Cemetery.[168]

From New London County Superior Court Papers by Subject: Indians: Mashantucket Pequot, located at the Connecticut State Library, dated March 30, 1875, the entry states:[169]

"Recd (Received) from R. (Robert) *Wilcox firewood $8.75"*

Robert Willcox 3rd died on January 11, 1885[170] in Ledyard. Mary Ann died on February 8, 1876[171] in Ledyard as well.

Robert and Mary Ann are buried in the Brown Peckham Main Cemetery on Iron Street in Ledyard in the Wilcox plot (see #34 on page 25).

Robert Willcox and Mary Ann Reed Gravestones
Brown Peckham Main Cemetery, Iron Street, Ledyard, Ct

ROBERT AND DEBORAH BROWN WILLCOX

Robert Willcox 2nd was born about 1783[172] probably in Westerly, RI. He was the son of **Robert Willcox 1st** and **Sarah Wilbur**. Robert married **Deborah Brown**, daughter of **Nathaniel Brown** and **Deborah Morgan**.

Deborah Brown was the sister to Hannah Brown Holdridge, mentioned in a later chapter and Aaron Brown and Nathaniel Brown, Jr. already mentioned. Deborah is another ancestor Noyes has to Nathaniel Brown and Deborah Morgan. Not through DNA, but through genealogy records. Nathaniel Brown died in 1821.[173] He names one of his daughters as Deborah Wilcox in his Probate Records.[174] Deborah Wilcox had been a widower, but by 1821 was married to Benjamin Wilcox, brother to her deceased husband Robert Wilcox.

The children of Robert and Deborah Wilcox are as follows (the children names are taken from the Distribution of the Estate of Robert Wilcox, filed in the Stonington Town Hall in the Probate Office in Volume 9 page 410, except Louisa Wilcox, see below):

1. **Erastus Wilcox**
2. **Robert Wilcox 3rd** was born in 1803 and he died in 1885. He married Mary Ann Reed. They are buried in the Brown, Peckham, Main Cemetery
3. **Nathaniel Wilcox**
4. **Raymond Wilcox**
5. **Deborah Wilcox**
6. **Louisa Wilcox** was born in 1810[175] and she died in 1811.[176] She is buried in the Brown, Peckham, Main Cemetery
7. **Robertson Wilcox**

Robert Wilcox 2nd and Deborah were living in Lyme when he bought 120 acres of land in North Groton off of Iron Street in

January of 1811. He bought the property from Jonas B. Avery of Groton, Ct. From the deed description, this property was bounded by a brook, to Nathaniel Brown property, to Jonas B. Avery property, to the heirs of Roger Williams property, to Capt. William Williams property, to James Heath land, to the said brook, by the land joining Capt. Christopher Morgan, and Comfort Brown and Nathaniel Brown land.[177] This became known as the Willcox Homestead in Ledyard, Ct.

On the deed mentioned above, it stated Robert Wilcox was from Lyme, Ct. He was buying 120 acres of land in Groton, Ct.

Robert Wilcox 2nd was listed on the 1810 Census for Lyme, Ct. He had the following number of people living with him on this Census:[178]

3 males 0 to 10 years of age
1 male 10 to 16 years of age
1 male 16 to 26 years of age
1 male 26 to 45 years of age
2 females 0 to 10 years of age
1 female 26 to 45 years of age

He died on September 1, 1811 in North Groton (Ledyard), Ct. He died a remarkable death. It was an accidental death from the records I have found. From Indian Colonial Research Center this is the account of what happened to Robert Willcox 2nd:

> *"have a cart full of stones – left tongue on stake - went into driving - lifted tongue – slid and stake driven through body, tongue drove him down on it"*[179]

There were receipts in Robert Wilcox 2nd Probate Records. One of those receipts was from Nathaniel Brown, Jr and Aaron Brown for a note payable by them to the estate. It was paid to the following heirs, Robert, Erastus and Deborah Wilcox, to their guardian Benjamin Wilcox.[180]

His wife Deborah Wilcox later married his brother Benjamin Wilcox and remained in North Groton until shortly after 1820. Benjamin and Deborah Wilcox became guardians for the minor children of Robert Wilcox, deceased.[181] She and Benjamin moved to Milan, Erie County, Ohio.

Robert Wilcox 2nd was the first to be buried in the Brown, Peckham, Main Cemetery with a tombstone (see # 34 on page 25).

Robert Willcox, Jr Gravestone
Brown Peckham Main Cemetery, Iron Street, Ledyard, Ct.

ROBERT AND SARAH WILBUR WILCOX

Robert Willcox was born in North Kingston, RI about 1753.[182] He was the son of **Jeremiah Wilcox**. He married **Sarah Wilbur** in Westerly, RI on April 9, 1777.[183] **Sarah Wilbur** was the daughter of **Joseph Wilbur** and **Sarah Hall.**

Children of Robert and Sarah Wilcox:

1. **Lucy Wilcox**
2. **Robert Wilcox 2nd** was born 1782 and he died in 1811. He married Deborah Brown. He is buried in the Brown, Peckham, Main Cemetery
3. **Susanna Wilcox** married Asa Gray[184]
4. **Hazard Wilcox** married Mary Wright in Lyme, Ct.[185]
5. **Charlotte Wilcox** married William Babcock[186]
6. **Nancy Wilcox** married Mr. Daniels[187]

7. **Benjamin Wilcox** married his brothers Widow Deborah Brown Wilcox

8. **Sally Wilcox** married Benjamin Wilbur[188]

9. **Mary Wilcox** was born in 1793[189] and she died in 1877.[190] She married Aaron Brown.[191] They are buried in the Brown, Peckham, Main Cemetery

10. **Jeremiah Wilcox** was born in 1794.[192] He died in Lebanon on May 23, 1893.[193]

11. **Delight Wilcox** married Gilod Waltrous[194]

Sarah Wilcocks was Received and Baptized on June 17, 1787 at the Groton Baptist Church, located on Cold Spring Road in Groton, Conn. On the Members List, she was listed as dead.[195]

Robert Wilcox 1st was in the Revolutionary War. From Abstracts from Rev. War Pension Files, page 3845 it states: [196]

"*...Willcox, Robert, RI line, Sarah, W18476, sol* (soldier) *was a son of Jeremiah Willcox & he lived at Westerly RI when he enl,* (enlisted) *sol* (soldier) *m* (married) *Sarah Wilbur at the home of her father (not named) in Westerly RI by one Isaiah Willcox an Elder of 1* (one) *of the Baptist Churches in Westerly RI (his relationship "if any" to sol (soldier)was not given) & they were m* (married) *9 Apr 1777, sol* (soldier) *d 11 Oct 1808 at Lyme in New London Co* (County) *CT & his wid app*(applied) *22 Apr 1842 at Ledyard in New London Co* (County) *Ct, sol* (soldier) *& his wife Sarah had 12 children of which the following survived their father, towit: Susan, Robert, Lucy, Hazard, Mary, Benjamin, Jeremiah, Delight, Charlotte, Sarah & Nancy (the other child was not named in this claim), in 1842 the daughter Susan (Willcox)Brown was aged 62 a res* (resident) *of Ledyard Ct & in 1842 sol's* (soldier's) *daughter Mary (Willcox) Brown was aged 51 & a res* (resident) *of Ledyard Ct, in 1842 wid's* (widow's) *sis* (sister) *Ruth Wilbur aged 78 was a res* (resident) *of East Lyme in New London Co* (County) *Ct & stated she was born at Westerly in Washington Co* (County) *RI & at age 18 she moved with her fathers family to CT, in 1842* *wid's* (widow's) *bro* (brother) *Daniel Wilbur aged 72 was a res* (resident) *of Norwich in New London Co* (County) *CT & was formerly of Westerly RI..."*

Robert Wilcox 1st was the son of Jeremiah Willcox who was living in Westerly, RI in 1774. The following was taken from the 1774 Inhabitants of the Colony of Rhode Island and Providence Plantations:[197]

Families	**Whites**				**Indians**	**Blacks**	**Total**
	Males		Females				
	Above 16	Under 16	Above 16	under 16			
Wilcox, Jeremiah	2		2		4	3	11
Wilbur, Joseph	1	5	1		4		11

Robert Wilcox 1st bought property in Stonington in 1783.[198] The property contained 89 acres of land, located on Wolf Neck Road. When he sold this property to Joseph Wheeler, in 1787 the deed stated that on one of the boundaries[199]

"...lived an Indian woman named Betty Sams..."

When Robert bought this property, there was no mention of any one living on any of the boundaries. I feel Robert had to have brought Indian Betty Sams with him in 1783.

There was a Betty Sams from the Narragansett Tribe of Indians. Betty Sam was one of the many signers of a petition against Thomas Ninigret of the Narragansett Tribe on June 16th, 1763.[200] Betty was not listed on the next petition in 1765. Betty Sams could have been one the Indians that Jeremiah Wilcox had living with him on the 1774 Census of Rhode Island shown above. Was Betty Sams of mixed blood herself or was she married to either a White or Black man? Was she one of the people that left the Narragansett Reservation? How did she get to Stonington, Connecticut? It was just 11 years before the 1774 Census, that Betty Sams was listed on the petition against Thomas Ninigret. Therefore, it is quite possible that Betty Sams was one of the 4 Indians living with Jeremiah Wilcox in Westerly, Rhode Island on the 1774 Census. Robert and Sarah were married in Westerly in 1777. Jeremiah Wilcox could have let his son Robert take Indian Betty Sams with him and his new wife to Stonington when Robert bought property in 1783. I feel this is a very logical explanation of how Indian Betty Sams came to be on the boundary of Robert Wilcox's property in Stonington.

On the 1790 Census in New London County, Robert Wilcox 1st had one free person living with him.[201]

In 1795, Robert Wilcox 1st moved to North Groton.[202] He bought 210 acres of property bordering Phinehas Holdridge, Indian Land, Capt. Henry Williams, John Packer, Joseph Williams, Jesse Barnes and Joseph Stanton. This would put him, behind Long Pond (see #19 on page 25). Thomas Main mentioned in a future chapter, bought this same property in the early 1800's. Robert Wilcox was on the 1800 Census for Groton.[203] The 1800 Census, did not list any other free persons living with him, but he had one slave. Robert sold the property in North Groton in 1804 and moved to Lyme.[204]

The map on the next page shows how Robert Wilcox 1st bordered Phinehas Holdridge (who will be discussed in a later chapter) and William Hempstead (who sold his property to Samuel and Abel Main, brothers to Thomas Main (who will also be discussed in a later chapter)) and the Western Pequot land:

Map of Robert Willcox 1st property along with Phinehas Holdridge property and William Hempstead property showing the Western Pequot Border [205]
Illustrated by Shirley H. Greene

Sarah Wilcox moved to Lebanon, Ct with her son Jeremiah after Roberts' death. She died there on March 13, 1854.[206]

Robert Wilcox 1st died October 11, 1808 in Lyme, Ct. [207] I found Robert Wilcocks Probate Records, recorded under New London Probate Records at the Connecticut State Library. He was from the Town of Lyme, Ct. His Inventory was taken in April of 1809.

From his Inventory I found the following information. He still had slaves with him in Lyme: [208]

"*...one Negro girl 16 years of age*	*63-00*
one Negro boy 14 years of age	*140-00*
15 tons of Ship timber	*7-50*
324 Acres of land at $12.00 per acre..."	

There was a good market for ship timber in those days. The ship building industry was very prevalent along the Connecticut coastline in this period. That is probably why he moved to Lyme, Ct. He lived near the Connecticut River and this was an area that would require his ship timber mentioned in his Inventory.

CHAPTER 6

MARY STANTON MAIN/PIERCE

Generation No. 4

Mary Stanton Main was born April 04, 1878, in Ledyard, Ct.[209] She died on November 29, 1939 in New London, Ct.[210] She was the daughter of **George Park Main** and **Sarah Eliza Brown**.

Chester Latham Pierce was born on February 27, 1880 in North Stonington, Ct.[211] He died February 5, 1946 at home in Ledyard, Ct.[212] He was the son of **Zachary T. Pierce** and **Almy Slocum**. He married **Mary Stanton Main** on November 15, 1899 in North Stonington, Ct.[213]

Mary Stanton Main **Chester Latham Pierce**

Courtesy of Goldie Ada Willcox Collins Robbins[214]

Children of Chester Pierce and Mary Main are:

1. **Mary Elvira Pierce** was born September 18, 1900 in Ledyard, Ct. She died on May 17, 1974 in Putnam, Ct. She married Ray Ernest Willcox

2. **Sadie Pierce** was born and died in 1902.[215] She is buried with her parents in the Brown Peckham Main Cemetery in Ledyard, Ct.

3. **Gertrude Maria Pierce** was born in 1903.[216]

4. **Clara Jennie Pierce** was born in 1906[217] and she died 2001.[218] She is buried at the Brown Peckham Main Cemetery in Ledyard, Ct. She married Harry Brewer.[219]

5. **Lucy Alma Pierce** was born in 1907[220] and she died in

1980.[221] She is buried at the Brown Peckham Main Cemetery, in Ledyard, Ct. She married Elmer R. Avery.[222]

6. **Mildred Annis Pierce** was born in 1909.[223]

7. **Chester Zachary Pierce** was born in 1915[224] and he died 1966.[225] He married Florence E.[226] He is buried at the Ledyard Center Cemetery in Ledyard, Ct

Mary Stanton Main

From the Census records of Mary S. Main parents, George P. and Sarah E. Main (see Chapter 7), Mary may have been born on Stoddards Wharf Road in Ledyard, Ct (see #6 on page 24). I was told that George and Sarah lived there for a very long time. Most of their children were born there. Mary probably went to school at the schoolhouse on Stoddards Wharf Road (see #15 on page 24). The farmhouse is no longer there, but when Noyes was a child, one of his friends lived in this house. His father had a farm there. It was near the Stoddard Avery Cemetery on Stoddards Wharf Road.

Chester Latham Pierce and Mary Stanton Main life

I know they lived on Hoot Owl Hill when they were first married because their daughter, Mary Elvira, was born there, which I have mentioned previously. Stephen Caswell owned the property at that time and they had to have been renting the house on top of Hoot Owl Hill from him. Noyes and I received permission to take a walk on the property to see where the house was.[227] From what I have been told, there were two houses. The older and bigger house was decaying and someone had built a smaller house next to it. They just let the bigger house drop to the ground. You can see where both foundations to these houses were. They were right on top of the hill in a grove of evergreen trees. Ezra Barnes owned this property in the late 1700 to early 1800's.[228] He and his family are buried in the Barnes Cemetery, which is just down the hill from where the houses were. My great-

great Grandfather Randall Holdridge married Nancy Barnes, daughter of Nathan Barnes who is buried in this cemetery.

Chester L. Pierce bought property on Center Groton Road near Ledyard Center in 1905.[229] This property was would be where they spent the remainder of their lives (see #20 on page 24). Chester had orchards and a cider mill on his property. On the Census Records he was listed as a farmer. I have been told he also did carpentry work as well.

Chester also bought another parcel of land which contained 6 acres of land and 4 acres of land.[230] His son, Chester Zachary Pierce, received these two plots from him. Chester Zachary Pierce sold these two plots of land to George and Sadie Greene.[231]

Chester Pierce was a farmer according to the Census records. His father Zachary was living with him on the 1900 and 1910 Censuses for Ledyard. His neighbor was Stephen Caswell, who owned the property on Shewville Road where Chester and Mary lived.

On the 1900 Census for Ledyard: [232]

Name	age	date of birth	occupation	born	
Pierce, Chester L.	20	Feb. 1880	farmer	Ct	rented
Mary S.	22	Apr 1878	none	Ct	
Zachary, father	52	Apr 1848	carpenter	Ct	
Caswell, Stephen					

On 1910 Census for Ledyard, Chester Pierce was living three houses from Shirley's Great Grandfather, Joseph E. Holdridge. They both lived on Center Groton Road at this time: [233]

2 2 **Pierce, Chester L.**	age 30, farmer
Mary S.	age 32
Mary E.	age 8
Gertrude M.	age 6
Clara J.	age 4

Lucy A.	age 3	
Mildred A.	age 7 months	
Zachary T. father	age 63	born Ct
Horatio S. cousin	age 45	born NY

3 3 Baudro, Thomas
4 4 Morgan, Frank W.
5 5 Holdridge, Joseph E.

On the 1920 Census for Ledyard, Chester Pierce was living in Henry Marsh house (now called), and his neighbors were Napolean Langevin and wife Martha (Hoxie, George). The next house up the list is Nathan Holdridge. This Nathan Holdridge was the brother to Joseph Enos Holdridge mentioned above and owned 140 acres near Blonders Park on Colonel Ledyard Highway. Shirley's grandfather, William Leeds Holdridge, inherited that property and sold it to Charles Lamphere. We believe that Napolean and Martha were living on the Nathan Holdridge property on this 1920 Census: [234]

235 244 **Holdridge, Nathan**	age 52, farmer
236 245 **Langevin, Napolean**	age 59, basket maker
Martha,	age 57
Ralph	age 16, son
Martha	age 14, daughter
Alice	age 17, daughter
237 246 **Pierce, Chester L.**	age 39, farmer
Mary	age 41
Gertrude M.	age 16
Clara	age 13
Lucy	age 12
Mildred	age 10
Chester	age 4, son

On 1930 Census for Ledyard, Chester and Mary are still at the same house, but as you can see two houses down lives Mary's mother Sarah E. Main: [235]

220 226 **Pierce, Chester** R.	age 53, farmer
Mary S.	age 52
Chester Z.	age 14
221 227 Crouch, Herbert G.	
222 228 **Main, Sarah E**., Head	age 83 widowed
Brown, Erastus J.	age 76 brother

Mary Main Pierce was a typical farmers wife. Some of her usual chores would include the cooking of the meals, raising her children and keeping house. Most women had wood stoves for kitchen stoves. The wood would have to be brought in daily and the stove was kept going all day. Water had to be brought up from the well located either on your property or from a community well. Most homesteads had their own wells. Some households used a hand pump that was at the sink. It looked similar to an old well hand pump, but smaller. Either way it was not like the modern world of today and just turn on a faucet. She also had to know how to take care of injuries and various ailments of her household. I am sure some of the remedies that Sadie Willcox told about came from her grandmother Mary Pierce. I am pretty sure, she probably even delivered a baby or two during her life span.

Chester and Mary are buried in the Brown Peckham Main Cemetery on Iron Street in Ledyard, Ct.

THE "PIERCE" ANCESTORS

This is the only line that does not relate to the Maternal Native American DNA. But this is the line that we have been told was Native American. I will just give a brief overview of this family.

ZACHARY TAYLOR PIERCE

Zachary T. Pierce was born on April 8, 1848[236], the son of **Freeman Pierce, Jr.** and **Eunice Babcock**. He was raised on Cossaduck Hill. Zachary married **Almy (Slocum) Gray,** the daughter of **Latham Slocum** and **Lucy Eccleston**, on November 26, 1879 in North Stonington. [237]
Children of Zachary and Alma Pierce:

1. **Chester Latham Pierce** was born on February 27, 1880. He married Mary Stanton Main
2. **Wallace Z. Pierce** was born in 1883.[238] He was a twin to Herbert Pierce. He married Jennie S. Main.[239]
3. **Herbert B. Pierce** was born in 1883.[240] He died in 1940,[241] and he is buried with his wife in the Brown, Peckham, Main Cemetery in Ledyard, Ct. He was a twin to Wallace Pierce above. He married Maria H. Main.[242]

The three Pierce brothers married three Main sisters. All of the above, Main sisters, were the daughters of George Park Main and Sarah Eliza Brown.

Zachary and Alma Pierce were divorced and she married Edwin Yerrington. I have never found when she died or where she was buried.

Zachary sold 60 acres to his father called Holmes Hole on Cossaduck Hill in North Stonington.[243] That was ½ interest in the property. The deed was dated in 1873.

On the 1880 Census for North Stonington, Ct. Zachariah Pierce and Almy were living on the same property as William H.H. Pierce, who was Zachary's brother. The entire entry states: [244]

117 123 **Pierce, William H.H.**	age 40 farmer
Sarah A.	age 39
Ezra E.	age 12

Nellie L.	age 11
Addie R.	age 9
Arthur	age 7
Ana B.	age 2
124 **Pierce, Zachary**	age 32 farming
Mialmy	age 22
~~Gray~~, Mary E.	age 2
Pierce, Chester L.	age under 1 year old

On the 1900 and 1910 Census, Zachary Pierce was living with Chester and Mary Pierce in Ledyard (see Chester Pierce for Census Record of 1900 and 1910).[245]

Zachary T. Pierce died on April 6, 1915 in Ledyard, Ct.[246] He is buried in the Eccleston Cemetery in North Stonington with his parents.

FREEMAN PIERCE, JR. AND EUNICE BABCOCK

Freeman Pierce, Jr was born in 1804, the son of **Freeman Pierce** and **Nancy Cook**.[247] He was raised in North Stonington, Ct. He married **Eunice Babcock.**[248]
They had the following children:

1. **Courtland Pierce** was born on September 13, 1830[249], and he died on January 5, 1874.[250] He is buried at the West Plains Cemetery in Norwich, Ct, with his wife Hannah.

2. **Elias F. Pierce** was born on December 16, 1833[251] and he died on December 4, 1901.[252] He married Lydia M. Main.[253] They are buried in the Eccleston Cemetery, North Stonington, Ct

3. **Elizabeth Pierce** was born in June 2, 1837 in North Stonington, Ct.[254] She died November 29, 1917 in Griswold, Ct.[255] She married Josiah Brown[256] and Russell M. Brown.[257] She and Russell Brown are buried in the Jewett City Cemetery in Griswold, Ct

4. **William H. H. Pierce** was born in 1841.[258] He died on April

29, 1888[259] in Griswold, Ct.

5. **Joseph Pierce** was born in 1842.[260] He died in April 15, 1899.[261] He is buried in the Rixtown Cemetery, Preston, Ct

6. **Samuel Pierce** was born in 1845.[262] He married Hattie Esther Pierce[263] Samuel and Hattie Pierce moved to Norwich, New York.

7. **Zachary T. Pierce** was born on April 8, 1848. He died on April 6, 1915. He married Alma Slocum.

8. **Ann S. Pierce** was born in 1846.[241] She married George W. Brown.[265]

9. **George F. Pierce** was born in 1850.[266]

Freeman Pierce bought 100 acres on the top of Cossaduck Hill in North Stonington in 1842.[267] He also bought another 60 acres from his son Zachary Pierce known as Holmes Hole(see Zachary Pierce). Freeman Pierces' borders were the North Stonington/Griswold Town Line and Billings Lake.

He was listed as a farmer on the Census records from 1850 to 1880.

On the 1850 Census for North Stonington, it states: [268]

312 325 **Pierce, Freeman**	age 50 farmer
Eunice	age 51
Courtland	age 20 laborer
Franklin	age 16 laborer
Elizabeth	age 13
William H.	age 12
Joseph	age 7
Samuel	age 5
Zachary	age 1 month

On the 1860 Census for North Stonington, page 42, it states: [269]

314 336 **Pierce, Freeman**	age 55 farmer
Eunice	age 55

William	age 19
Samuel	age 16
Zachary	age 11
George	age 9

On the 1870 Census for North Stonington it states: [270]

277 295 **Pierce, Freeman**	age 63 farmer
Eunice	age 64
Zachary	age 21 farm hand
Georg F.	age 19 farm hand

On the 1880 Census for North Stonington it states: [271]

114 120 **Pierce, Freeman** age 79, farmer Freeman was born in Ct; his father was born in RI; his mother was in born Ct

Eunice age 75, wife Eunice was born in Ct; her father was born in Ct; her mother was born in Ct

George age 28, son, farmer

Tacy age 22, wife

He died on September 2, 1898 at the age of 93 years.[272] Eunice Pierce died on July 31, 1890 at the age of 86 years.[273] Freeman and Eunice Pierce are buried in the Eccleston Cemetery, on the top of Cossaduck Hill, in North Stonington, Ct.

FREEMAN PIERCE, SR AND NANCY COOK AND ELIZABETH BROWN

Freeman Pierce Sr, was born about 1777[274], he died sometime between 1870 and 1880. He married **Nancy Cook**. Some family members have been told that Nancy Cook was a Native American. Possibly a Mohegan, but no proof through genealogy of this has ever been found to this date. **Freeman Pierce** then married for his second wife, **Elizabeth Wheeler**, widow of Lodowick Wheeler on

September 13, 1835[275] in North Stonington, Ct.
Children of the first marriage of Freeman and Nancy Pierce were:

1. **Freeman Pierce, Jr.** was born in 1804. He died on September 2, 1898. He married Eunice Babcock

2. **George W. Pierce** was born 1808 in North Stonington, Ct.[276] He died on December 26, 1891[277] in Griswold, Ct. He married Lydia Hurns in Norwich, Ct.[278] They are buried in the Robbins Cemetery, in Voluntown, Ct

9. **Samuel Pierce**, was born in 1811.[279] He moved to Norwich, New York.

10. **Joseph G. Pierce** was born in 1816.[280] He died 1893.[281] He married Lydia Stevens on March 17, 1845 Norwich, Ct.[282] They are buried in the Preston City Cemetery, Preston, Ct

5. **Nancy Ann Pierce** was born in 1820.[283] She married Capt. William A. Wilcox in Norwich, Ct on November 4, 1838.[284]

6. **Lucy E. Pierce** was born in 1822.[285] She married Edward Stevens in Norwich, Ct on January 19, 1843.[286] For her second husband, she married Charles Rogers in Norwich, Ct on November 14, 1847.[287]

7. **Elizabeth M. Pierce** was born in 1828.[288] She died on March 19, 1930 in North Stonington, Ct.[289] She married Asher D. Rathbone.[290] She is buried in the Union Cemetery on Route 49 in North Stonington, Ct

8. **Frances Pierce** was born in 1833.[291] She died on November 14, 1898[292] in Sterling, Ct. She married Albert C. Babcock[293]

The children of the second marriage of Freeman and Elizabeth Pierce were:

James M. Pierce was born on September 15, 1838.[294] He died on February 20, 1903.[295] He is buried in the Preston City Cemetery in Preston, Ct.

From Census records Freeman Pierce was either born in RI or CT. You will also see that Freeman was first listed on the Census

Records in North Stonington, then moved to Voluntown. From Voluntown he moved to Preston and finally lived with his daughter Lucy in Montville in 1870. Also, if you look on page 89, you will see his son Freeman, Junior, said his father was born in Rhode Island and his mother was born in Connecticut.

The following Census records are for Freeman Pierce, Sr.:

On the 1810 Census for North Stonington, Ct it states: [296]

One male under 10 years
One female 16 to 26 years

On the 1820 Census for North Stonington, it states: [297]

Three males 0 to 10 years old
One male 10 to 16 years old
One male 26 to 45 years old
One female 10 and under
One female 16 to years
One female 45 years and up

On the 1830 Census for Voluntown, Ct. it states: [298]

One male 5 to 10 years
2 males 10 to 20 years
1 male 20 to 30 years
1 male 50 to 60 years
1 female 0 to 10 years
1 female 5 to 10 years
1 female 10 to 20 years
1 female 50 to 60 years

On the 1840 Census for Voluntown, Ct, it states: [299]

One male under 5 years old
Three males 30 to 40 years old
One male 60 to 70 years old
One female 5 years old and under
Three females 10 to 20 years old
Two females 20 to 30 years old
One female 50 to 60 years old

On the 1850 Census for Voluntown, Ct it states: [300]

195 312 **Pierce, Freeman**	age 63 farmer	born RI
Elizabeth	age 55	born Ct
Wheeler, Emelia J.	age 20	
Pierce, James M.	age 13	

On the 1860 Census for Preston it states: [301]

358 430 **Pierce, Freman**	age 71 laborer	born Ct
Elizabeth	age 65	born Ct

On the 1870 Census for Montville, it states: [302]

136 141 **Pierce, Freeman**	age 84	born Ct
Rogers, Charles	age 50 laborer	
Lucy E.	age 48	
Rosa C.	age 20	
Maria	age 11	
Ida L.	age 9	

Nancy Cook Pierce, his wife was born in CT. This was taken from Census records of her children on where their mother was born. Also, on some of their children's death certificate it stated that their mother was born in Connecticut. She died before 1834 probably in Voluntown.[303] From the Census records of 1830 and 1840, Freeman Pierce was living in Voluntown during this time frame.

Freeman Pierce served in the War of 1812 in 1814 in Stonington under Commander Daniel Carr.[304]

Freeman also worked for Luther Palmer during 1816 –1820 doing various jobs for him. Luther Palmer also had a store and from his account books, many times Freeman Pierce would work for Luther to pay off his bill at Luther's store.[305]

Elizabeth Wheeler, Freeman's second wife, was the widow of Lodowick Wheeler. Quotes from Black Roots in Southeastern Connecticut 1650-1900 page 367.[306]

> *"SHANTUP*
>
> *Jeremiah, res. in North Stonington as early as 1825. (Dudley N. Wheeler, Account Book). He was in 1830 Census for North Stonington ae. 36-55; 2 in hsehd. Jeremiah, Thomas Ward and Giles Orchard were charged with the murder of Lodowick Wheeler of North Stonington, 1835. Jeremiah alone was tried and found guilty of murder, having beaten Wheeler fatally in a brawl outside a bar. He was sentenced to 8 yrs. in State Prison. Witnesses included Henry Shantup and Betsey Richards (N.L. Co. Sup. Ct. Sept 1835, File 106; CONNECTICUT GAZETTE, 1 July 1835)"*

We have many questions around this incident. Elizabeth had only been a widow for a very short time before she married Freeman. Freeman himself had only been a widower for a little over a year when he married Elizabeth. How they knew each other before they married, we will probably never know.

His wife Elizabeth bought a small piece of land with a house in Preston, Ct in 1856.[307] After her death, Freeman and Elizabeth's son, James M. Pierce, inherited the property. When he sold the property in 1871,[308] the deed it states it was known as "the Freeman Pierce place". Even though Freeman Pierce, himself never owned the property.

Freeman had to have died between 1870 and 1880. He was on the 1870 Census living with his daughter Lucy in Montville. But he was not on the 1880 Census. I have searched every Town and City Hall locally, but I could not find a death certificate for him. It is possible that he and his first wife Nancy Cook, could be buried in the Eccleston Cemetery on the top of Cossaduck Hill in North Stonington. The plot where Freeman and Eunice Pierce are buried is large enough for others from their family to be buried there. When Nancy died, she and Freeman, Sr. were living in Voluntown, but they had previously lived in North Stonington. Freeman, Sr. is not buried with his second wife Elizabeth. Elizabeth is buried with her daughter, Emelia J. (Wheeler) Pollard, in the Yantic Cemetery in Norwich, Ct.

CHAPTER 7

SARAH ELIZA BROWN/MAIN

Generation No 5

Sarah Eliza Brown was born in March 25, 1847[309] in Ledyard, Ct. She was the daughter of **Avery Wilbur Brown** and **Annis Holdridge**. She died in 1939.[310]

George Park Main was born in 1847.[311] He was the son of **Timothy Main** and **Mary Gay**. He died in 1929. [312] He married **Sarah Eliza Brown** on March 25, 1868[313] in Preston, Ct.

George Park Main

Sarah Eliza Brown

Courtesy of Vivian Williams[314]

Children of Sarah Brown and George Main are:

1. **Addie A. Main** was born in 1868.[315] She died in 1884.[316] She has a memorial in Brown Peckham Main Cemetery in Ledyard, Ct

2. **George E. Main** was born in 1870.[317] He died in 1928.[318] He is buried in the Brown Peckham Main Cemetery in Ledyard, Ct

3. **Timothy B. Main** was born on July 9, 1873.[319] He died on June 09, 1906.[320] He was married to Mary Corfey.[321] They are buried in the Ledyard Center Cemetery in Ledyard, Ct

4. **Erastus John Main** was born in 1874.[322] He died in 1960.[323] He is buried in the Brown Peckham Main Cemetery in Ledyard, Ct

5. Allyn T. Main was born in 1876.[324] He died in 1955.[325] He married Rosanna M. Rivers.[326] They are buried in the Ledyard Center Cemetery in Ledyard, Ct.

6. **Mary Stanton Main**, born April 04, 1878 in Ledyard, Ct.; died November 29, 1939 in New London, Ct. She married Chester Latham Pierce November 15, 1899 in No. Stonington, Ct

7. **Avery W. Main** was born in 1880.[327] He died in 1973.[328] He married Grace A. Taylor.[329] They are buried in the Avery Stoddard Cemetery in Ledyard, Ct.

8. Elmer O. Main was born in 1882.[330] He died in 1930.[331] He is buried in the Brown Peckham Main Cemetery in Ledyard, Ct

9. Amos G. Main was born in 1884[332]

10. Maria H. Main was born in 1885.[333] She died in 1964.[334] She married Herbert B. Pierce.[335] They are buried in the Brown Peckham Main Cemetery in Ledyard, Ct.

11. Jennie S. Main was born in 1887.[336] She died in 1923.[337] She married Wallace Pierce.[338] They are buried in the Brown Peckham Main Cemetery in Ledyard, Ct

12. Daniel P. Main was born in 1890.[339] He died in 1892.[340] He is buried in the Brown Peckham Main Cemetery in Ledyard, Ct

13. Annis B. Main was born in 1892.[341] She married Joseph Palmer Williams.[342]

Sarah Eliza Brown life

Sarah's father, Avery W. Brown, owned the property behind where the Up and Down Saw Mill is today. I believe that is where Sarah Eliza Brown was born (see #10 on page 20).

From an Article in the Day newspaper given to me by Vivian Williams: [343]

> *"Old Mystic,*
> *TOWN'S OLDEST RESIDENT CELEBRATES 93RD BIRTHDAY*

This community oldest inhabitant, Mrs. Sarah E. Maine, observed her 93rd birthday, and spent the day reading cards and messages of greeting sent by her many friends.

Born Sarah Eliza Brown in Ledyard in 1847, the daughter of Avery and Annis Brown, she lived in that town all her life until three years ago when she moved into a house owned by her son-in-law, Herbert B. Pierce, in this village, where she does all the housework for herself and her brother, John Brown, who will be 85 years old in April. She has lived an active life and during the past winter has pieced three quilt tops, sewing and threading her own needles without the aid of glasses; for her eyesight is remarkable for one of her years. She also knits and has completed six pairs of mittens this winter for members of her family.

She was married at the age of 21 to George P. Maine, and they were parents to 13 children, Erastus Maine, Avery Maine, Amos Maine, Mrs. Chester Pierce and Mrs. Joseph Williams, all of Ledyard. Mrs. Herbert Pierce of this village and Allen Maine of Fitchville are still living. In all she has 138 descendants, five more than last year including children, grandchildren and great grandchildren. Another brother William, lives in Rockville with one of his sons. He will be 90 years old a month from today."

I believe the Main Brown Reunion was started when Sarah celebrated her 93rd birthday. Those who have attended the Brown Peckham Main Reunion, over the years, always seem to be the descendants of Sarah Brown and George Park Main. Although any descendant of a Main or Brown is always welcome.

George Park Main life

George P. Main and Sarah lived in various places around town. I believe Mary Stanton Main was born on Stoddards Wharf Road heading to Gales Ferry. It would be just past the cemetery on your right. There used to be the Miller Farm there when Noyes was a child. He went to school with one of the sons. Vivian Williams also told me that she had heard that they lived there for a while. From the 1920 Census, they had to have lived on Shewville Road next to the Flower Cottage (see # 33 on page 25).[344] George and Sarah's neighbors were Fred and Jane Durfee. They probably lived at the Burns house at this time.

George Park Main was probably born off what is now known as Route 2 (see #7 on page 25). His father Timothy owned that property there for many years.

George Main never owned any property in the Town of Ledyard. He was a farm laborer most of his life and I believe he worked on the farms that other people owned.

George was a farmer from the Census Records I have found on him. I could not find George P. Main on 1870 Census.

On the 1880 Census for Ledyard: [345]

106 118 **Main, George P.**	age 32 farm laborer	born Ct
Sarah E.	age 33	born Ct
Addie A.	age 11	born Ct
George E.	age 9	born Ct
Timothy B.	age 6	born Ct
Erastus	age 5	born Ct
Allyn T.	age 4	born Ct
Mary	age 2	born Ct
Infant	age 2 months	born Ct

On 1900 Census for Ledyard: [346]

46 49 **Main, George P.**	age 52 farmer
Sarah E.	age 53
Avery	age 20 farm laborer
Elmer O.	age 18 farm laborer

Amos G.	age 16 farm laborer
Maria H.	age 14 at school
Jennie S.	age 12 at school
Anise B.	age 7 at school

After looking over the neighbors on both Census, it looked like George and Sarah lived on Stoddards Wharf Road or Route 214 in Ledyard, Ct.

On 1910 Census for Ledyard: [347]

7 7 **Main, George P.**	age 63 farmer, general farming
Sarah E.	age 63
Annis	age 17 daughter
Violet	age 9 granddaughter
Otis	age 3 grandson

On the 1910 Census, George P. and Sarah E. Main lived next to Phebe Willcox. Phebe Willcox lived on Iron Street, during this time frame. If you go four houses down from Phebe Wilcox, on the Census sheet, you will find that Frederick and Jane Durfee were living there.

On 1920 Census for Ledyard: [348]

321 330 **Main, George P.**	age 72 farmer, General Farm
Sarah	age 72 housekeeper
Elmer O.	age 38 son laborer Horse Farm
Otis	age 13 grandson
Violet	age 17 granddaughter
322 331 **Durfee, Fred**	age 75
Jane	age 65

This had to be when Fred and Jane lived in the Flower Cottage (see # 33 on page 25) on Shewville Road.

On the 1930 Census for Ledyard, Ct: [349]

222 228 **Main, Sarah E.**	age 83 widowed head of household
Brown, Erastus J.	age 76 single, general laborer, farm

George P. Main was named Administrator for his fathers, Timothy Main, estate. On July 13, 1901 per order of the Ledyard Probate Court, George sold his fathers estate to Ira D. Main. It consisted of 87 acres and the boundaries as follows: [350]

> "*...Northerly by Amasa M. Main*
> *Easterly by Mary E. Perkins and Amasa M. Main*
> *Southerly by Amasa M. Main and Col. George Ayers*
> *Westerly by Col. George Ayers estate to first mentioned bound...*"

The property had a house, barn and buildings on it.

George Park Main and Sarah Eliza Brown Main are buried in the Brown, Peckham Main Cemetery on Iron Street with Sarah parents (see #34 on page 20).

The "Main" Ancestors

This line is the second line that goes back to Nathaniel Brown and Deborah Morgan. This time it goes through their daughter Lois Brown who married Thomas Main. Their son Timothy was the father of George Park Main. The Main's lived all around the Western Pequot Reservation and along Lantern Hill Road. I have been told that parts of Lantern Hill Road were known as Main Town (it was like another section of the Town of Ledyard). The Main's interacted with the Western Pequot Natives over their lifetimes. Thomas Main himself bordered the reservation. Some of his children also owned property on at least three of the borders of the reservation as well.

TIMOTHY MAIN AND MARY GAY

Timothy Main was born on December 17, 1810 in Groton, Ct.[351] He died on September 13, 1889.[352] He married **Mary E. Gay**, daughter of **Jedidiah Gay** and **Dorothy Main**. **Mary E. Gay** was born on September 1807.[353] She died on May 20, 1901.[354]

Children of Timothy Main and Mary E. Gay:

1. **Mary Ann Main** was born in 1837.[355] She died on April 29, 1900.[356] She married Horatio Stillman.[357] They are buried in the Brown Peckham Main Cemetery, Ledyard, Ct.

2. **Thomas G. Main** married Mary H. Maine on October 10, 1865 in Preston Ct.[358] Mary H. Maine was the daughter of Nathaniel N. Maine and Mary A. Frink.

3. **Abby A. Main** was born in 1838.[359] She died October 6, 1871.[360] She married William D. Partelo.[361] They are buried in the Thomas Main Cemetery, Ledyard, Ct

4. **Timothy B. Main** was born in 1843.[362] He died on May 22, 1871.[363] He married Ann M. Crumb.[364] They are buried in the Thomas Main Cemetery, Ledyard, Ct

5. **George Park Main** was born in 1847. He died in 1929. He married Sarah Eliza Brown. They are buried in the Brown, Peckham, Main Cemetery, Ledyard, Ct.

6. **Jedidiah R. Main** was born in 1851.[365] He died March 1, 1879.[366] He is buried in the Thomas Main Cemetery, Ledyard, Ct.

7. **Dwight W. Main** was born in 1859.[367]

Timothy Main was born in Ledyard, probably at the Thomas Main Homestead off of Long Pond (see #8 on page 25).

Timothy was a farmer according to the Census Records below. You can see from the Map that Timothy was close to the northeastern boundary of the Western Pequot Reservation (see #30 on page 25). Timothy lived most of his entire life in the Lantern Hill area of Ledyard.

Timothy was listed on the 1840 Census in Ledyard, Ct: [368]

Timothy Main
One male 30 to 40 years old
Two females 0 to 5 years old
One female 10 to 14 years old
One female 20 to 30 years old

Some of his neighbors were:
Henry Hallett
Mary Hallett
Thomas Smith
Elisha Ayers
George Ayers
Wealthy Stoddard
William N. Scrantors
Timothy Main
Nathan Barns
Isaac Peckham

The Western Pequot Indians, were listed on this same page, before Henry Hallett's name. Timothy was living pretty close to the Northern boundary of the Mashantucket Reservation at this time.

Timothy Maine was listed on the 1850 Census in Ledyard, Ct: [369]

49 54 **Maine, Timothy**	age 37 farmer born Ct
Mary	age 37
Mary Ann	age 12
Abby	age 9
Timothy B.	age 7
Thomas G.	age 4
George P.	age 2

Jedediah R.	age 2/12 mos	

On the 1860 Census for Ledyard, Ct it states: [370]

243-264 **Main, Timothy**	age 47 farmer	born Groton, Ct
Mary,	age 47	born Stonington
Timothy B.	age 17	born Ledyard
Thomas G.	age 15	born Ledyard
George P.	age 13	born Ledyard
Jedediah R.	age 10	born Ledyard
Dwight W.	age 6	born Ledyard

On the 1870 Census for Ledyard, Ct it states: [371]

293 307 **Main, Timothy**	age 56, farmer
Mary	age 59
Dwight	age 17 works on farm

On the 1880 Census for Ledyard, Ct it states: [372]

Main, Timothy	age 67 farmer	
Mary L. wife	age 65	
Annis B. granddaughter	age 12	born Ct

While I was researching the New London County, Superior Court Papers by Subject: Indians, Mashantucket Pequot files at the Connecticut State Library, I found the following (It did not state why he was paid that money):

"*...May 2, 1836 Timothy Main was paid $9.50*" [373]

On the Abstract of a Ledyard Tax List for 1866, Timothy Main was listed as having one house with 50 acres of land. [374]

Timothy M. Main bought 55 acres of land from Thomas Main in Groton on January 5, 1836. The description reads as follows: [375]

> "*...Beginning at the southwest corner of the premises at a heap of stones.*
> *Thence easterly to land of Elisha Ayer to the end of a wall.*
> *Thence northerly by said wall to the highway crossing said road.*
> *Thence westerly by said road to Elisha Ayers land.*
> *Thence northerly by said Ayers land to Elijah Baileys land and bounded on the north wholly on land of said Bailey*
> *Easterly on said Baileys land till it comes to the land the said Joseph Ayer Bought of Samuel Whipple*
> *Thence by a stone wall southerly till it comes to the land of Ezra Stanton To the highway crossing said road*
> *Thence southerly by said road to the wall*
> *Thence westerly by said wall to a heap of stones at the corner of said wall*
> *Thence westerly to a heap of stones on the south side of an old Mill Dam*
> *Thence southwest to land of Amos Barns heirs to a Butternut sprout near the Brook*
> *Thence northwest by said Barns land and Elisha Ayers land to the first bound...*"

Timothy Main's Probate Records are at Ledyard Probate Court. He wrote his Last Will and Testament on March 7, 1887.[376] An abstract of this document is as follows:

Wife: Mary A.
Sons: George P. Main received $50
    Dwight W. Main received $25
    Thomas G. Main, deceased
    Jedediah R. Main, deceased
Daughters: Mary A. Stillman

Abby Partelo, deceased
Friends: James A. Billings, Executor
Witness: Miner Perkins
John E. Parks
James A. Billings

Timothy and Mary Main are buried in the Thomas Main Cemetery off Long Pond Road in Ledyard, Ct (see # 36 on page 25).

Timothy Main and Mary E. Gay Main Gravestones
Thomas Main Cemetery, Homestead Road, Ledyard, Ct.

THOMAS MAIN AND LOIS BROWN

Thomas Main was born about 1781 in North Stonington, Ct.[377] He died on February 10, 1864 in Ledyard, Ct.[378] He married **Lois Brown** on April 20, 1806 in Groton, Ct.[379] **Lois Brown** was the daughter of **Nathaniel Brown** and **Deborah Morgan**. **Lois Brown** was born about 1786.[380] She died on July 1, 1873.[381]
Children of Thomas and Lois Main:

1. **Thomas B. Main** was born on February 13, 1807 in Groton, Ct.[382] He died on January 11, 1896.[383] He married Lydia Hall November 15, 1835 in Groton, Ct.[384] They are buried in the Thomas Main Cemetery, Ledyard, Ct

From the New London County Superior Court Records, Papers by Subject: Indians, at the Connecticut State Library for the Eastern Pequot Tribe I found the following information about Thomas B. Main:

"...1. January 10, 1850 To this sum for Thos B. Main for keeping up fence by Shuntup Lot $1.50 [385]

2. June 20, 1851 To this sum for Thos. B. Main for potatoes 57c for Saml. Shuntup $.57 [386]

3. March 23, 1853, Thomas Main for work on chimney $.75 [387]

4. April 16, 1853 To Thos Main for 2 ½ Bu. Potatoes 50 S. Shuntup $1.25... [388] *"*

2. **Aaron Main** was born on May 14, 1808 in Groton, Ct.[389] He died February 19, 1893 in Noank, Ct.[390] He married Nancy Ashley on September 24, 1829 in Groton, Ct.[391] Aaron and Nancy had the following children:[392]

"...Andrew Main
Aaron Main, Jr. who married Happy L. Brown
Benjamin Main
John Tyler Main who married Katherine Williams of New Jersey
Annie Main who married Frank Charlton..."

From Genealogical Record of Nathaniel Babcock, Simeon Main, Isaac Miner and Ezekiel Main book under Aaron Main:[393]

"...Mr. Main was a farmer in early life; later, and for several years, was in Washington Market, New York City, until his health failed, when he followed the seas and became a captain for a number of years. He returned to Noank, where he owned large tracts of land which is now built upon. They attended the Baptist Church..."

3. **John Main** was born on August 20, 1809 in Groton, Ct.[394] He died on December 8, 1839.[395] He married Nancy Barnes, daughter of Nathan and Prudence Barns, February 1, 1835 in Groton, Ct.[396] John and Nancy Main had two children. One named John L. who died at four years of age and the other was Nancy Main.[397] Nancy married after John Main's death, Randall Holdridge in Norwich, Ct. (which is Shirley's ancestor) John Main is buried in the Thomas Main Cemetery. Nancy Barns, his widow is buried in the Ledyard Center Cemetery with her sons, Nathan and Joseph E. Holdridge

4. **Timothy Main** was born on December 17, 1810. He married Mary E. Gay, see previous section

5. ***William Leeds Main**, see * page 110

6. **Daniel Main** was born on October 18, 1813 in Groton, Ct.[398] He married Delia A. Roach, October 8, 1838 in Groton, Ct.[399] He married 2nd Emma Gay. He married 3rd Mary Main. Daniel Main's children were:

> "*...Delia, Catherine, Ellen and daughter Harriet who when young became deaf and after the death of her parents lived with her Uncle Amasa... Daniel and his three wives and daughter Catherine are buried in the Thomas Main Cemetery in Ledyard, Ct.*"[400]

7. **Louisa Main** was born on February 10, 1815 in Groton, Ct.[401] She died September 26, 1888.[402] She married Corridon Maine September 28, 1834 in Groton, Ct.[403] They are buried in the Thomas Main Cemetery, Ledyard, Ct.

From Genealogical Record of Nathaniel Babcock, Simeon Main, Isaac Miner and Ezekiel Main book under Louisa Main: [404]

> "*...They had fourteen children, seven of whom died young.*

John b. 1839, was accidentally killed by his gun, May 17, 1855...Those that came to maturity were: Lois, John and Jane (twins), Thomas, Mary, Sophia and Amasa..."

8. **Surviah B. Main** was born on May 11, 1817.[405] She died on January 10, 1876.[406] She married Albert Brown, son of Nathaniel Brown and Charlotte Wilbur, on September 6, 1835.[407] They are buried at the Brown, Peckham, Main Cemetery in Ledyard, Ct.
Children of Surviah and Albert Brown were: [408]

"Surviah L. Brown who married John O. Peckham
Albert M. Brown who married Nancy A. Peckham
Happy L. Brown who married Aaron Main, Jr.
Thomas M. Brown
Fannie E. Brown
Aaron A. Brown who married Deborah B. Perkins
Isreal W. Brown who married Annette Whipple
Seth L. Brown who married Margaret Cantwell
Fannie E. Brown who married Robert A. Peckham
Philetus W. Brown
Nathaniel S. Brown who married Lydia Stoddard
Charles T. Brown"

9. **Stanton Main** was born on February 9, 1819 in Groton, Ct.[409] He died on February 5, 1864.[410] He married Susan Gray, daughter of Asa Gray and Susannah Prosser, on September 4, 1842 in Ledyard, Ct. [411] Stanton is buried at the Thomas Main Cemetery, Ledyard, Ct
Stanton and Susan Main children are:[412]

"Sarah Ann Main who married William A. Main, son of Abel Main

Stanton Francis Main who married Julia A. (Stoddard) Ayer

Walter A. Main
Wilmot Holden Main who married Hattie E. Park"

From Genealogical Record of Nathaniel Babcock, Simeon Main, Isaac Miner and Ezekiel Main book under Stanton Main: [413]

"*...Susan Gray...daughter of Dr. Asa Gray of Ledyard, and Louisanna Prosser, of Rhode Island. The Gray Homestead in Ledyard is owned by George W. Gray, the youngest son and the only one living of the Gray family in 1909. The homestead was passed down to the fourth generation..."*

10. **Mary Esther Main** was born about 1820.[414] She died on October 22, 1902.[415] She married Miner A. Perkins.[416] Both are buried in the Thomas Main Cemetery, Ledyard, Ct
Children of Mary Esther Main and Miner Perkins are: [417]

"*Lydia E. Perkins who married Ishman Bromley*
Hannah M. (twin) Perkins who married Dwight C. Brown
Henry M. (twin) Perkins who married Mary E. Brown
Stephen F. Perkins
Eliza Ann Perkins, who resided with her brother Henry M. Perkins
Deborah Betsey Perkins married Aaron Alvah Brown"

11. **Nathaniel B. Main** was born about 1822.[418] He died on September 8, 1872.[419] He is buried in the Thomas Main Cemetery, Ledyard, Ct

12. **Seth Main** was born on September 13, 1824.[420] He died on August 13, 1903 in Preston, Ct.[421] He married Maryanna Stanton Woodward in North Stonington, Ct on August 27, 1848.[422] Children of Seth and Maryanna Main are: [423]

"*Seth Woodward Main who married (1) Ida Myers and (2)*

Hulda J. Gallup
Mary Rozilla Main who married Herbert H. Barlow
Cynthia Elvira Main who married Chauncey C. Pendleton
Appleton Main who married Isabelle Richardson
Nathaniel Main who married Nellie Holmes
Leonard Main who married Annie E. Richardson"

From the Genealogical Record of Nathaniel Babcock, Simeon Main, Isaac Miner and Ezekiel Main book under Seth Main: [424]

"*...They lived together to within fourteen days of fifty-five years of happy wedded life. Mr. Main was really a very successful business man. While farming was his principal business, he had other industries, conducting a gristmill a number of years. He owned a number of farms in Preston and No. Stonington, which he bought and sold. In 1894 he moved to the "Park Homestead Farm", which he had for some time owned a half interest. Three years later he became sole owner of this farm, which comprised in all about one hundred and fifty-four acres of excellent land. This beautiful farm became the care of his remaining days, and there he died. Politically he was a Democrat, and he took an active part in town affairs. In 1871 and again in 1884 he represented Preston in the State Legislature; among other offices, he was selectman for several years, member of the Board of Relief and Board of Assessors and tax collector. He settled a number of estates in his time. He was a member and liberal supporter of Elder Peckham's Baptist Church in Ledyard."*

In the New London Superior Court Records Papers by Subject: Indians at the Connecticut State Library, Seth Main was listed as an overseer for the Mashantucket Pequot Tribe on April 1, 1866 through April 1, 1871.[425] There was also the following entry for money due him from the new overseer:

..."January 1st 1874 Balance due Seth Main as former Overseer of Pequot Indians of Ledyard $9.45..."[426]

13. Hannah Main was born about 1827.[427] She died on August 3, 1860.[428] She married Paul Burrows.[429] Hannah Burrows is buried in the Thomas Main Cemetery. Hannah and Paul Burrows had two children:[430]

"Fannie Burrows
Isabella Burrows"

14. **Fannie E. Main** married George R. Parks on April 30, 1845 in Ledyard, Ct.[431] Children of Fannie and George Parks are:[432]

"Amasa Parks
Georgianna Parks
Fannie Parks"

15. **Amasa M. Main** was born on August 29, 1830.[433] He died on June 16, 1908 in North Stonington, Ct.[434] He married Lucy O. Frink, daughter of Zachary Frink and Phebe Holmes, on August 29, 1851.[435]
Children of Amasa and Lucy Main are:[436]

"Lucy M. Main
Ellen E. Main married Harban O. Whitford
Betsey Ann Main (twin) married Isaac Miner
Ada Ann Main (twin)
Amasa Everett Main married Kate L. Frye
Lillie A. Main who married Park B. Main
Lafayette F. Main who married Julia Emily Mather
Luther O. Main who married Edith Turpie
Fannie E. Main who married Otis Allen Chapman
Hattie B. Main who married Edward Jerry Duro"

From the Genealogical Record of Nathaniel Babcock, Simeon Main, Isaac Miner and Ezekiel Main book under Amasa M. Main: [437]

"...Mr. Main was a Republican, and held a number of offices in the gift of the people in the towns of Ledyard and No. Stonington. For four consecutive years he represented these towns in the State Legislature---- from 1895 to 1898. He was selectman, game and his warden. In his life he accumulated considerable wealth."

16. **Deborah B. Main** was born on August 17, 1831.[438] She married Joseph Morgan.[439] Deborah died on July 16,1884.[440] Deborah and Joseph Morgan are buried in the Morgan Pond Cemetery, Ledyard, Ct.
The children of Deborah and Joseph Morgan are: [441]

"Joseph Morgan, died young
Amasa Morgan
Mary Morgan
William Morgan
Nathan Morgan
Hannah Morgan"

THE LIFE OF THOMAS MAIN

From Genealogical Record of Nathaniel Babcock, Simeon Main, Isaac Miner and Ezekiel Main book under Thomas Main page 246: [442]

"He lived in Ledyard and made farming his life work. He was a man of large physique, of great muscular strength and was able to do a vast amount of work. He affiliated with the Democrat Party and was always active in town affairs, holding at different times, a number of offices in the gift of the people.

The house where he lived has all gone, and a portion of the land passed into other hands. He laid out the burying ground and walled it with a heavy stone wall, where he and his wife are interred and a number of his descendants. It is on a high hill one mile west of Lantern Hill..."

In 1801 Benajah Main and Samuel Main bought from Stanton Hewitt 100 acres of land.[443] This is the same property Stanton Hewitt bought from Robert Wilcox, Jr. and is shown on the map on page 41. Samuel Main sold a section of this property to Thomas Main in 1818.[444]

Thomas Main owned property bordering Long Pond in Ledyard, Ct (see #31 on page 25). He had bought many parcels over the years. One parcel he bought from Samuel Main was a farm of 72 ½ acres. This is the parcel mentioned in the above paragraph. It bordered Jesse Barns, Benjamin Wilbur, Phinehas Holdridge and a natural pond.

He also bought a farm of 40 acres from Stanton Hewitt in 1813, which bordered the Pequot Tribe, the late Jonathan Wood and Phinehas Holdridge.[445] He also bought another 35 acres of land from the same Stanton Hewitt, which border the Indian Land, Hewitts land, Jonathan Wood, Joseph Stanton and Henry Gallup.[446]

In 1828, Thomas Main bought 100 acres of land from Samuel and Abel Main.[447] The boundaries were Phinehas Holdridge and Rufus Fanning, the highway, Samuel and Abel Main. There was a lane to the land that Samuel and Abel Main purchased from William Hempstead. From this lane it went to the North Stonington border

In 1824, he also bought 32 acres from Rufus Williams of North Stonington.[448] It bordered Indian Town Pond, Thomas Main and Joseph Stanton.

On the 1810 Census for Groton under Th. Maine: [449]

Maine, Th.
3 males under 10 years
1 male 26 to 44 years
1 female 26 to 44 years

All neighbors are listed in the order they were on the Census record. Neighbors of Th. (Thomas) Maine were:
Jo. Stanton
Eunice Barnes
Asa Barnes
Ambrose Fish
Nehe. Barnes
Uriah Williams
Jesse Barnes
Ruf. Fanning
Th. Maine
Saml. Maine
Abel Maine
Shu. Whitney
Moses Smith
M. Smith Jr.
Amos Barnes
Elisha Ayers
Jo. Ayers
Elisha Bennett
Wm. Hempstead

On the 1820 Census for Groton, Ct under Thomas Main: [450]

Thomas Main
6 males 0 to 10 years
1 male 26 to 45 years
2 females 0 to 10 years

1 female 26 to 45 years

Neighbors of Thomas Main were:
John Packer 2nd
Benajah Packer
Susannah Gray
John Perkins
Abel Main
Saml Main
Thomas Main
Rufus Fanning
Gardner O. Worden
Phineas Holdredge
James Fanning
Latham Gray
Charles Chester

On the 1830 Census for Groton, Ct under Thomas Maine: [451]

Maine, Thomas
2 males 0 to 5 years
3 males 10 to 15 years
3 males 15 to 20 years
1 male 20 to 30 years
1 male 40 to 50 years
3 females 5 to 10 years
2 females 10 to 15 years
1 female 15 to 20 years
1 female 40 to 50 years

Neighbors of Thomas Maine were:
Russell Baggs
Samuel Maine
Saml Main, Ju.
Mary Barns

Lewis Tift
Nathan Swan
Russell Fitch
Phineas Holdredge
Wm. Bentley
Thomas Maine
Aaron Brown
John Packer 2nd
Benjah Packer
Deborah Brown
Andrew Gallup
Dennis Perkins

On the 1840 Census for Ledyard, Ct under Thomas Main: [452]

Main, Thomas
2 males 10 to 15 years
2 males 15 to 20 years
1 male 50 to 60 years
2 females 5 to 10 years
1 female 10 to 15 years
1 female 15 to 20 years
1 female 40 to 50 years

Neighbors of Thomas Main were:
Samuel Main
William Main
Samuel Main 2nd
Ephraim Williams
Nathan Swan
George Andrews
Thomas B. Main
Phineas Holdridge
Thomas Main
William L. Main

Coradon Main
Amos H. Mason
John Packer 3rd
Roger Williams
James B. Williams

On the 1850 Census for Ledyard, Ct under Thomas Maine: [453]

	Name	Age	Occupation	Real Estate
58 63	**Maine, Thomas**	70	farmer	$4000
	Louis female	65		
	Deborah M.	16		
59 64	Maine, William L.	37	farmer	
	Sarah	31		
	Sarah M.	11		
	John L.	8		
	Lucy	5		
	Phebe E.	3		
	Lury H.	11/12		

Neighbors of Thomas Maine were:
- George Andrews
- Phinehas Holdridge
- **Thomas Main**
- William L. Main
- John Packer
- Leander Holdridge
- Roger Williams
- James B. Williams

On the 1860 Census for Ledyard, Ct under Thomas Main: [454]

Name	Age	Occupation	Real Estate	Born
252 276 **Main, Thomas**				
	78	farmer	$1500 /$2703	North Stonington
Lois	78			Groton
Nathaniel	37	farmer		Groton
253 277 Main, William L.				
	47	farmer	$7000/$17,794	Groton
Sarah	42			North Stonington
John L.	18			Ledyard
Leeds	15			
Phebe E.	13			
Lura H.	10			
Ira	8			
Frances	5			
Alonzo	3 twin			
Melissa	3 twin			
1 not names	1/12 months			

From the above Census Records, Thomas Main lived in the Lantern Hill area of Ledyard, Ct. Some of Thomas Main's neighbors were also mentioned in the property description of his deeds when he bought his property. He and his wife, Lois, spent their entire married life on this property, where they raised their children.

In the Probate Records for Thomas Main in the Ledyard Probate Office, I found his Last Will and Testament along with his inventory. In his inventory, dated March 22, 1864, along with his personal belongings, it listed the real estate he owned.[155] The following is an abstract of the list of that real estate along with the value of each piece:

Home farm	$3000
Farm given to Mrs. Louisa Main	$ 250
Farm given to Mrs. Mary Esther Perkins	$ 300

Farm given to Mrs. Surviah Brown $ 400

The inventory also listed notes that were due to Thomas Main. The following is another abstract of some of those notes due (I did not include the amounts due):[456]

Est. of Stanton Main
Timothy Main
Daniel Main
Joseph Morgan
Robert and John Palmer
Aaron Main, Jr
Seth Main
Allen Denison
James Davis
Samuel L. Main
Miner Perkins
Albert Brown
Charles Stanton
Col. George Ayer
David W. Main
Lucius Witter
Phebe Frink
Elias R. Main

Some of these names you will recognize as husbands of some of Thomas Main's daughters. Other names I found familiar, because they bordered the various properties that he owned. And other names were his sons or other male relatives.

In Thomas Mains Last Will and Testament, I broke it down to each person mentioned as well as what they received. His Will was dated January 30, 1858 and was recorded March 18, 1864. The following is an abstract of his Last Will & Testament: [457]

Sons: (each received $1.00, plus anything he had already done for them previously)

Thomas B. Main
Aaron Main
Timothy M. Main
Daniel Main
William L. Main
Stanton Main

Seth Main
Amasa M. Main

Daughters:

Louisa Maine, received farm where she now resides (which it describes) (Louisa was married to Corridon Maine)…

It also lists Louisa's children who are:

Lois June Maine
Thomas C. Maine
Mary Elizabeth Maine
Surviah Maine
Amos Maine

Louisa also received $100

Surviah Brown, received three tracts of land (which it describes) (Surviah was married to Albert Brown)…

It also lists Surviah's children who are:

Surviah L. Brown
Albert M. Brown
Happy L. Brown
Thomas Brown
Aaron A. Brown
Isreal W. Brown
Fanny E. Brown
Seth L. Brown
Philetus Brown
Nathaniel Brown

Mary Esther, received tract lying in North Stonington (which it describes) (Mary Esther was married to Miner Perkins)…

It also lists her children:

Lydia E. Perkins
Hannah M. Perkins
Stephen F. Perkins
Eliza Ann Perkins
Deborah M. Perkins

Hannah (wife of Paul Burrows) received $300
Deborah (wife of Joseph Morgan)received $300

Grandson:

Amos Park received $100

Granddaughters:

Georgianna Park$100

Fanny Park $150

Nancy Main $ 50

Son:

Nathaniel Main received the home farm that I live on bounded as follows:

On the north by lands of Sarah Holdridge

On the east by lands of Amasa Main and William L. Main

On the south by lands of William L. Main and a lot to my daughter Louisa and James B. Williams

On the west by Seth Williams heirs and Jeffrey Brown, said demise is on the condition he pay to my executors within one year from my decease $350.

Wife:

Lois received 1/3 part of the house and some furnishings and some of the livestock

Grandsons:

Thomas, son of Surviah (Brown) $10

Thomas, son of Louisa (Maine) $10

Thomas, son of Timothy (Main) $10

William L. Main and **Seth Main** were appointed as Administrators of Thomas Main Estate.

From this Will of Thomas Main, I conclude that he was a man of great character and sensitivity. Three of his daughters were widowed and he made sure that they and their children had homes to live in. In the case of the Parks children, his daughter Fannie must have been deceased by 1858, when he wrote his Will, and he provided money for her children. His granddaughter, Nancy Main, was the daughter of his son John, who died in 1839. He also left her money. He paid each grandchild that was given the name Thomas, $10.00. I had found that over the years, he sold property to his sons that Thomas had previously owned. Four of his sons, William L., Aaron, Seth and Amasa M. were wealthy in their own right. His son, Timothy, bought his farm from Thomas Main in 1856. He did provide for his sons before his death. I think this Will shows Thomas Main was not a selfish man, but a man who instilled strong family and community values into his children.

Thomas and Lois Main are buried in the Thomas Main Cemetery off of Homestead Road in Ledyard, Connecticut (see #36 on page 25). Thomas and Lois Main gravestones are broken and buried, so we do not have pictures of the gravestones. Thomas Main built the wall around the cemetery. Below is a picture of the entrance to the Thomas Main Cemetery showing that wall.

Kayla Pendleton and Kelsey Greene standing in the entrance to the Thomas Main Cemetery[458]

*WILLIAM LEEDS MAIN

As you can see from the above list of Thomas and Lois Mains children, Timothy and William Leeds Main were brothers. Noyes and I have the same common ancestor at this point in the Main line with Thomas and Lois Main. William Leeds Main is my great-great grandfather.

Also, some of the descendants of William Leeds Main had dealings with some of Noyes's Ancestors as well. I hope this will help you relate to who these people are, as I will be discussing them throughout this book.

William Leeds Main was an interesting person. I feel he has bearing on this book because of the way he lived his life and his connection to both Eastern and Western Pequot Reservations, as well as he is my direct ancestor.

William Leeds Main was born July 4, 1812 in Ledyard, Ct.[459] William L. Main died June 22, 1890.[460] He married **Sarah A. Frink**, daughter of **Zachary Frink** and **Phebe Holmes** of North Stonington, Ct, on February 26, 1837.[461] Sarah was born April 11, 1818 in North Stonington, Ct.[462] Sarah died October 30, 1869.[463]

William Leeds Main[464]

The children of William L. and Sarah Main:

1. **Sarah Maria Main** was born on August 27, 1838.[465] She died on September 18, 1858.[466] She married David Boss.[467] Sarah is buried at the Brown, Peckham, Main Cemetery with her parents.

2. **John Latham Main** was born on August 2, 1841.[468] He married Phebe E. Frink[469]

3. **Leeds Main** was born on September 8, 1844.[470] He died on November 9, 1895.[471] He married Sarah Holdredge[472]

From Genealogical Record of Nathaniel Babcock, Simeon Main, Isaac Miner and Ezekiel Main book under Leeds Main: [473]

> *"...His home was in Ledyard, about two miles from the paternal homestead, which he purchased in 1876, where he successfully engaged in farming. Politically Mr. Main was a democrat. He was an attendant of the Baptist Church. The farm is pleasantly located in Ledyard, where the widow and two daughters reside..."*

4. **Phebe E. Main** was born on July 4, 1846.[474] She died on September 6, 1878.[475] She married John Finegan[476] and William Harrington[477]

5. **Lurie H. Main** was born on June 11, 1849.[478] She died on April 10, 1928.[479] She is buried at the Brown Peckham Main Cemetery in Ledyard, Ct. She never married.

A quote from the Genealogical Record of Nathaniel Babcock, Simeon Main, Isaac Miner and Ezekiel Main book under Lurie H. Main: [480]

> *"...resides on the old homestead, with a beautiful meadow in front of the house; easterly is the beautiful foliage of Lantern Hill, which gives the home a picturesqueness like the White Mountains in summer..."*

6. **Ira D. Main** was born on August 25, 1851.[481] He died on

February 15, 1909.[482] He is buried at the Brown Peckham Main Cemetery, Ledyard, Ct. He never married.

7. **Alonzo Main** was born on October 4, 1856.[483] He and Melissa Main were twins. He married Ethel Main.[484]

From Genealogical Record of Nathaniel Babcock, Simeon Main, Isaac Miner and Ezekiel Main book under Alonzo Main: [485]

> "*...Mr. Main since 1870 has lived at his present residence at the foot of Long Pond. For a number of years he has been boss of the silex mine at Lantern Hill. He is also interested in and owner in mines in New Mexico, Colorado, and California. He combines with his many industries also farming. He, being a man of marked executive ability, has been often sought by his fellow townsmen to public offices, but has always declined to serve. He has shown much interest in collecting family records. He places his father's picture in this genealogy...*"

8. ****Melissa Main** was born on October 4, 1856.[486] She was a twin with Alonzo Main. She died December 9, 1934.[487] She married Joseph E. Holdridge.[488] Melissa and Joseph Holdridge are buried in the Ledyard Center Cemetery in Ledyard, Ct

9. **Frances A. Main** was born on July 2, 1859.[489] She married William Richmond.[490]

10. *****Horace H. Main** was born on August 9, 1859.[491] He married Phebe M. Partelo.[492]

11. **Amos Main** was born on November 3, 1862.[493] He married Lucy Mathewson.[494]

LIFE OF WILLIAM LEEDS MAIN

From the Genealogical Record of Nathaniel Babcock, Simeon Main, Isaac Miner and Ezekiel Main book under William Leeds Main: [495]

> ... "*William Leeds, during this active life conducted a store,*

grist mill and a saw mill and financially prospered in all of his undertakings. He was a man of energy and good judgment and was a wise counselor to those in need of advice. In his friendships he was staunch and true and often lent a helping hand to those less fortunate. He was a conscientious official in public life and had a deep sense of responsibility of those elected to do the will of the people. He represented the Town of Ledyard for one term in the State Legislature. He was the largest land holder and the wealthiest man in Ledyard..."

William Leeds Main was born in Ledyard, probably on the Thomas Main Homestead off Long Pond (see #9 on page 20).

From the below Tax List, you will see what amount of property William L. Main owned in different Tax years. It is interesting to see that in his earlier years he had a store. In his later years, he owned four houses.

Year	**Property Owner**	**House**	**Acres**	**Mill**	**Store**
1839	William L. Main		32 [496]		
1851	William L. Main				Store [497]
1860	William L. Main	2	191		
		30 Indian Land			
		30 Indian Land.[498]			
1865	William L. Main	2	314.[499]		
1866	William L. Main	3	285 [500]		
1869	William L. Main	4&lots	346		
		100 acres of Packer and Indian Land [501]			
1871	William L. Main	4&lots	332		
		100 acres of Packer and Indian Land[502]			

On the 1850 and 1860 Census for Ledyard (see page 117 and 118), William Leeds Main lived next to his father Thomas Main. On the 1860 Census the value of his real estate was $7000, which was quite a bit of money for those days. His personal property was worth $17,794. As you can see from the above tax lists of Ledyard, he owned 2 houses and 191 acres of land, plus another 60 acres of Indian Land.

On the 1870 Census for Ledyard in the Mystic River District, listed under William Leeds Main, was the following: [503]

	Name	Age	Occupation	Real Estate	Pers. Prop.
273 286	Maine, Wm. L.	57	farmer	$13,000	$38,000
	Sarah M.	20	keeps house		
	Ira	17	works on farm		

On the 1880 Census for Ledyard, listed under William Leeds Main, was the following: [504]

	Name	Age	Relationship	Occupation
263 266	Main, William L.	66	self	farmer
	Julia A.	46	wife	
	Amos	18	son	
	Herrington, James L.	1	grandson	
	Main, Thomas B.	76	brother	farm laborer

At the Bill Library in Ledyard, I found the following in the School file: [505]

1858 Wood Bill for Schools
Charles H. Swan, Teacher, fireman
14th School for the year 1857-58
The following people paid for the schooling of their children:

Wm. Main	*23*
Daniel Main	*15*
Samuel Main	*52*
Betsey Wheeler	*93* (Betsey Wheeler as a Western Pequot Indian)

The school was where Lantern Hill Road meets Indian Town Road in Ledyard. It was located on the Main Property. (See #48 on the map on page 25)

From the New London County Superior Court Records, Papers by Subject: Indians, at the Connecticut State Library for the Mashantucket Pequot Tribe, I found the following information about William L. and Wm. L. Main:

"*1. 1846 Rent of land in cash in the year 1846 belonging to Pequot Indians in Ledyard Wm. L. Main $6.00* [506]

2. Jan. 25, 1855 by Wm. L Main & note for rent $34 (listed under credits) [507]

3. Dec. 25, 1855 Land Rented to William L. Main for $34 (listed under credits) [508]

4. March and April 1856, William L. Main saw bill 5248 ft, boards $17.49.

It was listed under: [509]

Expenses in erecting three dwelling houses on Pequot Reservation lands in the town of Ledyard

5. April 6, 1864 to cash for Wm. L. Main for school bill $.17. Listed under Jabez Niles[510]

From the New London County Superior Court Records, Papers by Subject: Indians, at the Connecticut State Library for the Eastern Pequot Tribe, I found the following information about William L. and Wm. L. Main:

1.Jan 30, 1850 to this__ Wm. L. Main for putting up house that blew down $5.00[511]

2. Elias Hewitt Overseer, was balancing his books on June 29, 1854 it stated: [512]

By this sum charged in my former acct. It being the amt of $4.00 Wm L. Main Bill which he refused to take By Interest on *the above since allowed .36*

3. August 1856 paid W.L. Main one dollar for plowing yards for said tribe [513]

4. Feb. 18, 1861, one lb. Candles .10 C, paid William L. Main 15C. moving Marun Duglus & Ned goods .80 [514]

5. Feb. 18, 1861 paid William L. Main 37.C Ea. Co. T .37
Paid William L. Main 15 for Codfish 7 .15 [515]

6. Jan. 30, 1871 To paid Wm. L. Main for plowing garden and 1 bushel potatoes the spring of 1871 for Eunice Cottrell or Fagins $2.88 [516]

7. Jan. 30, 1871 To paid Wm. L. Main for plowing garden and 1 bushel potatoes the spring of 1871 Leonard Brown or Nedson $2.87 [517]

William Leeds Main Estate was worth more than $100,000. From his Inventory, his Real Estate was listed as follows: [518]

1. Asa Gray place and Peter George lot
2. Hewitt place and Perkins and Pratt land
3. Herbert Spicer place
4. Whaley Place in Groton near Whipple House School
5. ½ acre tract of land near Lantern Hill Pond
6. David Mallory land in North Stonington
7. Dudley Main land in North Stonington
8. Thompson place in Montville
9. Cedar Swamp Lot #1, partly cut off
10. Cedar Swamp Lot #2
11. Cedar Swamp Lot #3, Samuel Main Lot
12. Cedar Swamp Lot #4 in dispute
13. Cedar Swamp Lot #5, Erasmus Avery Lot
14. Cedar Swamp Lot #6, Charles Woodmansee Lot
15. Home Farm as valued in Will
16. Bennett land and R.A. Stanton farm
17. Joe Tinker place in Milltown

William Leeds Main wrote his Last Will and Testament on June 28, 1887. The following is a list of his heirs and what they received: [519]

1. Wife, Julia A. Main, half the household goods and use, rents, interest and income of his farm and buildings known as Perkins and Pratt land
2. John L. Main, son, $5,000, received his April 2, 1891
3. Leeds Main, son, $5,000
4. Mrs. Sarah A. Holdredge, granddaughter, child of daughter Phebe Finnegan Harrington, deceased, $1,000, received April 2, 1891
5. John W. Finnegan, grandson, son of daughter Phebe (above) $1,000, received April 2, 1891
6. James L. Harrington, grandson, son of daughter Phebe (above) $1,000, on April 2, 1891 Julia A. Main received $1,000 for minor James L. Finegan.
7. Ira Main, son, $5,000, received $5,000 on April 2, 1891
8. Lury Main, daughter, $3,000, received $3,000 on April 2, 1891
9. Frances A. Richmond, daughter, has use, rent and income of lot and buildings situated in Milltown, North Stonington
10. Melissa Holdridge, daughter, $3,000, received $3,000 on April 2, 1891
11. Alonzo Main, son, $5,000, received the following on April 2, 1891:

Note	$1800.00
Interest	240.00
Samuel Main Cedar Swamp Lot	145.00
David Mallory Lot, lease 99 years	108.00
Hay, N. E. Perkins barn	20.00
Hay in Packer barn	17.00
Goods at auction	40.66
Margaret Brown note	2500.00
Interest	37.50

Book account	51.50
Deposit in Norwich Saving Society	100.00
Carpet and Arbor	5.00
Cash	35.34
Total	$5100.00

12. Horace H. Main, son, use, rent and income of the Robert Stanton farm and Bennett land and all the buildings thereon standing, where he now lives in the Town of Ledyard. Also $1,500

13. Amos Main, son, the Homestead Farm and buildings where I now live formerly known as the Jeffrey Brown farm valued at $5,300

14. Worthy friends, Mr. George Fanning and Mr. Jacob Gallup were named executors.

15. $150 to be put in trust to keep my family burial lot and gravestones in Brown Burying Ground of Ledyard in good condition.

On William Leeds Main death certificate it states that he was a counselor which goes along with the quote from the Genealogical Record of Nathaniel Babcock, Simeon Miner, Isaac Miner and Ezekiel Main book. William Leeds Main and Sarah A. Frink are buried in the Brown, Peckham, Main Cemetery on Iron Street in Ledyard, Ct (see #34 on page 25).

**MELISSA MAIN

****Melissa Main**, the daughter of **William L. Main** and **Sarah A. Frink**, married **Joseph E. Holdridge**, son of **Randall Holdridge** and **Nancy Barns**.
Children of Joseph and Melissa Main Holdridge: [520]

Marion M. Holdridge
Randall L. Holdridge
Joseph Nelson Holdridge
Estella I. Holdridge
William Leeds Holdridge
Gladys Holdridge

My grandfather was their son, William Leeds Holdridge. William Leeds Holdridges son Joseph Fairfield Holdridge is my father. As you know from this chapter, Melissa Main was the daughter of William Leeds Main. William Leeds Main was the son of Thomas Main and Lois Brown. Lois Brown was the daughter of Nathaniel Brown and Deborah Morgan. Noyes and I have the same common ancestors through Nathaniel Brown and Deborah Morgan and through Thomas and Lois Brown Main (myself through William Leeds Main and Noyes through Timothy Main) and Nathan and Hannah Brown Holdridge (myself through Randall Holdridge and Noyes through his sister Annis Holdridge).

Joseph Enos Holdridge and Melissa Main wedding picture[521]

***HORACE H. MAIN

*****Horace H. Main**, son of **William L. Main** and **Sarah A. Frink**, married Phebe M. Partelo.
Children of Horace and Phebe Main: [522]

Florence B. Main, married Philetus Brown
Lure E. Main
Phebe M. Main,
Horace W. Main
Harry C.W. Main

From Genealogical Record of Nathaniel Babcock, Simeon Main, Isaac Miner and Ezekiel Main book under Horace Main: [523]

> *"...Mr. Main was a farmer, and combines with it carpenter work and other industries. Mrs. Main is an expert in poultry-raising and gives much attention to that industry..."*

I am showing this line, because Ray Ernest Willcox bought property from two of Horace's children, Harry C.W. and Lure E.

Main, which I have already mentioned in the Ray Willcox section. Also, Avery W. Brown and Albert Brown, sons of Nathaniel Brown and Charlotte Wilbur were brought up in the house that Harry C. W. Main lived in, on Iron Street in Ledyard, Ct.

On the 1930 Census for Ledyard, Jane Durfey was listed as a lodger at Lurie Mains home: [524]

233 303 **Main, Luretta** Head of household age 43 born Ct
Main, Lure H. daughter age 9 born Ct
Durfey, Jane Boarder age 86 Indian Pequot Mixed Blood
Johnson, Willis A. Lodger age 54 born Maine
house carpenter

Jane Durfee was mentioned earlier in the George Park Main section along with her husband Frederick Durfee. George P. and Sarah A. Main lived next door to Jane in 1920 according to the Federal Census Records.

Jane Wheeler Durfey is buried with Frederick Durfee and his first wife Annie Sinclair in the Holdridge Cemetery on Indian Town Road in Ledyard, Ct (see #35 on page 25).

CHAPTER 8

ANNIS HOLDRIDGE/BROWN

Generation No 6

Annis Holdridge was born on July 08, 1812 in Groton, Ct. [525] She was the daughter of **Nathan Holdridge** and **Hannah Brown.** She died on June 05, 1901 in Ledyard, Ct. [526] She married **Avery Wilbur Brown** on July 21, 1833 in Ledyard, Ct.[527]

Avery Wilbur Brown was the son of **Nathaniel Brown** and **Charlotte Wilbur**. He was born on December 05, 1805 in Ledyard, Ct.[528] He died on August 08, 1885 in Ledyard, Ct.[529]

Avery W. Brown and Annis Holdridge Gravestones
Brown Peckham Main Cemetery in Ledyard, Ct.

The birth dates of all the children of Annis Holdridge and Avery Brown are recorded in the Ledyard Town Clerk office in Family Records.[530] Below are their children:

1. **Nathaniel Brown** was born on August 05, 1835 in Ledyard, Ct. He died in infancy.[531]

2. **Cynthia Brown** was born on May 22, 1836 in Ledyard, Ct. She married Elias D. Comstock on November 20, 1853[532] in Ledyard, Ct

3. **Hannah F. Brown** was born on July 11, 1836 in Ledyard, Ct. She died in her infancy.[533]

4. **Elias S. Brown** was born on August 27, 1838 in Ledyard, Ct. He died on March 16, 1877 in Ledyard, Ct. [534] He married Sarah Norman.[535]

5. **Daniel H. Brown** was born on October 11, 1840 in Ledyard, Ct. He married Mary. [536]

6. **Nancy A. Brown** was born on April 29, 1843 in Ledyard, Ct. She married Isaac E. Norman on November 21, 1865 in Ledyard, Ct.[537]

7. **James A. Brown** was born on March 25, 1845 in Ledyard, Ct. He married Eliza Stanton.[538]

8. **Sarah Eliza Brown** was born on February 27, 1847 in Ledyard, Ct. She died on October 09, 1939 in Ledyard, Ct. She married George P. Main on March 25, 1868 in Preston, Ct.

9. **William N. Brown** was born on March 27, 1849 in Ledyard, Ct. He married Julia E. for his first wife. His second wife was Lucy A. White.[539] William N. Brown along with his wife Julia and Lucy A. White are buried in the Brown Peckham Main Cemetery in Ledyard, Ct.

10. **Fanny F. Brown** was born on March 28, 1851 in Ledyard, Ct. She married John H. Godfrey on September 29, 1872 in Ledyard.[540] He was the son of George & Aedelia (Howard) Godfrey of Norwich. Mr. Godfrey was a blacksmith, Mystic, Ct.[541]

11. **Erastus J. Brown** was born on April 04, 1854 in Ledyard, Ct.

12. **Lillie A. Brown** was born on August 30, 1858 in Ledyard, Ct. She died on December 21, 1891 in Ledyard, Ct.[542]

Avery W. and Annis Holdridge Brown life

Avery Wilbur Brown was born on Iron Street in Ledyard, Ct. (see #11 on page 25). As I was researching the Brown family, I found this paragraph at the Bill Library in Groton, Ct. in the book History of New London. Albert Brown and Avery Wilbur Brown were brothers, so this helps explain where they were born and who their parents were: [543]

"BROWN, ALBERT MORGAN.... Nathaniel Brown, grandfather of Albert M. Brown of the town of Ledyard, New London county, Conn. was born on the old Brown farm in the town of Ledyard, as was his son, Albert Brown and the laters son Albert M. Brown. The house in which Nathaniel Brown was born was not the one in which his son and grandson were born, but belonged to an earlier day Nathaniel Brown married Lottie Wilbur, and both spent their lives on the farm in Ledyard, where he passed away, his wife died in Waterford.

Their son Albert Brown, was born, lived and died on the same farm, and most of his life was spent in cultivating its acres. He, however, was a skilled wheelwright and built houses. He was school committeeman, and a man of a good deal of influence in his town. He married Surviah Main, who was born, lived and died in Ledyard. They were the parents of Albert Morgan Brown, of Ledyard, now too passed to his reward..."

I believe that Annis Holdridge was born on Colonel Ledyard Highway in Ledyard, Ct. I will discuss more on why Annis could have been born there, in the Holdridge section, which will be in the next chapter.

The Family Records of Avery and Annis Brown are recorded in the Ledyard Town Hall, in the Town Clerks office. It stated the following: [544]

"Avery W. Brown born December 5, 1805 and Annis Holdridge born July 8, 1812 and were married July 21, 1834. Children:

Nathaniel Brown	*born August 15, 1835*
Hannah Brown	*born July 11, 1836*
Cynthia Brown	*born May 22, 1836(1837)*
Elias Brown	*born August 27, 1838*
Daniel Brown	*born October 11, 1840*
Nancy A. Brown	*born April 29, 1843*
James A. Brown	*born March 25, 1845*
Sarah E. Brown	*born March 25. 1845*
William N. Brown	*born February 27, 1847*
Fanny F. Brown	*born March 27, 1849*
Erastus J. Brown	*born April 4, 1854*
Lillie A. Brown	*born August 30, 1858*

Received and recorded May 15, 1874"

At the Bill Library in Ledyard on Ledyard Abstract on Tax Levy of 1866: [545]

Name	***House/Value***		***Acres/Value***		***Store/Mill***		***Cows***	***Sheep***
Brown, Avery W.	*1*	*$200*	*45*	*$67*	*1*	*$25*	*2*	*1*

On the 1869 Ledyard Tax List for Avery W. Brown is the following: [546]

"Brown, Avery W.
1 house and lot
40 acres of land at $15 per A. (acre)
1 Saw Mill
2 Oxen
2 three year old
2 three years old heifers

1 poll (paid for the right to vote in elections)"

From these tax lists, you can see that Avery Brown had a small saw mill on his property in Ledyard. He and Annis must have had a small farm on this property as well. As you will see in the Census Records he was listed as a farmer. His property is located near a brook and also in the same valley as Robert Willcox 3rd. This valley was known to be of very fertile ground, so Avery could have had orchids or vegetable gardens. Two cows and one sheep would be enough to help feed the household, but not to make a living from. Also, as you will see from the Mashantucket Pequot Overseers Report, Avery was paid for teaming. On the 1869 Tax List he had 2 oxen. The oxen were used for teaming in this time frame, not horses. As a matter of fact on the tax list, horses are not mentioned at all. Most people from this area used their oxen for plowing and pulling logs from the woods and other tasks that we associate with a horse doing today.

Avery and Annis Brown were also members of the 1st Baptist Church of Groton. Avery W. Brown was received and baptized Nov. 1831. He was on Members List March 2, 1843. Annis Brown was a Member on Oct. 15, 1842.[547] Annis Holdridge was received and baptized Aug 1831. Annis Brown was dismissed Mar. 2, 1843. I believe they went to the 2nd Baptist Church (see # 45 on page 25) on Iron Street after that point.[548]

From the New London County Superior Court Records, Papers by Subject: Indians, at the Connecticut State Library for the Mashantucket Pequot Tribe I found the following information about Avery W. Brown and Albert Brown:

"Expenses in erecting three dwelling houses on Pequot Reservation lands in the town of Ledyard:

March and April 1856 Avery W. Brown was paid for teaming $3.73 [549]

(Avery's brother) *Albert Brown bought land in 1855 for*

$191.27 [550]

January 27, 1837 Albert Brown was paid for a coffin for Maryann Deshon boy $1.25 [551]"

Avery Wilbur Brown and Annis lived off of Iron Street in Ledyard, Ct (see #21 on page 25). If you look at the Census Records for Avery and Annis Holdridge Brown, you will notice they lived in Ledyard their entire married life.

On 1850 Census for Ledyard: [552]

117 135 **Brown, Avery** age 46 farmer born Ct. property $1000

Annis	age 36
Cynthia	age 16
Elias S.	age 12
Daniel	age 11
Nancy	age 7
James I.	age 6
Sarah E.	age 3
William E.	age 1

On the 1850 Census, Avery Brown's next neighbor was his brother Albert Brown. The neighbor after Albert was Robert Willcox. So they were living off Iron Street at this time.

On 1860 Census for Ledyard: [553]

222 239 **Brown, Avery W.**	age 55 farmer	born Groton
Annis	age 46	born Groton
Elias W.	age 21 Fisherman	born Ledyard
Daniel H.	age 19 farming	"
Nancy A.	age 17	"
James A.	age 15	"
Sarah E.	age 13	"
William A.	age 11	"

Fanny F.	age 9	born Ledyard
John E.	age 6	"
Lillie A	age 1	"

Again, on the 1860 Census, Avery and Annis Brown had same neighbors as mentioned above in the 1850 Census.

On 1870 Census for Ledyard: [554]

231 241 **Brown, Avery**	age 65 farmer 3500 1000
Annis	age 58 keeps house
James	age 25 Lumberman
Fanny	age 19
John	age 16
Lillie A.	age 12

On the 1870 Census, Avery Brown's neighbor was Robert and Mary Wilcox on this Census as well.

On 1880 Census for Ledyard: [555]

241 264 **Brown, Avery W.**	age 76 farmer
Anis wife	age 68 keeping house
John E. son	age 26 farm laborer
242 265 **Brown, Albert M**.	age 41 farmer
Nancy A. wife	age 39 keeping house
Ella N. daughter	age 16 at home
Philetus A. son	age 14
Emma B. daughter	age 9
Minnie A. daughter	age 5
243 266 **Main, William L.**	age 66 farmer
Julia A. wife	age 46 keeping house
Amos son	age 18
Herrington, James L. grandson	age 1
Main, Thomas B. brother	age 74 farm laborer

On the 1880 Census, Avery and Annis Brown's neighbor was Avery's brother, Albert M. Brown. Albert Brown's neighbor was William L. Main, which still puts Avery and Annis on Iron Street in Ledyard, Ct.

In Avery Browns Probate records, they had to sell the property during the Probate process. William Leeds Main bought this property on February 16, 1887. This property consisted of 3 tracts or parcels of land: [556]

"#1 Homestead Farm with 20 acres
#2 wood lot had 12 acres
#3 lot with 5 acres"

In Probate Records for Annis Brown I found the following bills in the Inventory section, which were taken on March 24, 1902:[557]

"...Undertakers Bill	*$57.70*	
Rev. John Avery		*$ 5.00*
Raymond Wilcox (digging Grave)		*$11.00*
Headstone	*$18.00*	
Probate Fees	*$ 3.00*	
Admin Fees	*$ 3.00*	
E. John Brown	*$ 6.22"*	

Avery Wilbur Brown and Annis Holdridge are buried in the Brown Peckham Cemetery on Iron Street in Ledyard, Ct. (see #34 on page 25)

BROWN ANCESTRY

This is the third line that goes back to Nathaniel Brown and Deborah Morgan. This time it is through their son Nathaniel Brown who married Charlotte Wilbur. I will be discussing the parents of Nathaniel Brown who married Charlotte Wilbur along with his sisters, Hannah, Lois and Deborah Brown in Chapter 9.

NATHANIEL BROWN AND CHARLOTTE WILBUR

The following information is from the Brown Genealogy: [558]

Nathaniel Brown was born 1773 and died July 2, 1836. He is the son of **Nathaniel Brown** and **Deborah Morgan**. He married **Charlotte Wilbur**. She was born 1781 and died March 24, 1866, aged 85 years. They lived near the Peckham Church (which is the 2nd Baptist Church, see #45 on page 25) and are buried there. (Nathaniel and Charlotte Browns house is #25 on page 25)

Children of Nathaniel and Charlotte Brown:

1. **Nathaniel Brown** m. Eliza Brockway
2. **Gurdon Brown**, unmarried, He was a mariner. He went to Utah, and all record of him was lost.
3. **Avery Wilbur Brown**, born December 5, 1805, married Annis Holdridge
4. **Albert Brown**, born September 1, 1811, married Surviah B. Main, daughter of Thomas and Lois Brown Main (already mentioned in the last Chapter)
5. **Alvah Brown**, married Frances
6. **John Brown**, married Sarah Fox. They lived in Waterford, Conn. Both deceased. No issue.
7. **Samuel Brown**, was a mariner and died at sea; unmarried
8. **Calvin Brown**, unmarried. He lived at Waterford and died there, aged 45 years
9. **Frank Brown**, unmarried

CHAPTER 9

HANNAH BROWN/HOLDRIDGE

Generation No 7

Hannah Brown was born about 1779.[559] She died on December 07, 1843.[560] She was the daughter of **Nathaniel Brown** and **Deborah Morgan.**(See next Chapter for possible discrepancies on parentage of Hannah Brown) She married **Nathan Holdridge** on February 14, 1799 in Groton, Ct.[561]

Nathan Holdridge was the son of **Phinehas Holdridge** and **Mary Thompson**. He was born on July 10, 1760 in Groton, Ct.[562] He died on November 18, 1817 in Groton, Ct.[563]
Children of Hannah Brown and Nathan Holdridge are:

1. **Hannah Holdridge** was born about 1799.[564] She married (1) Benjamin Pettis.[565] She married (2) Stephen Comady.[566]

2. **Nathan Holdridge** was born about 1801.[567] He married Jane Wright October 11, 1829 in Groton, Ct.[568]

3. **Mary Holdridge** was born on July 02, 1802 in Groton, Ct.[569] She died September 18, 1892.[570] She married James Stanton October 20, 1841 in Groton, Ct.[571]

4. **Betsey Holdridge**[572]

5. **Phinehas Holdridge** was born about 1805.[573]

6. **Stephen Holdridge** was born on March 29, 1807 in Groton, Ct.[574] He died September 08, 1891.[575] He married Hannah Sterry.[576] They are buried in the Colonel Ledyard Cemetery, in Groton, Ct.

7. **Eneas Holdridge**, born about 1808.[577] He died on October 19, 1832 in Lisbon, Ct.[578] He married Sarah Sullivan March 04, 1832 in Lisbon, Ct. [579] Eneas Holdridge is buried in the Holdridge Cemetery on Indian Town Road in Ledyard, Ct. (See #35 on page 25)

8. Randall Holdridge was born on August 22, 1808 in Groton, Ct.[580] He died on January 15, 1885 in Ledyard, Ct.[581] He married (1) Emeline F. Reed on March 25, 1832 in Groton, Ct.[582] Emeline F. Reed was born about 1814.[583] She died on January 23, 1854.[584] He married (2) Nancy Barnes on July 09, 1854 in Norwich, Ct.[585] Nancy Barnes was born May 11, 1817 in Ledyard, Ct.[586] She died on February 02, 1900.[587]

9. Annis Holdridge was born on July 08, 1812 in Groton, Ct. She died on June 05, 1901 in Ledyard, Ct. She married Avery Wilbur Brown.

10. Almira Holdridge was born about 1814. [588] She died on March 14, 1880.[589] She married Rev Stephen Hazard Peckham September 02, 1850 in Ledyard, Ct. [590] Rev. Stephen H. Peckham was born 1805.[591] He died December 18, 1863. [592] Almira and the Rev. Stephen Peckham lived off Shewville Road (see #49 map on page 25) on the west side of the Western Pequot Reservation. Rev. Stephen Peckham and his wives are buried in the Brown, Peckham Main Cemetery on Iron Street in Ledyard, Ct. Rev. Peckham was the Pastor at the 2nd Baptist Church on Iron Street. [593] He also was listed in the New London County Superior Court Records, Papers by Subject: Indians, at the Connecticut State Library for the Mashantucket Pequot Tribe:

> "*1859, February 23, To cash to S.H. Peckham for drawing 7 loads of wood $4.20* [593]
>
> *1859, September 23, Paid Elder S. Peckham for attending funeral (E. Deshon) $1.00* [594]
>
> *1860, November 28, paid, Stephen Peckham for drawing wood $2.00* [595]"

11. Daniel Holdridge was born on March 30, 1814 in Groton, Ct.[596] He died on March 27, 1888. [597] He married Eliza Jane Maine September 11, 1845 in Ledyard, Ct.[598]

Life of Nathan Holdridge

Nathan Holdridge lived a very short married life. Nathan had to have been born in Stonington, Ct. I believe he was born on the James Thompson farm, his grandfather, or possibly somewhere in that vicinity. The James Thompson property is located on Route 49 in North Stonington, Ct. Nathan's father, Phinehas Holdridge, did not buy any property in Groton until 1784, and he was of Stonington, Ct when he bought this property. So it would make sense that Nathan was born in Stonington, seeing he was born in 1760.

At the Connecticut Historical Society, Punderson Account Book Vol 14, 1797 July – 1797 Nov[599]

> *"July 13, 1797, Nathaniel Holdridge d. 2 pencils, 1 pen knife, 20 eggs*
> *July 22, 1797, Nath'l Holdridge, 2 1/2 yd. Satten*
> *July 29, 1797, Nath'l Holdridge, horse whip"*

The Punderson Store was owned by Ebenezer Punderson and was located in Preston. There are many account books for this store at the Connecticut Historical Society.

When Nathan Holdridge went to the store, he was not married to Hannah Brown yet. My question is, "Is he buying the Satten (Satin) for Hannah or for one of his sisters or his mother?" Hannah and Nathan were married 1½ years later. It could have been for Hannah's wedding dress.

When Nathan Holdridge went to Punderson store, if you look at #37 on pages 24 and 25, and follow that route, you may feel the same as we feel that Nathan Holdridge took this route in 1797. It would be one of the straightest routes to take. It seems like the most logical way to go from his fathers, Phinehas Holdridge property.

The following is the route Nathan Holdridge could have

followed:

If you started at the Phinehas Holdridge house and went up through William Hempstead property (see map on page 79) this would take you near where they found the location of the Fort at Mashantucket at the Mashantucket Pequot Museum and Research Center.

You would have to cross the backside of the reservation (there were many cart paths through this area) to Kate Swamp Road. After crossing Kate Swamp Road, you would follow another cart path to Shewville Road. Follow Shewville Road to Fanning Road and Fanning Road to Churchill Road. It would be just a short distance on Churchill Road then on to Thomas Road to Route 117. You would follow Route 117 to the store.

That would be one of the shortest routes to take to Punderson Store. The Punderson Store was located in the Poquetanuck section of Preston on the water.

Census Records for Nathan and Hannah Holdridge

On 1800 Census for Groton[600]

Nathan Holdridge
1 male 0 to 10 years
1 male 16 to 26 years
1 female 16 to 26 years

Neighbors:
Ephraim Wailey
Zachariah Watrous
Nathan Holdridge
Elias Miner
Sarah Stark
William Alexander
Henry Gallup
Henry Gallup Jr

Nehemiah Gallup
Joseph Stanton

On the 1800 Census, Nathan and Hannah Holdridge were living near the Shewville Road section of the Town of Ledyard. Henry Gallup lived on Shewville Road in this time frame.

On 1810 Census Groton[602]

Nathan Holdridge
4 males under 10 years
1 male 26 to 45 years
1 female under 10 years
2 females 10 to 16 years
1 female 26 to 45 years

Neighbors:
Isaac Avery
Russel Perkins
Jonathan Chapman
Nathan Holdridge
Stephen Billings
Aaron Lamb

On the 1810 Census, seeing Stephen Billings was Nathan's neighbor, Nathan and Hannah Holdridge were living on Colonel Ledyard Highway.

On 1820 Census for Groton, page 815:[603]

Hannah Holdridge:
3 males under 10 years old
2 males 10 to 16 years
1 male 16 to 18 years old
1 male 18 to 26 years old

2 females 10 to 16 years old
1 female 26 to 45 years old

Neighbors:
James Etheridge
Thomas Hull
Benj. Pettis
Hannah Holdridge
Timothy Tuttle
Dan King
Joseph S. Avery

On 1830 Census for Groton:[604]

Hannah Holdridge
1 male 15 to 20 years
1 male 20 to 30 years
2 females 15 to 20 years
1 female 50 to 60 years

Neighbors:
Samuel Newton
Stephen Billings
Enos Morgan
Stephen Holdridge
John Chapman
Hannah Holdridge
Russel Gallup
Charles Gallup
Eber Chapman
John A. Williams
Gurdon Bill

On 1840 Census Ledyard[605]

Hannah Holdridge
1 male 30 to 40 years old
2 females 15 to 20 years
1 female 60 to 70 years

Neighbors:
Egbert Bailey
Christopher C. Brand
Washington Avery
Hannah Holdridge
Stephen Holdridge
Daniel Clark

On the 1820, 1830 and 1840 Census, Hannah Holdridge was still living on Colonel Ledyard Highway in Ledyard, Ct. After Nathan Holdridge died, I did not find that Hannah ever remarried. She spent her remaining days on Colonel Ledyard Highway. (See #24 Map on page 24)

Nathan Holdridge did not have a Last Will and Testament, but the distribution of his property is recorded in the Stonington Probate office. Stephen Billings and Samuel Newton were appointed to divide the property between all the children of Nathan and Hannah Holdridge.[606] Their son, Phinehas Holdridge Jr chose Christopher Newton as his guardian on March 25, 1825.[607]

Nathan and Hannah's son, Randall Holdridge, is my great-great Grandfather by his second wife, Nancy Barns. I am not going to get into great detail on Randall, but the property Randall owned stayed in the Holdridge name until about the 1930's. (See #32 on Map on page 24) Randall was a farmer and surveyor.[608] He also signed the Petition to start the 2nd Baptist Church along with his 1st wife Emeline Reed.[609]

I checked the Probate Records in Ledyard and Stonington and there are no Probate Records for a Hannah Holdridge in either town. Hannah was not given any land in the Distribution of Nathan Holdridge Estate. I believe she lived with her children, but she was listed as Head of Household on the Census records because she was the oldest person living in the house.

Nathan Holdridge was buried next to his parents in the Holdridge Cemetery on Indiantown Road in Ledyard, Ct. (See #35 on the map on page 25) Hannah Brown Holdridge is also, buried in the Holdridge Cemetery. (See #35 on the map on page 25) Hannah Holdridge gravestone says she died December 5, 1843, aged 64 years. As you saw from the list of the children of Nathan and Hannah Holdridge, their son Eneas Holdridge is also buried in this same cemetery.

There is a Pequot Indian known as Jane Wheeler Durfee who is buried there as well with her husband Frederick Durfee and his first wife Annie Sinclair. From a previous chapter, I discussed that Jane Wheeler Durfee was known as a Pequot Indian. The three gravestones for Annie Sinclair Durfee, Frederick Durfee and Jane Durfee are all exactly alike. Frederick Durfee must have had them all put in at the same time. He wanted to make sure his wife Jane had a place for her burial, or he would not have put in the third stone. There are no death dates on Frederick and Jane Durfees' stones.

Hannah and her son Eneas Holdridge are Native American through Noyes's Maternal DNA testing. So there are three Native Americans buried in the Holdridge Cemetery, Jane Durfee and Hannah and Eneas Holdridge.

The Holdridge Ancestors

I will be discussing this line because of the relationship that Phinehas Holdridge had with one of the Western Pequot Indians as well as his western boundary was referred to as Indian Land in this deed.

Phinehas Holdridge 1st was born about 1738.[610] He died on January 1, 1815 in Groton, Ct.[611] He may have been the son of **Nathaniel Holdridge** and possibly **Lydia Holdridge**. It is written in other genealogies, that he was the son of Samuel Holdridge and Sarah Fellows. I believe there is sufficient evidence that he could very possibly be the son of Nathaniel Holdridge and not Samuel Holdridge. He married **Mary Thompson**, daughter of **James Thompson** and **Mary Dixon**. I have never found a marriage record for Phinehas and Mary Holdridge. Mary Thompson was born in Stonington, Ct on December 16, 1746.[612] She died on November 9, 1814 in Groton, Ct.[613]
Children of Phinehas and Mary Holdridge:

1. **Nathan Holdridge** was born on July 10, 1760. He died on November 18, 1817 in Groton, Ct. He married Hannah Brown.

2. Nancy Holdridge was born on February 13, 1770.[614] She died on June 7, 1856.[615] She married James Etheridge. James and Nancy Etheridge are buried in the Spicer Cemetery on Colonel Ledyard Highway in Ledyard, Ct.

3. Phinehas Holdridge 2nd was born about 1771.[616] He died on June 22, 1854.[617] He married Fanny Starr on June 26, 1828 in Griswold, Ct.[618] He is buried in the Holdridge Cemetery on Indiantown Road in Ledyard, Ct.

4. **Thompson Holdridge** was born 1775.[619] He married his cousin Betsey Thompson.[620]

5. Mary Holdridge was born about 1779.[621] She married Amos Mason.[622]

6. **Phebe Holdridge** married William Sisson February 27, 1806 in Groton, Ct.[623]

7. Cynthia Holdridge was born about 1787.[624] She died October 21, 1853.[625] She never married. Cynthia is buried in the Holdridge Cemetery on Indiantown Road in Ledyard, Ct

8. Amos Holdridge was born about 1791.[626]

9. Sarah Holdridge was born about 1792.[627] She died on March 8, 1860.[628] She never married. She is also buried in the

Holdridge Cemetery.

Cynthia and Sarah Holdridge lived with their brother Phinehas Holdridge 2nd after their father died in the homestead on Indiantown Road in Ledyard, Ct.

Life of Phinehas Holdridge

The first mention of Phinehas Holdridge that I found was when his wife Mary Thompson Holdridge was given personal items from the Estate of her father James Thompson of North Stonington, Ct. This is also when I found that Phinehas Holdridge wife's, Mary, last name was Thompson. James Thompson Last Will and Testament stated:[629]

> "... *I give to my three daughters viz: Mary Holdridge, Sarah Crandall & Rebeckah Larkin five shillings cash which with what I have already given them is in full of their part of my estate ...*"

This was dated October 25, 1801. Among James Thompson personal items, it listed his daughter Mary Holdredge, wife of Phinehas Holdridge.[630]

(Phinehas Holdridge, the son of Nathan and Hannah Holdridge, and grandson to Phinehas Holdridge, moved to North Stonington. He owned property on Route 49, up the road from his Thompson relatives in North Stonington. He bought this property from Gershom Eccleston in 1838 and one of the borders was Alexander Thompson, son of James Thompson. One tract was 10 acres, the other tract was 30 acres.[631])

In the Groton Land Records are the following transactions:

> "*...Phinehas Holdridge, late of Groton, now of Stonington...*"

Phinehas Holdridge sold 15 acres of land in Groton on January 19, 1771 to Benjah Packer.[632] The description of the land, is as follows:

> "*...Beginning at a heap of stones being the northeast corner bound of the Land Capt. Henry Williams bought of Mr. John Dean of Stonington thence N. 8 degrees E. measuring fifty eight rods to a merestone thence West 8 N. measuring 40 rods and 23 Links to a merestone thence SW measuring 64 rods to two Ash Trees Standing on the East side of a small brook in the North line of said Capt. Williams Land thence Easterly bounding with said Williams Land 40 rods and 23 links to the Bound first mentioned, it being the Land I took by Execution of John Packer...*"

On November 12, 1771, Phinehas Holdredge of Stonington bought from Samuel Newton of Groton, 60 acres of land. The description is as follows: [633]

> "*...Beginning at a merestone standing nine rods southerly from Mr. Johnson southeast corner in the line of Samuel Williams Land and said Newton own Land thence southerly one hundred and three rods bounding on said Williams Lands to his southeast corner thence East 22 ½ South one hundred and four rods to a great Rock with stones on it, thence North east one hundred and twenty five rods to a merestone, thence westerly to the first mentioned bound, measuring about one hundred and thirty rods...*"

On December 25, 1786, Phinehas Holdridge, of Groton, bought 220 acres from Jedediah Leeds and Nathan Morgan of Groton, Ct.[634] This is the property he lived on until his death in 1814 (see #23 on Map on page 25).

The following is the description of this property:

"...Beginning at Lanthornhill pond low water mark in a line with Robert Stoddard Land. Thence running westerly by said Stoddards Land bout one hundred and sixty rods more or less to a heap of stones near a black oak tree which is the northwest corner of said Stoddards Land. Thence south by said Stoddards and Matthew Barns Land about seventy rods more or less to a heap of stones which is the Northeast corner of William Williams Land. Thence west by said Williams Land about one hundred and ten rods more or less to a heap of stones in a line of the Indian land. Thence running on the line of said Indian Land northerly about two hundred rods more or less till it comes to Lands the Estate of John Winthrop, Esq. Deceased, being said Winthrop's southwest corner. From thence Easterly two hundred rods by said Winthrop's Land to a heap of stones and crossing a highway. Thence Southerly by said Winthrops Land thirty two rods to a white oak tree formerly a heap of stones round it which makes a corner. Thence running Easterly by said Winthrop Land one hundred and sixty rods to said Lanternhornhill Pond low water mark to a heap of stones support to be now covered with water by the following of said ***pond to erect a Mill*** *on the same. Thence running by said Pond at low water mark, southerly about thirty rods to the first mentioned bound or however other ways butted and bounded together also with the Mansion or dwelling house and all other Buildings thereon now standing and being as also all the Ways, Woods, Walls, Waters, Fences, Trees, Brush or appertaining Improvements..."*

In this deed, it stated that ...a mill to be erected... I believe this mill would have been a cloth mill on Lantern Hill Pond (see #40 on Map on page 25). As you read on, you will see why from the evidence I have found on Phinehas Holdridge through an account book and his Inventory in his Probate Records.

In Punderson Account Book, located at the Connecticut Historical Society, I found the following: [635]

"*...Jan. 3, 1797, Phinehas Holdridge, Debt 10 ¼ 16 homemade full'd and shear'd redish brown cloth to be sold*
Jan 14, 1797, Phinehas Holdridge, Debt to sand P. to Daniel Billings sons special desire
Feb. 2, 1797, Phinehas Holdridge, sent 14 ¾ yds, white flannel by Dan Toby to be Sold
Feb. 16, 1797, Phinehas Holdridge by lender
Mar. 8, 1797, Phinehas Holdridge cloth sold to Jonathan Brewster..."

From the above entry dated February 2, 1797, it shows that Phinehas Holdridge trusted Dan Toby to take his wares to market (see #38 on Map on pages 24 and 25). In a deed recorded in the Town of Groton, dated December 16, 1830 from Peter Williams of Groton to John Williams of Groton, one of the landmarks they used as a border was Toby Orchard. The description reads as follows: [636]

"*...Commencing at the northwest corner being a pond hole, butting to lands of said John Williams and formerly owned by Thomas Mallison. Thence southerly a piece by said Mallison land. Thence connecting with land of the said John Williams formerly owned and occupied by Isaac Williams. Thence on said Lands tile it strikes the northeast corner of a lot of land which was set off to Isaac Williams, Jun., from the estate of Isaac Williams deceased. Thence westerly to land of Charles Allyn. Thence southerly by said Allyn Land. Thence easterly til it comes to a wall with the east end of the last, westerly course. Thence southerly to lands of James Fanning. Thence east by said Fanning to land belonging to the Pequot Tribe of Indians. Thence northerly by said Indians to the easternmost northeast corner of the Crucker field, so called.*

*Thence westerly and northerly by a number of short distinct courses, to a piece of Land known by the name of the **Toby Orchard**. Thence southerly to the southeast corner of said **Toby Orchard**. Thence westerly on a direct line to the first mentioned bound..."*

When Dan Toby went to the Punderson Store, he could have very easily gone by the Toby Orchid to get there (see above mentioned #38 on Map on pages 24 and 25). He would have taken pretty much the same route that Nathan Holdridge did when Nathan went, but I believe Dan Toby started from the Mill on Lantern Hill Pond. Dan Toby was an Indian living on the Western Pequot reservation at that time. Dan Toby could have been not only a worker for the Holdridge family, but a friend as well.

On the New London County Superior Court Records, Papers by Subject: Indians, at the Connecticut State Library, the Town of Lebanon billed the Agent of Indian Affairs of the Town of Groton for the following: [637]

*"**1820** Jan 4th to Charles Lathrop Esq. For boarding and nursing Dan alias **Daniel Toby** 1 week in sickness $2.00*
*Feb. 7th to Caleb Stark for Boarding and nursing sd. **Toby** in sickness 5 weeks @ $2 per fo week $10.00*
*15th to Doct Erastus Osgood for medical attendance on sd **Toby** is sd. sickness $4.25*

Lebanon March 1st 1821
Test Elisha Waterman
Selectman"

I believe that once Phinehas Holdridge died, Daniel Toby left this area and went to Lebanon, Ct.

From the Punderson Account Book, Phinehas Holdridge made cloth and flannel to sell. Also after looking over Phinehas Holdridge's Inventory, you will notice that Phinehas also had quite a few sheep, which would be his supply of wool. He also had enough weaving items to make a large amount of cloth. Phinehas had to have had a cloth mill on Lantern Hill Pond I am sure there are other account books that I have not read yet, where Phinehas Holdredge had them sell his wool and cloth.

From Phinehas Holdridge Inventory of his Estate, he had the following listed: [638]

"...1 Dye tub	*6 lbs 8 of wool*
1 woolen wheel	*19 lbs of wool*
1 linen wheel	*27 lbs of sole leather*
1 reel	*1 calf skin dressed*
1 pr of cards	*1 cow hide*
2 pr shears	*1 calf skin*
2 Razors	*6 sheep skin with wool on*
1 old loom	*...37 sheep*
1 quill wheel with spindle	*...5 swine*
13 spools	
2 old shuttle	
1 pr of sheep sheers"	

On Phinehas Holdridge Last Will and Testament, dated May 12, 1814, he left his son Nathan the following: [639]

"...I give & bequeath unto my beloved son Nathan Holdridge all the tract of land & buildings where the sd. Nathan now lives during his natural life & after his decease to his heirs forever & I Likewise give unto my sd Son Nathan the one half of the residue of my cattle sheep & hogs & half of my farming tools & all my wearing apparel forever And I further give unto my sd Son Nathan & order my Executor herein

named to pay yearly unto the sd. Nathan the sum of whole $10 a year for 6 years after my Decease which will be as the whole $110.

I give & bequeath unto my Loving Son Phinehas Holdridge all my homestead farm & Buildings where I now live & improve being under the incumberance of his mothers right of thirds & a further incumbrance hereafter in this Will to be made to him the said Phinehas his heirs & forever..."

From the above Will of Phinehas Holdridge, he well provided for his son Nathan Holdridge. His son Phinehas Holdridge received the homestead farm, which is the deed with 220 acres described above.

Phinehas and wife Mary are buried in the Holdridge Cemetery on Indiantown Road in Ledyard, Ct (see #35 on Map on page 25).

Nathan Holdridge recorded his parents deaths at the Groton Town Hall and while he was there he recorded his birth date as well. All three entries were done on the same day.

There is no record of the parents of Phinehas Holdridge that I have been able to find. Some places put him with Samuel Holdridge and Sarah Fellows. But Phinehas Holdridge was never baptized and I found baptismal records for Samuel and Sarah's other children. Phinehas may also be the son of William Holdridge and Sarah Parker, but I have never found any information on any of their children. As I was researching, and I was finding more information on Nathaniel Holdridge, it is very possible Phinehas could have been his son, but as of this writing, there is no real conclusive evidence that Phinehas Holdridge is the son of Nathaniel Holdridge. But the places where I found Nathaniel Holdridge, coincide with how Phinehas could have met his wife and why he bought in Groton in the area he did. Also, Nathaniel named a son Amos, who was older than Phinehas. Phinehas also named a son Amos. So in the next section of this chapter, you will be reading about Nathaniel Holdridge as Phinehas Holdridges father.

Life of Nathaniel Holdridge

Nathaniel Holdridge, the son of **William Holdridge** and **Deborah Elliot** was born May 30, 1715 in Stonington, Ct.[640] He died 1761 in Preston, Ct.[641] He married **Lydia Holdridge** on October 9, 1735 in Stonington, Ct. [642] He also had a second wife **Elizabeth**. Elizabeth was the mother of his two children born in Groton, Ct. He married 3rd **Prudence Parke** on November 7, 1751 in Stonington, Ct.[643] Prudence Parke was the daughter of **Thomas Parke** and **Hannah Witter**. She was married 1st Isaac Kimball of Preston, Ct.[644]

Children possibly by Lydia:

1. **Phinehas Holdridge** was born about 1738. He married Mary Thompson.

Children by Elizabeth:

1. **Daniel Holdridge** was born on April 13, 1741 in Groton, Ct[645]

2. **Zeborah Holdridge** was born on March 25, 1743 in Groton, Ct.[646]

No children were born of the third marriage.

From Jonathan Wheeler Account Book, located at the Connecticut Historical Society, was the following: [647]

Date ***Account***

"3/8/1735 ***Nathaniel Holdridge*** *for sundrys*

12/8/1735 ***Nathaniel Holdridge***

1/61737/8 ***Nathaniel Holdridge*** *and remainth duc to me 4 lost days in March and 3 lost days in April and 4 days in May and 4 days in June and their remaineth due to me upon balance of compto for the first year rent of my place*

5/10/1739 ***Nathaniel Holdridge*** *2nd year rent, also credit to Nathaniel Holdridge for work done in 1738*

7/13/1739 ***Nathaniel Holdridge*** *borrowed money*

1739 When building the little house Jonathan Wheeler paid ***Nathaniel and Thomas Holdridge****, Daniel Stanton and George for boarding house in 98 work days, also rum for the completion of the house*

5/9/1740 ***Nathaniel Holdridge*** *holding due to me for cash that I paid Indian Stephen*

8/2/1740 ***Nathaniel Holdridge*** *for riveing 4 thousand and a half of stave 21-16-0, Sawing 3 thousand and half of frame*

9/18/1740 ***Nathaniel Holdridge*** *rent of house for 4th year and use of my former pasture for 4th year*

6/4/1741 ***Nathaniel Holdrig*** *debt to me for boarding him four days and boarding Obediah Stark 8 days*

6/15/1741 charged ***N. Holdridge*** *debt to me 2 dinners and keeping his hogs*

1/8/1741/2 ***Nathaniel Holdridge*** *to balance*

3/12/1742 ***Nathaniel Holdridge*** *worked*

3/8/1743 ***Nathaniel Holdridge*** *worked*

1/3/1745/6 ***Nathaniel Holdridge*** *to balance books*

7/14/1746 ***Nathaniel Holdridge*** *one day worked*

4/16/1747 ***Nathaniel Holdridge*** *riveing of staves*

4/19/1748 ***Nathaniel Holdridge*** *galviring and bolting and riveing 11 or 12 hognut staves*

4/29/1749 ***Nathaniel Holdridge*** *for goods, paid him for shaving shingles"*

At the same time Nathaniel Holdridge was working for Jonathan Wheeler, Stephen Mason an Indian was also working for Jonathan Wheeler.

From the Preston Land Records, I found that Nathaniel and Prudence Holdridge sold to son John Kimball of Preston 1/3 of Estate of his father, Isaac Kimball of Preston dated December 12, 1754. The witnesses on the deed was William Witter and Josiah Park.[648]

Nathaniel Holdridge Probate records are in Norwich, but he

lived in Preston when he died. From the Estate of Nathaniel Holdridge, his Inventory, was taken in May of 1761, by Roswell Park and Ebenezer Witter, Jun.[649]

CHAPTER 10

Hannah Brown, which Brown, if any, does she come from?

Up to this point, the genealogy I have found has proven to be pretty accurate to Hannah Brown. Each female ancestor, in each generation, has at least one primary source record for their birth, death or marriage along with enough secondary sources to make a very educated statement that they belong to the stated parents. On the other hand, Hannah Brown was born in 1779. There were very few primary sources during this time frame and the few that were available, Hannah Brown is not mentioned. There is no birth record for a Hannah Brown daughter of Nathaniel Brown and Deborah Morgan. As a matter of fact, there is no recorded birth record of any of Nathaniel and Deborah Brown's children. When she married Nathan Holdridge in 1799, you did not have to give your parents names, so her parents were not listed on this record either. She died on December 5, 1843, and the only death record I have is from the Avery History of Ledyard book other than her gravestone, which have almost identical dates for her death. In the History of the Town of Ledyard book, it only says she is the widow of Nathan Holdridge and her age, which was 64 years old and the date she died. She is listed on Census Records from 1820 to 1840, but she was only listed as a head of household, it does not give where she was born or even who was living in the household with her. To find her parents, you would have to rely on secondary sources, which I will be discussing in each of the scenarios.

One of the reasons I have questioned whether Hannah Brown was the daughter of Nathaniel Brown and Deborah Morgan, is because I have never found a primary source stating that Hannah Brown the wife of Nathan Holdridge was the daughter of Nathaniel Brown and Deborah Morgan. Everything I have found about Hannah Holdridge has been written in books and it shows that

Hannah, wife of Nathan Holdridge was their daughter. As I have been studying how to find the preponderance of the evidence through genealogy, I have questioned this relationship. I feel that this is where I need to stop and take a good look at what has been written and see if there could be another set of parents for Hannah Brown.

Another reason I questioned whether this Hannah belonged to Nathaniel and Deborah Brown was there were two Hannah Holdridges on the 1820 census. It could be possible that she is the same person, but at different locations, when the Census was taken. But I feel I have found enough evidence that there were two different Hannah Holdridge's during this time.

Below are listed some of differences between the two Hannah Holdridge's:

Hannah, wife of Rufus Holdridge	**Hannah, wife of Nathan Holdridge**
Born 1766[650]	Born 1779
Died February 23, 1848[651]	Died December 7, 1843
1820 Census in South Groton	1820 Census in North Groton
Owned Property in South Groton	
Rufus Holdridge died Sept. 17, 1836[652]	Nathan Holdridge died Nov. 18, 1817
Was **not** a widower in 1820	Was a widow in 1820
Buried Wightman Cemetery, Groton	Buried Holdridge Cemetery, North Groton

Both Hannah's were born just a few years apart. They also died only a few years apart from each other. They were both married to Holdridge men.

But the biggest issue I have is with Nathaniel Browns Last Will and Testament (which will be brought in Scenario #1), where he lists his married daughters. The first daughter he lists is his daughter Mrs. Hannah Holdridge. He did not say who she was the wife of, but she was listed as being married. The Hannah that married Nathan Holdridge was widowed for three years previous to the writing of this Will. It would seem to me that Nathaniel

Brown would have known that his daughter was a widower and not still married and listed her separately. This leads me to believe that the Hannah Holdridge Nathaniel was talking about, could have been Mrs. Rufus Holdridge, who also had the first name Hannah. Mrs. Hannah Holdridge was still married to Rufus Holdridge in 1820 during the writing of Nathaniel Browns Will.

It would also seem that Nathaniel Brown would have provided something for his orphaned Grandchildren or at least some of them. There were three children under ten years of age that Mrs. Nathan Holdridge had to take care of. There were also four more children under the age of fifteen years of age. Mrs. Rufus Holdridge in 1820 (see Census on next page), did not have any young children living with her. She did not have to raise and feed young children. I feel this is another good reason why Mrs. Rufus Holdridge could very well be the daughter of Nathaniel Brown and Deborah Morgan.

Nathan Holdridges wife, Hannah, lived in North Groton. One of her neighbors was James Etheridge. James Etheridge married Nancy Holdridge. She was the sister to Nathan Holdridge. James Etheridge lived on Route 117. (See #46 on map on page 24) Dan King lived where the Ledyard Center School is today. So, that would put this Hannah Holdridge in North Groton, which became Ledyard.

If you notice on the next page, the second Hannah Holdridge is mentioned on the 1820 Census for Groton. She lived in South Groton, in the area called Burnett's Corner or close to the vicinity. I made this judgment by her neighbors names such as Haley, Burnet and Wightman. This is also the area the Wightman Cemetery is (see list on previous page). If you will notice, she did not have any young children living with her on the Census.

1820 Census for Groton, page 781[653]

Holdridge, Hannah
1 male 16 to 26 years
2 females 45 and over
1 person engaged in Agriculture

Neighbors:
Stephen Haley
Stephen Brightman
John Thompson
Richard Burnet
Mary Burnet
Hannah Holdridge
Phebe Avery
Abigail Avery
Elisha Haley
Jesse Wightman

I found that **a** Hannah Holdridge who had bought 21 acres of land in Groton on May 5, 1815.[654] She bought this piece from Lucy Fellows of Stonington. She also bought 3 acres of land from Elisha Haley on February 3, 1821.[655] Hannah Holdridge bought a third piece of property in Groton from Jesse and Maria Starr of Stonington which consisted of 1 acre with a dwelling house on this property.[656] The border of this property was the Mystic River (then spelled Mistick River) as well as Jeremiah Haley. I believe this one acre of property was down by the Burnetts corner area in Groton, Ct. Burnetts Corners is located off Route 184 in Groton, Ct on what is now called Cow Hill Road. This is the same area that the above second Hannah Holdridge on the 1820 Census lived in South Groton. Some of the neighbors listed in the 1820 Census are also mentioned as landowners of some of the boundaries mentioned in all three deeds. It was very uncommon for a woman to buy property in her name alone, in this time frame. Usually the husband was listed on the property transactions as well.

In the following three sections, I will be discussing the below three scenarios on possibly who the parents of Hannah Brown are. I will start with what has already been written and the evidence I found to support that statement. Scenario #1 will represent Hannah's mother as Deborah Morgan. In each of the other scenarios, I will state the other evidence I have found to support why I feel that she may be the daughter of someone else:

Scenario #1	Nathaniel Brown and Deborah Morgan
Scenario #2	Nathaniel Brown and Hannah Alexander
Scenario #3	A family other than Brown

CHAPTER 11

Scenario #1
Nathaniel Brown and Deborah Morgan ARE the parents of Hannah Brown, wife of Nathan Holdridge

The first scenario I will be discussing will be Nathaniel Brown and Deborah Morgan were the parents of Hannah Brown, who married Nathan Holdridge.

It is very easy to go along with this scenario, because everywhere you look, you will find that Hannah Brown Holdridge has been placed with these parents in various books such as the "History of the Town of Ledyard" and the "The Brown Genealogy". By genealogy standards, both of these books are considered secondary source information. Secondary source information, is not a birth record, baptismal record or a marriage record, these are all primary source information, because the person you are speaking about was present during the event. I have not found any primary source information to confirm the fact that Hannah Brown was born to Nathaniel and Deborah Brown. Again by genealogy standards, a primary source is something where the person themselves were there for the event that occurred, such as a birth, marriage or death. The parents would record their children's birth records. Also, if a child was baptized that could give you an approximate date of birth. When two people were to marry, they themselves gave any information for their marriage record. A death record is not always a primary source. But it can give you some vital information on the individual you are looking for.

In Hannah Brown's case, there is no recorded birth record I have been able to find or a Family Bible with her name in it. I have also not been able to find any baptismal record of a daughter of Nathaniel and Deborah Brown by the name of Hannah.

As far as her marriage record, it does not state who her parents were. During this time frame of 1799, not many marriage records stated who the parents were of the couple. But in Hannah's case, it did state both she and Nathan Holdridge were from Groton.

There is no official death record for Hannah Holdridge, with her parents name on it. But the History of the Town of Ledyard by Avery, states her date of death and that she was the widow of Nathan Holdridge. The only primary source I have found that Hannah Holdridge was the daughter of Nathaniel and Deborah Brown, was the Last Will and Testament of Nathaniel Brown in 1821. He did state he had a married daughter, Hannah Holdridge.

I will start off by giving you the birth, marriage and death information that I have found from the above mentioned secondary sources, on Nathaniel and Deborah Brown, as well as their children's information. After each married child's information, such as their birth, death and who they married, I will also include the names of all the children of that marriage or marriages. So you can see for yourself the naming patterns that I feel they could have used when naming their children. I feel that probably almost all of the children listed below belong to Nathaniel and Deborah, but with the naming pattern and other evidence, I don't believe Hannah Holdridge, wife of Nathan Holdridge fits into this family.

The naming pattern I most often use is a combination of different patterns. But I always include the first two or three sons and first two or three daughters. It depends on the family whether the eldest son is named after his father or his fathers father or his mothers father. The same holds true for the first three females born. Also during this time frame, many children would be named after their mothers maiden name, such as Avery Wilbur Brown, the Wilbur comes from his mothers maiden name. Sometimes, there is no rhyme or reason how they came up with the names of their children, but if a pattern is started, then I assume they followed it through the first two or three boys and first two or three girls. If the father or mother has the same name as a grandparent, such as **Nathaniel** Brown and **Nathan** Holdridge, the son **Nathan** could have been named after both men, so then only the first two sons could have been involved in a naming pattern. After that point, they could have named their children after anyone including people who were famous at that time, such as the President of the United States or even a famous artist or author. Sometime they named children after a close friend or neighbor.

Deborah Morgan and Nathaniel Brown

Deborah Morgan was born on March 01, 1750/51.[657] She died on December 25, 1830.[658] She was the daughter of **Timothy Morgan** and **Deborah Leeds**.

Deborah Morgan married **Nathaniel Brown**, son of **Comfort Brown** and **Temperance Brown**. He was born about 1753.[659] He died on January 17, 1821.[660]

Nathaniel Brown and Deborah Morgan Brown gravestones
Brown Peckham Main Cemetery on Iron Street in Ledyard, Ct.

Children of Nathaniel Brown and Deborah Morgan are:

1. Nathaniel Brown was born 1773 in North Groton, Ct. He died July 02, 1836 in Ledyard, Ct. He married Charlotte Wilbur. Charlotte was born June 12, 1782 in Westerly, RI. Charlotte died March 24, 1866 in Waterford, Ct., which I have already discussed. I will be listing all children, so you will be able to see some of the naming patterns that could have been used by each family.

Children of Nathaniel Brown and Charlotte Wilbur were:

1. *Nathaniel Brown (is named after father)*
2. Gurdon Brown
3. Avery Wilbur Brown (is named after mothers maiden name Wilbur)
4. Albert Brown
5. **Alvah Brown**
6. **John Brown**
7. **Samuel Brown**
8. Calvin Brown
9. **Frank Brown**

2. Temperance Brown was born about 1777.[661] She died in June of 1785 in Ledyard, Ct.[662] She had no children and died young.

3. Hannah Brown was born about 1779. She died on December 07, 1843. She married Nathan Holdridge February 14, 1799 in Groton, Ct., which we are currently discussing. Children of Hannah Brown and Nathan Holdridge were:

1. Hannah Holdridge (named after mother)
2. Nathan Holdridge (named after father & possibly Hannah's father)
3. Mary Holdridge (named after Nathan's mother)
4. Betsey Holdridge
5. Phinehas Holdridge (named after Nathan's father)

6. Stephen Holdridge
7. Eneas Holdridge
8. Randall Holdridge
9. Annis Holdridge
10. Almira Holdridge
11. Daniel Holdridge

4. Aaron Brown was born on November 25, 1781.[663] He died November 03, 1870.[664] He married Mary Wilcox. Mary was born about 1793.[665] She was the daughter of Robert Wilcox and Sarah Wilbur. Mary Brown died on November 28, 1877.[666] Aaron and Mary Brown are buried in Brown Peckham Main, Cemetery on Iron Street in Ledyard, Ct.

Children of Aaron and Mary Willcox Brown were:[667]

1. Robert Brown (named after Mary's father)
2. Eleazer Brown
3. Sabrina Brown
4. Laura Brown
5. Allura Brown
6. Theophilus Brown
7. Jeffrey Champlin Brown

5. Deborah Brown was born about 1784. She married (1) Robert Willcox, Jr. He died September 01, 1811 in Ledyard, Ct. She married (2) Benjamin Willcox. I have already discussed Deborah's line in the Willcox section of Chapter 4. I am showing the children again so you can see the naming pattern of Deborah's children.

Children of Deborah Brown and Robert Wilcox were:

1. Erastus Wilcox
2. ***Robert Wilcox(named after father & Robert's father)***
3. ***Nathaniel Wilcox (named after Deborah's father)***
4. **Raymond Wilcox**

5. ***Deborah Wilcox(named after mother & Deborah's mother)***

6. Louisa Wilcox

7. **Robertson Wilcox**

Children of Deborah and Benjamin Wilcox were:

1. ***Benjamin Wilcox (named after father)***

2. Susan Wilcox

3. ***Sarah Wilcox (named after Benjamin & Robert's mother)***

6. Lois Brown was born about 1786. She died on July 01, 1873. She married **Thomas Main** April 20, 1806 in Groton, Ct. I have already discussed Lois and Thomas in Chapter 6 under the heading of the "Main" Ancestors. As with Deborah Brown, I am including the names of the children so you can see any naming patterns they might have used.

Children of Lois Brown and Thomas Main were:

1. Fannie E. Main

2. ***Thomas B. Main (named after father)***

3. Aaron Main

4. John Main

5. ***Timothy Main (named after Lois's grandfather)***

6. ***William Leeds Main (his middle name after Lois's grandmothers maiden name Leeds)***

7. **Daniel Main**

8. ***Louisa Main (named after mother, but with different spelling)***

9. Surviah B. Main

10. **Stanton Main**

11. ***Mary Esther Main (named after Thomas's mother)***

12. ***Nathaniel B. Main (named after Lois's father)***

13. Seth Main

14. **Hannah Main**

15. Amasa Main

16. ***Deborah B. Main (named after Lois's mother)***

7. Matilda Brown was born about 1790.[668] She died in 1844.[669] Matilda married John Main.[670]
Children of Matilda Brown and John Main were:[671]

1. David Morgan Main (named after Matilda's mother maiden name, Morgan)
2. Jesse M. Main
3. Mary Matilda Main (named after John's mother and after Matilda)
4. Nathaniel Main (named after Matilda's father)
5. Sabrina Main
6. Deborah Main (named after Matilda's mother)
7. Hannah Elizabeth Main
8. John S. Main (named after father)

8. Sabrina Brown was born about 1793.[672] She died in April of 1812.[673] She had no children. She died young.

9. Zerviah Brown was born about 1795.[674] She died on April 04, 1869.[675] She never married. She is buried in the Peckham Brown Main Cemetery in Ledyard, Ct

10. Temperance Brown was born about 1796.[676] She died on May 18, 1865.[677] She married Prentice Lewis. Temperance and Prentice Lewis are buried at the Packer Cemetery, in Canterbury, Ct.

Children of Temperance Brown and Prentice Lewis were:

1. Temperance E. Lewis (named after mother) [678]
2. Caroline Lewis[679]
3. Prentice Lewis (named after father)[680]
4. Priscilla Lewis[681]
5. George W. Lewis[682]
6. Richard Lewis[683]
7. Hannah Lewis[684]

Nathaniel Brown and Deborah Morgan lived on Iron Street in Ledyard, Ct. If you look at the 1790 census record below, some of their neighbors were located in that area during that time frame. I have included the neighbors here, so you will see who was living nearby. If you look at #26 on the map on page 25, you will see the area that I believe Nathaniel and Deborah Brown lived in. If you notice that Phinehas Holdridge was 5 houses down from Nathaniel Brown. I know Phinehas lived on the east boundary of the Western Pequot Reservation. John Packer owned property on the southern border of the Reservation and in one deed, Nathaniel Brown bordered John Packer.

1790 Census for New London County: [685]

Nathaniel Brown, Jr

Male over 16 years old	1
Male under 16 years old	2
All females	6

Neighbors:
Increase Stoddard
Roger Williams
Nathaniel Brown, Jr.
James Brown
Simeon Barns
Easter Barns
John Packer 3rd
Phinehas Holdridge

Males over 16 years old	3
Males under 16 years old	2
All females	5

Jesse Barnes 2nd
Jesse Barns

1800 Census for Town of Groton:[686]

Nathaniel Brown
2 males 10 to 26 years
1 male over 45 years
3 females under 10 years
3 females 10 to 15 years
1 female 45 and up

Neighbors:
Comfort Brown
Nathaniel Brown
Prince Cutwater
Nehemiah Barnes
John Packer
Robert Forsyth
Jonathan Dewey
Benjamin Peckham
Elizabeth Park
John Enos
Joseph Lee
Mary Hilliard

On the 1800 Census, Nathaniel Brown was still living in the same neighborhood as in the 1790 Census. John Packer lived on the southern border of the Western Pequot Reservation. Benjamin Peckham lived on the Western border of the same reservation.

On 1810 Census for Town of Groton:[687]

Nathaniel Brown
1 male 16-18
1 male 45 and up
1 female 45 and up

Neighbors:
Ephr. Allyn
Ben Gray
Latham Gray
th.B. Gray
Seabury Perkins
Nathaniel Brown
Aaron Brown
Nathaniel Brown Jun
Asa Gray

On the 1810 Census, Nathaniel Brown, was living on Iron Street. He lived next two his two sons. He also owned land all the way to Shewville Road and bordered the Grays.

On 1820 Census for Town of Groton:[688]

Nathaniel Brown
1 male 1 to 10 years
1 male 16 to 26 years
1 male 45 and up
2 females 10 to 16 years
1 female 26 to 45 years
2 females 45 and up

Neighbors:
Ezra Geer
Charles Allyn
Nathl. Brown
Nathl. Brown, Jr
Aaron Brown
Andrew Gallup
Squire Lee
Ann Morgan

1830 Census for the Town of Groton:[689]

Deborah Brown
1 female 10 to 15 years
1 female 20 to 30 years
1 female 70 to 80 years

Neighbors:
Phineas Holdridge
Wm. Bentley
Thomas Main
Aaron Brown
John Packer 2nd
Benjah Packer
Deborah Brown
Andrew Gallup
Desire Perkins

On the 1820 Census, Andrew Gallup lived on Iron Street, so that would put Nathaniel Brown on Iron Street then. On the 1830 Census, Deborah Brown lived again next to Andrew Gallup and Benjah Packer, who lived on Indiantown Road near where Shewville and Kate Swamp Road (see #39 on map on page 25) meet.

I found that Nathaniel Brown was in the Iron Street area between 1790 and 1805, from the book, Historic Ledyard Volume 1, Gales Ferry Village:[690]

> *"...Nathaniel Brown was operating a sawmill on this site in 1790 and presumably operated it until 1805 at which time Philip Gray bought the mill, which was standing on the property of Joseph Lee. It was stipulated that, "...the said Philip Gray build a new mill on the spot where the old one now stands on the farm where the said Lee now lives" with rights to repair the dam and the "privilege of flowing a pond of water"*

on the land " as much as necessary for the use of said mill..." In turn Lee received the privilege of having 700 foot of board cut if he brought the lumber to the mill during the cutting season, which ran from April to November. Gray was given right to keep the gate shut on the dam "from the first of November until the thirteenth of April every year" as this was the lumbering season, before and after the farming season..."

Nathaniel Browns Probate Records were very important in why it seems like Hannah Holdridge, wife of Nathan Holdridge was the daughter of Nathaniel Brown and Deborah Morgan. To me, Probate Records are a primary source. The person themselves are writing this type of record, especially when it is the Last Will and Testament. In Nathaniel Brown's Last Will and Testament in Stonington Vol 11 page 133, he lists as one of his married daughters Hannah Holdridge. The Will was dated in 1820. This is the only official document that lists the children of Nathaniel and Deborah Brown.

Below is a list of Nathaniel Browns heirs that was abstracted from his Last Will and Testament: [691]

"...Wife Deborah
Daughter Zerviah, never married
He has a brother James Brown
Married Daughters:
Hannah Holdridge
Deborah Wilcox
Lois Main
Matilda Main
Temperance Lewis
Sons:
Nathaniel Brown
Aaron Brown"

Nathaniel Brown left his two sons, Nathaniel and Aaron his real estate. If you look on the map on page 25 #27, you will see where Aaron Brown lived. His brother Nathaniel lived at #25 on the same page. That does help put this Nathaniel Brown between Shewville Road and Iron Street in Ledyard.

If you use this document alone, it would make sense that Hannah Holdridge, wife of Nathan Holdridge would be the daughter of this Nathaniel and Deborah Brown. But also, when you include that Nathan Holdridge was a neighbor, it would be easy to conclude that the Hannah Holdridge mentioned in the Will of Nathaniel Brown was the wife of Nathan Holdridge.

Nathaniel Brown and his wife Deborah Brown are buried in the Brown Peckham Main Cemetery on Iron Street in Ledyard, Ct.

Deborah Morgan Ancestry

From this point on, I will be discussing the female line through Deborah Morgan. If I assume this is the correct female line, that Hannah Brown Holdridge is the daughter of Nathaniel and Deborah Brown, then Deborah and Timothy Morgan would be the next logical generation to follow.

I feel that there is some proof that Deborah Morgan is the daughter of Timothy Morgan and Deborah Leeds. I could not find any primary source records that Deborah was the daughter of Timothy and Deborah Morgan other than the Probate Records (which will be discussed under Deborah Leeds and Timothy Morgan).

Was Deborah Morgan the daughter of Deborah Leeds and Timothy Morgan?

Deborah Leeds was born on October 21, 1729 in Groton, Ct.[692] She died on August 22, 1794.[693] Deborah was the daughter of **Thomas Leeds** and **Mary Williams**. She married **Timothy Morgan**. He was the son of **Samuel Morgan** and **Hannah Avery**.

Children of Deborah Leeds and Timothy Morgan are: [694]

1. **Experience Morgan**
2. **Deborah Morgan** married Nathaniel Brown
3. **David Morgan**
4. **Elizabeth Morgan**
5. **Theophilus Morgan**
6. **Samuel Morgan**
7. **Timothy Morgan**
8. **Jesse Morgan**
9. **Hannah Morgan**

Timothy Morgan Last Will and Testament (listing of heirs only): [695]

"Wife Deborah
Daughters: Experience Brown
Deborah Brown (from receipts wife of Nathaniel Brown Jun(Junior)*)*
Elizabeth Williams (from receipts wife of Samuel Williams)
Hannah Packer
Sons: David Morgan
Theophilus Morgan (Executor)
Samuel Morgan (refused his share)
Timothy Morgan
Jesse Morgan"

From Timothy Morgan's Inventory, which was taken November 30, 1795, by Park Avery, Jr. and Nathan Morgan, I found the following: [696]

"*...Due from Peleg Brown as per receipt*
Due from Nathaniel Brown , Jr
Due from Samuel Williams
Due from Hubbart Packer"

I found the following receipts recorded with Timothy Morgan Probate records: [697]

"...Groton September the 16 AD1796 then received thirteen pounds eight shillings of Theophilis Morgan Executor to Timothy Morgan Late Deseast Estate it Bearing in full which My father gave Me in his Will and intestate Estate & Say received in full by the

*Signed, **Deborah Brown***
Nathaniel Brown Junr **(Junior)**

*Another receipt was from Colchester, dated April 27, 1795 where **Elizabeth Williams** received thirteen pounds eight shillings from Timothy Morgan, Estate. It was signed by **Elizabeth Williams** and **Samuel Williams***

*Another receipt was from Groton, dated September the 16, AD1796 where **Hannah Packer**, was paid nine pounds from the estate of Timothy Morgan. It was signed by **Hannah Packer** only."*

There were other receipts in Timothy Morgans Probate records to his sons as well. But the above receipts were the only ones where his daughters names were mentioned. Deborah and Elizabeth signed their names along with their husbands. Hannah Packer was the only one to sign her receipt. It could have been her husband was deceased by this point in time.

In this time frame, a woman did not sign any legal documents unless she was related to the deceased person somehow. If she was married, her husband had to sign the document as well. I have seen this in deeds as well as Probate records. When I saw the signature of Nathaniel and Deborah Brown on the receipt, I felt that Timothy's Probate records, shows more evidence that Deborah was the daughter of Timothy Morgan and also the wife of Nathaniel Brown.

Timothy and Deborah Morgan are buried in the Packer Burrows Cemetery #18, Groton, Ct. On Deborah Morgan's gravestone it says she died August 22, 1794 age 69, this would give her a birth date of about 1725. Timothy Morgan's gravestone says he died October 13, 1795 age 72, which would make his birth date about 1723.

Deborah Morgan Gravestone, Packer Burrows Cemetery, Groton, Ct.

Was Deborah, wife of Timothy Morgan the daughter of Mary and Thomas Leeds?

The next female in this line would be Mary Williams, wife of Thomas Leeds.

Mary Williams married **Thomas Leeds** April 17, 1717 in Groton, Ct.[698] All their children were born in Groton, Ct.
Children of Mary Williams and Thomas Leeds are: [699]

1. **Jedediah Leeds** was born on October 10, 1717.
2. **Cary Leeds** was born on May 15, 1720. He died on April 10, 1722.

3. **Sarah Leeds**, was born on February 28, 1720/21.

4. **Thomas Leeds** was born on September 24, 1724.

5. **Mary Leeds** was born on June 17, 1727.

6. **Deborah Leeds** was born on October 21, 1729 in Groton, Ct. She died on August 11, 1786 in Groton, Ct. She married Timothy Morgan

Thomas and Mary Leeds definitely had a daughter Deborah born in Groton, but her birth date does not coincide with Deborah, the wife of Timothy Morgan. Here are reasons that Timothy Morgans wife Deborah may not be the daughter of Thomas Leeds and Mary Williams:

1. From Deborah Morgans gravestone, it said she was born about 1725, which is four years difference.
2. I also could not find any Probate Records for Thomas Leeds in Stonington or New London. Those would be the only Towns that had Probate Records for Groton in that time frame.
3. Timothy Morgan and wife Deborah has no marriage record as well, which would have given her maiden name. But without that marriage certificate, there is no real evidence that Deborah is a Leeds at all. She may belong to any family in the Groton/New London area.
4. Also, looking over the children of Timothy and Deborah Morgan, there were no children with the names Thomas or Mary. It is possible they children with those names and those children died, but I feel they would have renamed other children to carry on those names:

Samuel was named after Timothy's father Samuel Morgan
Hannah was named after Timothy's mother Hannah Avery
Timothy was named after Timothy Morgan
Deborah was named after Deborah wife of Timothy Morgan

It would seem that they would have also named children after his wife's Deborah side of the family. The names of their children that remain are:

Males	Females
David	Experience
Theophilus	Elizabeth
Jesse	

These above names do not fit into the Thomas and Mary Leeds family.

With such a discrepancy and with no other paperwork supporting that Deborah, wife of Timothy Morgan, was the daughter of Thomas Leeds and Mary Williams, I feel that this female line ends at Deborah, wife of Timothy Morgan.

CHAPTER 12

More Discrepancies

To introduce the 2nd Scenario, I feel there are enough discrepancies that there was more than one Nathaniel Brown alive during this time frame. Also, there were two Hannah Holdridge's very close in age, during this time frame. One married to Rufus Holdridge and the other to Nathan Holdridge. If you look at the paragraph below, it goes into more detail on the Hannah Holdridge, wife of Rufus Holdridge. I feel that there is a strong possibility that there is confusion on which Nathaniel Brown had a daughter, Hannah Holdridge, wife of Nathan.

After going over the Probate Records for Nathaniel Brown who married Deborah Morgan, and his statement that *"...his **married** daughters, Hannah Holdridge, Deborah Wilcox, Lois Main, Matilda Main and Temperance Lewis...",*[700] this leads me to believe that it is **possible** that Hannah Holdridge may not be his daughter.

I feel because there is so little evidence available during this time frame, it is easy to assume that Nathaniel Browns daughter, Hannah Holdridge, was the wife of Nathan Holdridge from reading his Will.

Let's take it from Nathaniel Browns Last Will and Testament:

Nathan Holdridge died in 1817. Hannah had been widowed for three years previous to the actual writing of Nathaniel Browns Last Will and Testament. It seems to me, he would have known that his daughter Hannah Holdridge was a widower and no longer married. It would also make sense that Nathaniel Brown could have provided something for any or all of Hannah's children, which he did not do.

Nathaniel Brown also said he had a married daughter, Deborah Wilcox. Deborah, whom I have already discussed earlier, had lost her husband Robert Wilcox nine years previous to her father,

Nathaniel Browns, death. She had remarried Robert Wilcox's brother Benjamin Wilcox. So she would still have the Wilcox name when her father died in 1820. It makes sense to me, that between the Will and the naming patterns, Deborah was the daughter of Nathaniel and Deborah Brown.

All of the other daughters were married at the time of his death. If you look at Thomas and Lois Main, the naming pattern of their children goes along with this theory as well. So up to this point, I believe that at least two or three of Noyes ancestors really belongs to Nathaniel and Deborah Brown. Lois and Deborah Brown more than likely belong to Nathaniel and Deborah Brown.

As I explained earlier, there was another Hannah Holdridge during this time frame (as I mentioned on pages 130 and 131). She married Rufus Holdridge and was still married to Rufus when Nathaniel Brown died in 1821. She was not a widower, so she, too, could fit into the category of a married daughter. If Hannah Holdridge, wife of Rufus Holdridge, was the daughter of this Nathaniel Brown and Deborah Morgan, then who does Hannah Brown who married Nathan Holdridge belong to?

There were at least two Nathaniel Browns alive during this time frame. One Nathaniel Brown had married Mary Morgan and the other was his nephew, Nathaniel Brown who married Deborah Morgan. From the deeds I have researched, there could have been two or three Nathaniel Browns buying and selling property from 1780 to 1820. At one point in time, during the late 1700's and very early 1800's, there were three Nathaniel Browns living in North Groton.

One of the Nathaniel Brown's, owned the property, which was located next to the Wilcox Homestead on Iron Street. The other Nathaniel Brown was on Fanning Road on the north end of Shewville Road. (See #28 on map on page 20) We will be discussing the Nathaniel Brown who married Mary Morgan and lived on Fanning Road, during this scenario.

Also from the Census records for Groton in New London County the Census shows two Nathaniel Browns living in Groton on each Census:

Census Year	**Name**
1790	Nathaniel Brown
	Nathaniel Brown Jun
1800	Nathaniel Brown
	Nathaniel Brown
1810	Nathaniel Brown
	Nathaniel Brown Jr.
1820	Nathaniel Brown
	Nathaniel Brown Jr.

I decided to make a list of all the Nathaniel Browns living in Groton, to help determine which Nathaniel it was showing on the Census records. This list also helped determine which Nathaniel Brown owned certain pieces of property. The following is a list of all the Nathaniel Browns:

PERSON	**BORN**	**DIED**	**WIFE**	**PARENTS**
Nathaniel Brown 1st	1660	1731	Mary Wheeler	Charles & Mary Brown
Nathaniel Brown 2nd	1690	1770	Anna Haynes	Nathaniel &Mary Brown
Nathaniel Brown 3rd	1716	1807	Mary Morgan Hannah Alexander	Nathaniel &Anna Brown
Nathaniel Brown 4th			Rhuhannah Holdridge married 1803	Parents unknown
Nathaniel Brown	1753	1821	Deborah Morgan	Comfort & Temperance Brown
Nathaniel Brown	1773	1836	Charlotte Wilbur	Nathaniel & Deborah Brown

Nathaniel Brown 2nd on the previous list was the father to Nathaniel Brown 3rd and also Comfort Brown. Comfort Brown was the father to the Nathaniel Brown who was born in 1753, listed above. Nathaniel Brown 2nd also lived in North Groton. If you look at #29 on the map on page 20, you will see the area where the Nathaniel Brown 2nd lived.

After looking over the 1790 Census and the list, I determined that Nathaniel Brown 3rd and Nathaniel Brown born 1753, were the two Nathaniel Browns on the 1790 Census. On the 1800 Census, it would have been the same two people. On the 1810 and 1820 Census, it would have been Nathaniel Brown born in 1753 and who was married to Deborah Morgan. The other Nathaniel Brown was born in 1773 and was married to Charlotte Wilbur.

It was very difficult to tell in some instances, which one of the Nathaniel Brown's the land record was discussing. Other times there was a Nathaniel Brown listed as the second or third or as Jun (Junior), which taking into consideration the time frame, helped place which Nathaniel it was. The above list, also helped determine who was buying or selling property, because the date of deed or record and the dates of birth and death of each Nathaniel Brown.

But looking over the Census records along with the land records, it places the Nathaniel Brown born in 1753 in the Iron Street area of Ledyard. It is very possible that Hannah Brown, daughter of this Nathaniel Brown, could have met Nathan Holdridge. He lived very close by. She would have been raised on the western border of the Western Pequot Reservation on Iron Street and Shewville Road and Nathan Holdridge lived on the eastern border of the Western Pequot Reservation. It would seem likely that their paths would cross at sometime or another.

But from the 1800 Census and other land records, there was another Nathaniel Brown living somewhere in the Fanning Road area of North Groton (see #29 on the map on page 20). This area is closer to the Preston border and also very close to the northwestern border of the Western Pequot Reservation. If this Nathaniel Brown had a daughter Hannah, she too would have been a neighbor of Nathan Holdridge as a young girl and she would be living along the route that Nathan Holdridge took to Punderson's Store in 1797 (see #37 on Map on pages 24 and 25). This Nathaniel Brown was married to Mary Morgan and possibly Hannah Alexander. Both names, Mary and Hannah, would fit the naming pattern of the eldest females of Nathan and Hannah Holdridge.

Which leads us into the next scenario.

CHAPTER 13

Scenario #2
Or are Nathaniel Brown and Mary Morgan or Hannah Alexander, the parents of Hannah Brown, wife of Nathan Holdridge

When Hannah married Nathan Holdridge, on the marriage record I found it stated the following: [701]

> *"Mr. Nathan Holdridge and Miss **Hannah Brown** both of sd Groton were married February 14, 1799..."*

This marriage was performed by Amos Gere, Justice of the Peace, for the Town of Groton, Conn. (now Ledyard)

So we will assume the above Hannah Brown was a Brown.

If you take the naming pattern of Nathan and Hannah Holdridge's children, they did name a son Nathan. Of course, he is named after his father Nathan Holdridge, but it could also mean that Hannah's fathers name was also Nathaniel.

With the two facts mentioned above, one of which is the marriage record to Nathan Holdridge and the other naming pattern of Hannah Holdridges children, I believe she is probably the daughter of **a** Nathaniel Brown, but is she the daughter of Deborah Morgan?

There was a Nathaniel Brown who married a Hannah Alexander, which I found in the marriage records of William Williams, Justice of the Peace in 1773: [702]

> *"New London Ct, Groton March the 28th Adommi 1773 Nathaniel Brown and Hannah Alexander both of Groton aforesaid were married by me Wm. Williams Justice of Peace..."*

The following is the evidence I have found on Nathaniel Brown and Mary Morgan and Hannah Alexander:

Nathaniel Brown was born June 6, 1716[703] and he died July 1807.[704] Nathaniel was the son of **Nathaniel Brown** and **Anna Haynes**. Nathaniel married **Mary Morgan**, daughter of **William Morgan**. Mary possibly died October 1771 age 53,[705] Nathaniel could have married for his second wife, **Hannah Alexander** on March 28, 1773.[706] Hannah died August 1804.[707]

The Historic Ledyard Book, Volume II, has the Brown Genealogy on page 136.[708] On this page, from the Brown Genealogy, it does not list any children for Nathaniel Brown. But I have found evidence that it is very possible this Nathaniel Brown did have children.

Hannah Brown was born about 1779, so it is possible that she could be the daughter of this Nathaniel Brown and Hannah Alexander.

I do not know the ages of either Nathaniel Brown or Hannah Alexander from this marriage record. It is possible that this Nathaniel Brown who was married to Mary Morgan first, remarried Hannah Alexander after Mary's death. Also from Tuttles Catalog of Deaths, Hannah Brown wife of Nathaniel Brown died in August 1804. It did not give an age for her, but it also did not say she was a widower either. In July of 1807, Nathaniel Brown, age 93, died.

If Hannah Alexander was the wife of this Nathaniel Brown, was she young enough to have children? Nathaniel Brown would have been 63 years old in 1773. He could still produce children at that age, but the age of Hannah Alexander is more significant. They were married six years previous to Hannah Brown's birth, and if Hannah Alexander was even in her late forties early fifties, she still could have produced children.

The History of the Town of Ledyard, states the following about James Fanning and his wife Elizabeth:[709]

"...He married Miss Elizabeth Williams and located in Preston, where five children were born to them, viz: George, James, Phebe, William and Isaac.

This family later on, moved into North Groton (now Ledyard), and settled on a farm purchased of one Nathaniel Brown, his wife's grandfather, being the same place now occupied by Lyman A. Latham, about one mile and a half northeasterly from the Bill Parsonage. On this farm he lived during the remainder of his life..."

From this above entry, Nathaniel Brown did have a daughter who married a Williams and this daughter had a daughter, Elizabeth Williams, who married James Fanning.

On the 1790 Census for New London County: [710]

Nathaniel Brown

Males over 16 years	1
Males under 16 years	1
All females	2

Neighbors:
Thomas Giles
Nathaniel Bellows
John Bellows
James Allen
Nathaniel Brown
Ann Brown
Thomas Malleson
Richard Williams

On this Census Nathaniel Brown had one male over 16 years of age, which would be Nathaniel Brown. Nathaniel also had one male under 16 years of age and 2 females. I believe one female is Hannah Alexander, his wife and the other female could be Hannah Brown.

On the 1800 Census for Groton, New London County: [711]

Nathaniel Brown
1 male 16 to 18 years
1 male 16 to 26 years
1 male 45 and up
1 female 10 to 16
1 female 26 to 44 years
1 female 45 and up

Neighbors:
Samuel Stanton
Cary Latham Jr
Gershom Brown
Cary Latham
Nathaniel Brown
John Brown
Richard Williams
Theophillus Haley
Isaac Williams
Anna Williams
Peter Williams
Thomas Hallet

This Nathaniel Brown died in 1807, so he would not be on the 1810 Census.

I also found some Probate Records in Stonington for a Nathan Brown. The records were in the year 1808. This Nathan Brown was from Groton. If you look at the list I used to determine which Nathaniel Brown was which, the Nathaniel Brown 3rd died in 1807, which would make him the logical choice for the Probate Records recorded in 1808. Nathan Brown did not have a Last Will and Testament. The Administrators for his Estate were Israel Brown, William F. Brown and Samuel A. Brown.[712] Also there was a citation from Elijah Partridge, husband of Prudence, late Brown, daughter of Nathan Brown, late of Groton deceased.[713] Israel Brown was the Administrator who witnessed this document. Isreal Brown was of Norwich, Ct.

If you look at the above information, these were some of the children of Nathan Brown:

Israel Brown
William F. Brown
Samuel A. Brown
Prudence Brown, married Elijah Partridge
Daughter, who married Williams, child, Elizabeth Williams who married James Fanning

Nathaniel Brown and Deborah Morgan did not have any daughters that were married to a Williams. So this helps substantiate that there was another Nathaniel Brown, who had a daughter, who married a Williams and a granddaughter, Elizabeth, who married James Fanning. If this other Nathaniel Brown had one daughter, it is entirely possible that there were more children. I feel Hannah Holdridge could fit into the family of Nathaniel and Hannah Alexander.

Hannah Holdridge named a daughter, Hannah after herself and possibly her mother (which would be Hannah Alexander). And as I explained earlier, Hannah and Nathan Holdridge never named a daughter Deborah. I feel the possibility is present that she could be the daughter of Nathaniel Brown and Hannah Alexander.

I have never found any information on Hannah Alexander. Alexander was not a common last name in this area in that time span. Even in the entire state of Connecticut in 1790 there were only 3 men with the last name of Alexander and they all lived in Voluntown in Windham County.[714] Their names were: James, John and Joseph Alexander. More research would need to be done on the Alexander line.

From the 1790 Census in the New London County area, there were no Alexanders. But there were two Elexanders, one was William and the other was James. James Elexander probably lived in Stonington (I made this judgment from his neighbors on the 1790 Census).[715] William Elexander probably lived in Groton, Ct. (again, using his neighbors as a reference).[716] The 1790 Census for New London County did not tell which town anyone lived in. But, if you look at the surrounding neighbors, you can pretty much pinpoint the towns where the Census was taken. Also in Groton Land Records, there were no land records recorded under the name Alexander in the late 1700's. I also checked Probate Records and could not find any Probate Records in either Stonington or New London for any Alexanders.

CHAPTER 14

Scenario #3 Other parents

The 3rd scenario will be based on the assumption that Hannah Brown was not the daughter of either of the Nathaniel Brown's, but from a different family all together. When Hannah married Nathan Holdridge she was 20 years of age. In this time frame, if you reached 20 years of age and were not married, it would be considered that this female was an old maid. Hannah also married a man 12 years her senior. This was not uncommon in those days, but the majority of people did marry people that were closer to their own age.

Hannah and Nathan Holdridge did follow a naming pattern for their children as most people did in that time frame:

The eldest son was named Nathan after his father
The second son was named Phinehas after Nathan's father Phinehas
The third son was named Stephen
The eldest daughter was named Hannah after her mother
The second daughter was named Mary after Nathan's mother
The third daughter was named Betsey

Is the name Stephen after Hannah's father? Is the name Betsey after Hannah's mother? If so, the first names of her parents would have been Stephen and Betsey.

In researching North Stonington Land Records, I found a Phinehas Mason Holdridge on some of the land records there. I can not be sure if he, Phinehas Mason Holdridge, was the son of Nathan and Hannah Holdridge or if Phinehas Mason Holdridge was the son of Phinehas Holdridge (Nathan and Hannah son). Does the name Mason play a role in the maiden name of Phinehas' mother Hannah Holdridge?

Hannah and Nathan's son Phinehas Holdridge, chose Christopher Newton as his guardian after his fathers death.[717] He was the only child to chose a guardian. Eventually, he ended up back in North Stonington buying property next to his great grandparents the Thompson family. He did not marry a Mason. He married Mary Slocum, so the name Mason would not have anything to do with the Slocum side of the family.

Which would bring us back to Phinehas Holdridge's parents, Nathan and Hannah. Nathan father, Phinehas Holdridge, named a son Thompson after his wife's maiden name. So it is possible that Nathan and Hannah did the same with the name Mason.

Let us assume that Hannah's maiden name was Mason and her parents were Stephen and Betsey Mason. I have taken the names Stephen and Betsey because they were the third eldest male and female children of Nathan and Hannah Holdridge.

I have checked into the Mason family name and I could not find a Stephen Mason during this time frame. I also checked the names of Phinehas and Nathan Mason in the local Mason history. I could not find either of these names was well, with a daughter Hannah born in 1779.

There was a Stephen Mason and Joanna Newkuchuse. They were Indians from Stonington. They married in Stonington[718] in 1741 and Stephen worked for Jonathan Wheeler the same time Nathaniel Holdridge did in the 1740's.[719] I believe it could be possible that Hannah Holdridge could have been the daughter or granddaughter of Stephen and Joanna Mason. If she is not their daughter, she could be the daughter of one of their children.

This is only hypothetical, because I have very little evidence to show that is what happened.

Another possibility could be that Nathaniel Brown and Mary Morgan had a son, Nathaniel Brown and he was the one that married Hannah Alexander. I am going to show you the chart again, but this time it includes another Nathaniel Brown who married Hannah Alexander:

PERSON	BORN	DIED	WIFE	PARENTS
Nathaniel Brown	1660	1731	Mary Wheeler	Charles and Mary Brown
Nathaniel Brown	1690	1770	Anna Haynes	Nathaniel and Mary Brown
Nathaniel Brown	1716	1807	Mary Morgan	Nathaniel and Anna Brown
Nathaniel Brown	about 1740 ?		Hannah Alexander	Parents unknown
Nathaniel Brown	1753	1821	Deborah Morgan	Comfort and Temperance Brown
Nathaniel Brown	1773	1836	Charlotte Wilbur	Nathaniel and Deborah Brown
Nathaniel Brown 4th			Rhuhannah Holdridge	Parents unknown

If you go with this scenario, Hannah would have been named after her mother, Hannah Alexander. So Betsey could have been Hannah Alexanders mother's name. There is nothing I can find to substantiate this statement. It is purely conjecture on my part. But the possibility is still there.

Of course, Hannah Brown Holdridge could have been anyone's daughter. I may never be able to find her parents through genealogical records. I do not think there is enough evidence showing who Hannah Browns parents are. It may well be that her parents are Nathaniel Brown and Deborah Morgan, just as history has written it. But I feel there is enough evidence to show some doubt to that fact. The only way, I feel I am going to find out, is through more DNA testing. The more people who do their direct maternal DNA test, the more likely to find which family Hannah Brown Holdridge truly belongs to.

CHAPTER 14

MY CONCLUSION

This is our legacy to our grandchildren. Mitochondrial DNA is in its infant stages at the moment. There are so many changes being done to the Mitochondrial DNA on a weekly, monthly and yearly basis. But the progress is still slow. I believe in the next 10 to 20 years, there will be major developments with this type of DNA. Noyes and I may never see the outcome of his direct Maternal line through DNA. We are hoping to find this female ancestor before we leave this earth, but if we don't, at least someone can continue on with what we have found to this point.

There is an abundance of information available about our white ancestors. But with this particular line being Native American and dating so far back, there is very little recorded information available.

I hope this book, will have people check their attics and read some of the old letters, diaries or whatever has been saved over the years from previous ancestors. Take the time to talk to older relatives and see if they know of any information that may have been passed down through generations.

I may not be correct in some of my assumptions as you go back into the 1700's. I feel very confident about the information I have found through Hannah Brown who married Nathan Holdridge. But I am hoping either someone has some primary source evidence that shows who the real parents of Hannah Brown was; or as more people do Maternal DNA's, I am hoping that Noyes will match more people and we can find out who the real parents of Hannah Brown was.

If you know your ancestry and you have a **direct** Maternal line to Nathaniel Brown and Deborah Morgan. Also, if your maternal ancestry goes back directly to one of their daughters Deborah Brown, Lois Brown, Matilda Brown or Temperance Brown, you may want to consider doing a Maternal DNA test. If someone can match Noyes's Maternal DNA test, then the likelihood of Nathaniel Brown and Deborah Morgan as being the parents of Hannah Brown, who married Nathan Holdridge, would be greatly increased. If you do not match Noyes's DNA, then Hannah Brown may not have come from the family of Nathaniel Brown and Deborah Morgan.

Remember to keep in mind, before you decide to do a Maternal DNA, do not do it because you think you will come back Native American. You really need to do it because you want to know your oldest ancestor, no matter who it is. Also, contact different companies who are doing the Mitochondrial DNA testing and talk to them before you make any decisions. They are doing many different types of testing all the time and they could help you decide what is right for you. In some cases a DNA Print would be the best answer. You can find out what percentage you are as far as Asian, European, Native American and African American.

Genealogy can bring ancestors back to life if you take the time to thoroughly research not just for genealogy, but also to find out about your Ancestors history.

I did not include all the information that I have on all of the ancestors in this book. I have much more information, but not all of it has been proven. Also, if I could not get written permission to use certain information, it was excluded from this book. My primary reason for writing this book was to show the direct female line and her ancestry.

I am still doing research and as I find new facts, some of this information in this book will change. I will keep searching any and all records I can find to hopefully solve who are the parents of Hannah Brown. I am only human, and I am the first one to admit I do make mistakes. If you find something you think is wrong, I will be more than willing to discuss it with you.

I am hoping that some people will contact me with information to either shed new light on any ancestry mentioned in this book, as well as any pictures that they may have that they would like to share. I would like to hear any comments or suggestions on whatever is written in this book. Please contact me at greenholow@aol.com.

I would like to get to know you, my Grandmother
I have so many questions and not enough answers

Once I started this journey
I had to follow many paths to find the right direction
Now I have only one journey left
That is to find you, Grandmother
I know you are a part of me and I feel proud that you are

I have learned about some of the Native American culture
But very little about you
I would like to pass down to my grandchildren
The Native American culture of days gone by
As well as who you are

I have spent many moons looking for you
I will keep looking until there are no more moons left for me
Until our paths cross in the Spirit World, Grandmother
Your spirit will remain within me

Grandmother, I will not give up this journey

Shirley Holdridge Greene

ABBREVIATIONS

Avery Stoddard Cemetery, Route 214, Ledyard, Ct	ASC
The Brown Genealogy, by Cyrus H. Brown	BG
Brown Peckham Main Cemetery, Iron Street, Ledyard, Ct	BPMC
City Clerk Office	CCO
Colonel Ledyard Cemetery, Meridan Street, Groton, Ct	CLC
Connecticut Historical Society	CHS
Connecticut State Library Hartford, Ct.	CSL
Eccleston Cemetery #10, Route 201, Cossaduck Hill, North Stonington, Ct	EC#10
Elm Grove Cemetery, Greenmanville Avenue, Mystic, Ct	EGC
Genealogical Abstracts from Revolutionary War Pension File Volume III N-Z	GARWPF
Genealogical Records of Nathaniel Babcock, Simeon Main, Isaac Miner, Ezekiel Main by Cyrus H. Brown	BMMM
Griswold Town Hall Jewett City, Ct	GrTH
Groton Town Hall, Route 1 Groton, Ct	GTH
Holdridge Cemetery, Indiantown Road, Ledyard, Ct.	HC
Jewett City Cemetery, Griswold Ct.	JCC
Judge Williams Cemetery, Shewville Road, Ledyard, Ct	JWC
Land Records	LR
Ledyard Center Cemetery, Center Groton Road, Ledyard, Ct	LCC
Ledyard Historical Society Ledyard, Ct	LHS
Ledyard Town Hall, Colonel Ledyard Highway, Ledyard, Ct	LTH
Morgan Pond Cemetery, Sandy Hollow Road, Ledyard, Ct.	MPC
New London City Hall, State Street New London, Ct	NLCH
New London County Superior Court Papers by Subject: Indians (CSL)	NLCSCPSI
North Stonington Town Hall North Stonington, Ct	NSTH

Norwich City Hall Norwich, Ct.	NCH
Preston City Cemetery, Route 165 Preston, Ct	PCC
Preston Town Hall, Route 2 Preston, Ct	PTH
Probate Office	PO
Spicer Cemetery, Colonel Ledyard Highway, Ledyard, Ct	SC
Stonington Town Hall Stonington, Ct	STH
The History of the Town of Ledyard by Rev. John Avery	HTL,Avery
Thomas Main Cemetery, Homestead Road, Ledyard Ct	TMC
Town Clerk Office	TCO
U.S. Federal Census, State of Connecticut, New London County-1790	USFC-1790
Roll #M32_3, U.S. Federal Census, State of Connecticut, New London County-1800	USFC-1800
Roll #M252_3, U.S. Federal Census, State of Connecticut, New London County-1810	USFC-1810
Roll #M33_2, U.S. Federal Census, State of Connecticut, New London County-1820	USFC-1820
Roll #M19-10, U.S. Federal Census, State of Connecticut, New London County-1830	USFC-1830
Roll #M704_29, U.S. Federal Census, State of Connecticut, New London County-1840 Town of Ledyard	USFC-1840 Ledyard
Roll #M704_30, U.S. Federal Census, State of Connecticut, New London County-1840 Town of North Stonington	USFC-1840 North Stonington
Roll #M432_49, U.S. Federal Census, State of Connecticut, New London County-1850 Town of Ledyard and Town of Griswold	USFC-1850 Ledyard USFC-1850 Griswold
Roll #M432_48, U.S. Federal Census, State of Connecticut, New London County-1850 Town of Bozrah, Montville, North Stonington And Norwich	USFC-1850 Bozrah USFC-1850 Montville USFC-1850 North Stonington USFC-1850 Norwich

Roll #M653_90, U.S. Federal Census, State of
Connecticut, New London County-1860
Town of Ledyard and Town of Groton
USFC-1860 Ledyard or USFC-1860 Groton

Roll #M653_91, U.S. Federal Census, State of
Connecticut, New London County-1860
Town of North Stonington and Town of Preston
USFC-1860 North Stonington or USFC-1860 Preston

Roll #M593_113, U.S. Federal Census, State of
Connecticut, New London County-1870
Towns of Ledyard, Montville and North Stonington USFC-1870

Roll #T9_108, U.S. Federal Census, State of
Connecticut, New London County-1880
Town of Ledyard and North Stonington USFC-1880

U.S. Federal Census, State of
Connecticut, New London County-1900 USFC-1900

Roll #T624, U.S. Federal Census, State of
Connecticut, New London County-1910 USFC-1910

Roll #T625_196, U.S. Federal Census, State of
Connecticut, New London County-1920 USFC-1920

Roll # T626_282, U.S. Federal Census, State of
Connecticut, New London County-1930 USFC-1930

Voluntown Town Hall, Route 138
Voluntown, Ct VTH

Westerly Town Hall, Route 1
Westerly, RI WTH

ENDNOTES

1. Dr. Bryan Sykes, "The Seven Daughters of Eve", (New York, W. W. Norton & Company, 2001)
2. Oxford Ancestors, Ltd, The World Clans DNA Certificate, (University of Oxford, England, Received July 19, 2002)
3. Candida Checksfield, Letter to Noyes P. Greene pertaining to his MatriLine chart for above Certificate, (United Kingdom, Oxford Ancestors 2002)
4. Oxford Ancestors, Ltd., Interpreting Your World Clans Certificate, (2001)
5. Doug George Kanentiio, "Iroquois Culture and Commentary", (Santa Fe, New Mexico, Clear Water Publications, 2000)
6. Goldie Ada Willcox Collins Robbins, written permission to use her test results from Oxford Ancestors, (permission given January 8, 2004)
7. Family Tree DNA, Native American Ancestry – Female DNA, Certificate, (Houston, Texas, March 6, 2003)
8. Wheeler, Richard Anson, "History of Stonington, Conn", (New London, Conn, Press of The Day Publishing Company, 1900), pg 175
9. Avery, Rev. John, "History of the Town of Ledyard 1650-1900", Norwich, Conn., Press of the Bulletin Co., 1901), pg 251
10. Wheeler, Richard Anson, pg. 193
11. Wheeler, Richard A., "The Pequot Indians an Historical Sketch," not dated, page 8 and 9
12. Indian Colonial Research Center (hereinafter listed as ICRC), Old Mystic, Ct., Eva Butler Collection, "Local Indian Lore", Chapter IV, The Curse of Cuppacommock, page 9
13. Wheeler, Richard Anson, "History of Stonington, Conn", pg.194
14. Ibid, pg. 194
15. New London City Hall, (hereinafter listed as NLCH), City Clerk Office (hereinafter listed as CCO), Births Book 1945
16. Stonington Town Hall (hereinafter listed as STH), Town Clerk Office (hereafter listed as TCO), Marriages Book 1970
17. Westerly Town Hall, (hereafter listed as WTH), TCO, Births, 1950
18. Connecticut State Library, (hereinafter listed as CSL), 60 State Street, Hartford, Ct
19. Ledyard Historical Society, (hereinafter listed as LHS), Map of The Town of Ledyard, (this is only a section of the entire map)
20. Birth of Ray Ernest Willcox, taking into account that he was born in 1897, Raymond and Phebe Wilcox were living at the Willcox Homestead at this time
21. Birth of Raymond Willcox, taking into account that he was born in 1844, Robert Wilcox was living on Iron Street at that time
22. Birth of Mary Stanton Main, from Census records and neighbors of her father
23. Birth of George Park Main, from where his father Timothy Main lived at the time of George P. Main birth, and Census records of Timothy Main when George P. Main was still very young
24. Birth of Timothy Main, from where Thomas Main lived
25. Birth of William Leeds Main, he is a brother to above Timothy Main and was probably born in the same house
26. Birth of Sarah E. Brown, where Avery W. Brown lived when she was born

27. Birth of Avery Wilbur Brown, an educated guess on my part, from the information we have found from Avery's brother Albert Brown
28. Ledyard Town Hall (hereafter listed as LTH), TCO, Land Records (hereinafter listed as LR), Volume 8 page 756, September 10, 1926, Harry C. W. Main to Ray Ernest Wilcox
29. Groton Town Hall (hereafter listed as GTH), LR, Volume 19 page 59, May 16, 1827, Nathaniel B. Wilcox to Robert Wilcox
30. Ibid
31. LTH, TCO, LR, Volume 8 page 151, May 2, 1903, George B. Jones to Chester Pierce
32. LHS, Map of The Town of Ledyard, A.W. Brown, (Avery Wilbur Brown)
33. Ibid, A. B. (Albert Brown)
34. GTH, LR, Volume 11 page 24, December 25, 1786, Jedidiah Leeds and Nathan Morgan to Phinehas Holdridge
35. STH, Probate Office (hereafter listed as PO), Volume 4 page 145, Distribution of the Estate of Nathan Holdridge
36. "A Modern History of New London County Connecticut", Editor in Chief Benjamin Tinkham Marshall A.M.D.D., President of Connecticut College, New London, Connecticut, Lewis Historical Publishing Co., New York City, NY; 1922; Volume III; page 268; description of where Albert Brown was born, house of Nathaniel & Charlotte Brown
37. Ibid
38. LHS, Map of the Town of Ledyard, A. Brown(Aaron Brown)
39. GTH, LR, Volume 16 Page 10, dated June 30, 1806, Nathaniel Brown to beloved daughter Anner Williams
40. LHS, Historic Ledyard Volume II, Ledyard Center, 1987, page 62
41. LTH, PO, Journal Book 2 page 515, dated September 19, 1889, under Estate of Timothy Main, authorized to sell Timothy Main, deceased, property at Public Auction
42. GTH, LR, Volume 16 page 88, dated March 19, 1813, Stanton Hewitt to Thomas Main
43. LHS, Map of The Town of Ledyard, R. Holdridge, (Randall Holdridge)
44. Noyes Greene, memories of his childhood, Location of the Flower Cottage
45. Ibid, most logical route for Nathan Holdridge to take to get to Punderson's Store
46. Ibid, most logical route for Dan Toby to take to get to Punderson's Store
47. Ibid, memories from his childhood, for location of Kate Swamp Road
48. GTH, LR, Volume 11 page 24, December 25, 1786, Jedidiah Leeds and Nathan Morgan to Phinehas Holdridge, deed mentions "...*mill to be erected*..."
49. LHS, Tax Records, 1858, 1859, 1860, 1871, Grain mill under Robert Willcox
50. Ibid, Map of The Town of Ledyard, SM (Saw mill)
51. GTH, LR, Volume 19 Page 140, dated December 16,1830, Peter Williams to John Williams; in the description of the property it mentions, "... a piece of Land known by Toby Orchid..." as one of the boundaries
52. LHS, Map of The Town of Ledyard, Second Baptist Church
53. Ibid, J. Etheridge (James Etheridge)
54. Ibid, S. Billings (Stephen Billings)
55. Ibid, School House #14

56. Ibid, Mrs. A. Peckham (Mrs. Almira Peckham)
57. Written permission from James L. Williams
58. Written permission was given by Kimberly Pendleton, dated December 19, 2003
59. Written permission was given by Goldie Ada Willcox Collins Robbins, dated January 8, 2004
60. STH, TCO, LR, Volume 11 page 132, dated October 22, 1787, William Williams the second to Ephraim Williams, 120 acres
61. LHS, Fanning Map, location of William Williams Saw Mill
62. LTH, TCO, birth 1924
63. NLCH, CCO, Death Book 1992
64. East Lyme Town Hall, TCO, Birth Book 1919
65. Norwich City Hall (hereafter listed as NCH), CCO, Death Book 1960
66. GTH, TCO, Marriage Book 1943
67. Written permission was given by Sadie Louise Greene, dated December 18, 2003
68. Ibid
69. LTH, TCO, LR, Volume 19 page 253, dated October 24, 1951, Chester Z. Pierce and Florence E. Pierce husband and wife to George F. Greene and Sadie A. Greene, husband and wife
70. Ibid, Volume 2 page 174 Births Mary Elvira Pierce
71. Putnam Town Hall, TCO, Deaths, 1974, Mary Elvira Willcox
72. LTH, TCO, Volume 2 page 163, Birth Ray Ernest Willcox
73. Ibid, 1951, Deaths, Ray Ernest Willcox
74. Ibid, TCO, 1916 Marriages Ray Ernest Willcox and Mary Elvira Pierce
75. Written permission was given by Goldie Ada Willcox Collins Robbins to use pictures, dated January 8, 2004
76. Ibid, marriages
77. Brown Peckham Main Cemetery, (hereafter listed as BPMC), Iron Street, Ledyard, Ct
78. Ibid
79. Ibid
80. Ibid
81. LTH, TCO, Volume 8 page 40, dated December 18, 1898, William H. Williams to Stephen Caswell
82. Written permission was given Goldie Ada Willcox Collins Robbins to use pictures, dated January 8, 2004
83. Noyes Greene, memories of his childhood, Location of the Flower Cottage
84. ICRC, Western Pequot Indians, "Eva Butler Collection"
85. U.S. Federal Census for the State of Connecticut, New London County. (hereafter listed as USFC), 1900, Town of Ledyard, Martha Langevin and USFC-1910, Town of Ledyard, Martha Langevin
86. USFC-1920 Ledyard, George P. Main
87. Ibid, -1900, Town of Ledyard, Jane Wheeler Durfee and USFC-1910 New London County, Town of Ledyard, Jane Wheeler
88. LTH, TCO, LR, Volume 15 page 290, dated August 12, 1949, Cedar Swamp Property
89. Ibid, Volume 16 page 323, dated November 11, 1938, distribution of the Estate of Horace H. Main to Harry C.W. Main and Lurie Main, the Cedar Swamp property

90. Ibid, PO, Volume 3 page 689, 1895, Estate of William Leeds Main, son Horace Main inheritance
91. Ibid, TCO, LR, Volume 14 page 293, dated January 4, 1930, James C. Adams to Ray Ernest Willcox
92. USFC-1930 Ledyard, Ray and Mary Willcox
93. BPMC, Willcox, Raymond, date of birth
94. Wilcox, Robert N., "Reminiscences Of California Life being An Abridged Description of Scenes which the Author has passed through in CALIFORNIA and other Lands"; Willcox Print; 1897; Library of Congress, Rare Book Room, F864W64, 478870, My 18, 38
95. GTH, TCO, Volume 4 page 25, Marriages, Raymond Willcox and Phebe Waite
96. Ibid, Deaths, dated October 17, 1935, Birth date of Phoebe Wilcox from death certificate
97. West Greenwich Town Hall, TOC, Cemetery Records, Tillinghast Waite Cemetery, Historical #1, Hannah P. Waite
98. GTH, LR, Volume 26 page 121, dated April 4, 1855, Henry W. Avery to Warren Haley and George R. Waite
99. USFC-1860 Groton, George Waite, occupation millwright
100. ICRC, Elmer Waite Collection, pictures of Phebe Elizabeth Waite and George Reynolds Waite
101. BPMC, Willcox, George R; date of birth
102. Ibid; date of death
103. Union Cemetery, North Stonington, Ct; Crumb, Julia A. Willcox, date of birth
104. Ibid; date of death
105. BPMC, Willcox, Jeremiah, date of birth
106. Ibid, date of death
107. Jewett City Cemetery (hereafter listed as JCC), Griswold, Ct; Miner, Bernice Willcox, date of birth
108. Ibid; date of death
109. Ibid; marriage to George G. Miner
110. USFC-1880 Ledyard, under Raymond Wilcox; Willcox, Charity A., estimated birth year
111. BPMC, Willcox, Arthur; date of birth
112. Ibid; death
113. USFC-1880 Ledyard, under Raymond Wilcox; Willcox, Mary Ann, estimated birth year
114. JCC, Willcox, Benjamin; date of birth
115. Ibid; date of death
116. USFC-1900 Ledyard; under Willcox, Raymond; Willcox, Frances, birth year
117. USFC-1900 Ledyard; under Willcox, Raymond; Willcox, Grover C., birth year
118. BPMC, Willcox, Betsey; date of birth
119. Ibid; date of death
120. Ibid; Willcox, Fairy, date of birth
121. Ibid; date of death
122. USFC-1900 Ledyard; under Willcox, Raymond; Charles Willcox birth year
123. USFC-1870 Ledyard, abstract of Raymond Wilcox family
124. USFC-1880 Ledyard, abstract of Raymond Willcox

125. LHS, Ledyard Tax List, 1871, Raymond Willcox
126. LTH, TCO, LR, Vol 5 page 300, dated February 27, 1869, Robert Wilcox to Raymond Wilcox
127. LTH, PO, Volume 3 page 210, dated October 8, 1885, Raymond inherited half of the Real Estate of his deceased father, Robert Willcox
128. LTH, TCO, LR, Volume 5 page 249, dated February 10, 1885, Robert N. Wilcox, of the Town of Milane, County of Erie, State of Ohio, to Raymond Wilcox Of Ledyard, Ct
129. Ibid, Vol 5 page 253, dated March 18, 1885, Martin Wilcox of The Town of Lehigh, County of Jasper, State of Missouri and Mollie F. Wilcox, his wife to Raymond Wilcox of Ledyard, Ct
130. LHS, Town Meetings, 1867, Elector, Raymond Wilcox
131. Ibid, , 1867, Poundkeeper, Raymond Wilcox
132. LTH, TCO, Deaths, Volume 2 page 226, dated March 29, 1904, Raymond Wilcox
133. LTH, LR, Volume 8 page 362, dated March 15, 1913, Phebe Willcox sold property
134. GTH, TCO, Deaths, dated October 17, 1935, Phoebe E. Wilcox; death date
135. LTH, TCO, Deaths, Volume 2 page 207 dated January 11, 1885; Robert Willcox, III; birth date was recorded on death certificate
136. Avery, Rev. John, History of the Town of Ledyard 1650-1900, (hereafter listed as HTL, Avery),1901, Reprinted 1986 under the auspices of the Ledyard Historic District Commission and the Ledyard Historical Society; page 303, Deaths: Robert Wilcox 1811
137. STH, PO, Volume 8 page 316, dated October 1, 1811, Guardianship of minor children of Robert Wilcox
138. GTH, TCO, Volume 1 page 12, Marriages, dated April 4, 1824; Robert Willcox/Mary Ann Reed
139. BPMC; Willcox, Mary Ann Reed; wife of Robert Wilcox, date of birth from gravestone
140. Ibid, Willcox, Robert, date of birth from gravestone
141. Ibid, date of death of gravestone
142. LTH, PO, Volume 3 page 210, Estate of Robert Wilcox, Last Will and Testament, dated October 8, 1883; daughter, Mary Ann Chapman
143. BPMC; Palmer, Frances Willcox, wife of Charles H. Palmer; birth date from gravestone
144. Ibid; Palmer, Frances Wilcox; death date from gravestone
145. Ibid; Frances Willcox marriage to Charles Palmer; husband and wife on gravestone
146. LTH, PO, Volume 3 page 210, Estate of Robert Wilcox, Last Will and Testament, dated October 8, 1883; daughter Betsey Turner
147. BPMC, Willcox, Amos, birth date from gravestone
148. Ibid; Willcox, Amos; death date from gravestone
149. USFC-1850 Ledyard; under Robert Wilcox; birth year for son, Robert N. Willcox
150. BPMC; Willcox, Robertson; birth date from gravestone
151. Ibid; death date from gravestone
152. USFC-1850 Ledyard; under Robert Wilcox; birth year for son, Martin Willcox
153. BPMC; Willcox, Chauncey; birth date from gravestone
154. Ibid; death date from gravestone
155. Ibid; Willcox, Reuben; birth date from gravestone

156. Ibid; death date from gravestone
157. STH, PO, Volume 9 page 410, dated May 2, 1815; Distribution of the Estate of Robert Willcox, of Groton, Ct
158. GTH, LR, Volume 19 page 59, dated May 16, 1827; Nathaniel Wilcox to Robert Wilcox
159. Ibid, Volume 19 page 52, dated March 13, 1829; Joseph and Deborah Crandall to Robert Wilcox
160. Ibid, Volume 20 page 363, dated December 16, 1832; Robertson Wilcox to Robert Wilcox
161. LHS, Abstract of Ledyard Tax Records
162. USFC-1850 Ledyard, abstract of Robert Wilcox family
163. Ibid, -1860 Ledyard, abstract of Robert Wilcox family
164. LHS; Town Meetings for Ledyard; Robert Wilcox, years he was elected to be a surveyor of the highways
165. Fee, Janet; "A Portion of the Descendants of Edward Wilcox of Rhode Island" page 16
166. LHS; Abstract of the 1st Baptist Church of Groton Records; Wilcox/Willcox
167. Ibid
168. HTL,Avery; page 59
169. New London County, Superior Court Papers by Subject: Indians, 1743-1907 (hereafter listed as NLCSCPSI), CSL, Hartford, Ct; RG 3 Box 2, Mashantucket Pequot 1758-1887, March 1875; R. Wilcox
170. LTH, TCO, Volume 2 page 207; Robert Willcox death date
171. Ibid, Volume 2 page 198; Mary A. Willcox death date
172. HTL,Avery; page 303; Robert Willcox, Jr., birth date came from age at death
173. Ibid; page 307; Nathaniel Brown death date
174. STH, PO, Volume 11 page 133; dated March 14, 1820; Estate of Nathaniel Brown, Last Will and Testament
175. BPMC; Wilcox, Louisa, date of birth
176. Ibid, Wilcox, Louisa, date of death
177. GTH, LR, Volume 16 page 14, dated January 18, 1811, Jonas B. Avery to Robert Wilcox of Lyme, Ct, 120 acres of land
178. USFC-1810 Lyme, Robert Wilcox
179. ICRC, Family Histories, Willcox Family, Robert Willcox, Jr, cause of death
180. STH, PO, Volume 10 page 285, dated December 15,1817, Notes Payable for the Estate of Robert Willcox
181. STH, PO, Volume 8 page 316, dated October 1, 1811, Deborah Wilcox appointed guardian to minor children of Robert Wilcox, deceased
182. ICRC, Family Histories, Willcox Family, Robert Wilcox, Sr., birth
183. White, Virgil D.; "Genealogical Abstracts from Revolutionary War Pension Files, Volume III: N-Z" (hereafter listed as GARWPF); The National Historical Publishing Company, Waynesboro, Tennessee, 1992; page 3845, under Wilcox/Willcox, Robert, RI line, marriage of Robert Wilcox to Sarah Wilbur
184. ICRC, Family Histories, Willcox Family, Robert Wilcox, daughter Susanna Wilcox marriage to Asa Gray
185. Ibid, son Hazard Wilcox marriage to Mary Wright
186. Ibid, daughter Charlotte Wilcox marriage to William Babcock

187. Ibid, daughter Nancy Wilcox marriage to Mr. Daniels
188. Ibid, daughter Sally Wilcox marriage Benjamin Wilbur
189. BPMC, Brown, Mary Wilcox, date of birth
190. Ibid, date of death
191. ICRC, Family Histories, Wilcox Family, Robert Wilcox, daughter Mary Wilcox marriage Aaron Brown
192. Ibid, Jeremiah Wilcox year of birth
193. Ibid, date of death
194. Ibid, Delight Wilcox marriage to Gilod Waltrous
195. LHS, Abstract of the 1st Baptist Church of Groton Records, Wilcocks, Sarah
196. GARWPF, Willcox, Robert, page 3845
197. Bartlett, John R., "CENSUS of the Inhabitants of Rhode Island and Providence Plantations 1774", Originally published Providence, 1858, Reprinted for Clearfield Company, Inc. by Genealogical Publishing Company, Inc. Baltimore, Md 1990, 1999, page 74
198. STH, LR, Volume 10 page 425, dated April 2, 1783, John James of Preston to Robert Wilcox of Stonington
199. Ibid, Volume 11 page 178, dated June 8, 1787, Robert Wilcox of Stonington to Joseph Wheeler of Stonington
200. Rhode Island Historical Society, Paul Campbell Research Notes, Box 1, Folder 10, Photocopy of original document from the Rhode Island State Archives
201. USFC-1790, under Robert Wilcox
202. GTH, LR, Volume 12 page 100, dated March 16, 1795, William Williams of Groton to Robert Wilcox of Stonington, 210 acres, a farm
203. USFC-1800 Groton, under Wilcox, Robert
204. GTH, LR, Volume 14 page 119, dated March 9, 1804, Robert Wilcox of Groton to Stanton Hewitt of Stonington, Ct, 210 acres
205. Greene, Shirley, Map of Robert Willcox Property, taken from deed descriptions from the following deeds filed in the Town of Groton, Land Records office:
    1. Phinehas Holdridge, Volume 11 page 24, dated December 25, 1786
    2. Robert Wilcox, Volume 12, page 100, dated March 16, 1795
    3. William Hempstead , Volume 14 page 15, dated March 27, 1801, 270 acres,
Daniel Deshon of New London to William Hempstead of Groton
206. Exeter Cemetery, Goshen Society, Lebanon, Ct.; Wilcox, Sarah, date of death
207. GARWPF, page 3845, date of death, Robert Wilcox
208. Microfilm of Estate Papers to 1880: Town of New London, CSL, Robert Wilcocks, Town of Lyme,1809, File #5715
209. NLCH, CCO, 1939, Deaths, dated November 29, 1939; death certificate gives birth date of April 4, 1878 and birthplace was Ledyard, Ct. for Mary Stanton Pierce
210. Ibid; date of death for Mary Stanton Pierce
211. North Stonington Town Hall (hereafter listed as NSTH), TCO, Book 1852-1920 page 54, Births, dated February 27, 1880, Chester Pierce
212. LTH, TCO, 1946. Deaths, dated February 5, 1945; Chester Latham Pierce
213. NSTH, TCO, Volume 1 page 37, Marriages dated November 15, 1899; Chester L. Pierce/ Mary S. Maine
214. Written permission was given by Goldie Ada Willcox Collins Robbins to use pictures, dated January 8, 2004

215. BPMC, Avery, Lucy Pierce, birth date from gravestone,
216. Ibid, death date from gravestone
217. Ibid; marriage Lucy Pierce/Elmer R. Avery
218. Ibid, Pierce, Sadie, date of birth and date of death from gravestone
219. USFC-1910 Ledyard, under Chester L. Pierce, daughter Gertrude M. Pierce year of birth
220. BPMC, Pierce, Clara J., birth date from gravestone
221. Ibid, death date from gravestone
222. Ibid, Clara Pierce marriage to Harry Brewer
223. USFC-1910 Ledyard, under Chester L. Pierce, daughter, Mildred A. Pierce year of birth
224. Ledyard Center Cemetery (hereafter listed as LCC), Center Groton Road, Ledyard, Ct; Pierce, Chester Z., birth date from gravestone
225. Ibid, death date from gravestone
226. LTH, TCO, LR, Volume 19 page 253, dated October 24, 1951, Chester Z. Pierce and Florence E. Pierce, husband and wife of Ledyard to George F. Greene, Jr and Sadie A. Greene, husband and wife of Ledyard. Shows that Chester Z. Pierce was married to Florence E. (does not give maiden name)
227. Oral permission from Henry Morgan in 1999, to cross his property to see Barns Cemetery and old cellar holes from the houses that were once there
228. GTH, LR, Volume 8 page 11, dated February 28, 1775, George Fanning to Ezra Barns, property on Hoot Owl Hill, in Ledyard, Ct
229. LTH, TCO, LR, Volume 8 page 151, dated May 2, 1903, George B. Jones to Chester Pierce
230. Ibid, Volume 8 page 641, dated December 21, 1922, Mary E. Whipple, Administrator to the Estate of Samuel A. Whipple of Ledyard to Chester Pierce; 6 acres 4 acres
231. Ibid, Volume 19 page 253, dated October 24, 1951, Chester Z. Pierce and Florence E. Pierce, husband and wife of Ledyard to George F. Greene, Jr and Sadie A. Greene, husband and wife of Ledyard. Two tracts of land 6 acres and 4 acres
232. USFC-1900 Ledyard, under Chester L. Pierce; lists who was living with Chester Pierce at this time as well as the next neighbor Stephen Caswell
233. USFC-1910 Ledyard, under Chester L. Pierce; lists the children of Chester Pierce as well as some of the closest neighbors
234. USFC-1920 Ledyard, under Chester L. Pierce; again lists the children as well as neighbors of Chester Pierce
235. USFC-1930 Ledyard, under Chester R. Pierce, lists child and neighbors, one of which is his mother in law Sarah E. Main
236. NSTH, TCO, Births, Volume page, Pierce, Zachary date of birth
237. Ibid, Marriages, Volume page, Pierce, Zachary marriage to Almy Gray
238. BPMC, Pierce, Wallace, date of birth from gravestone
239. Ibid, marriage to Jennie S. Main from gravestone
240. Ibid, Pierce, Herbert B, date of birth from gravestone
241. Ibid, date of death
242. NSTH, TCO, 1852-1920, Marriages, dated 1904, Herbert B. Pierce to Maria H. Main
243. Ibid, LR, Volume 10 page 341, dated June 15, 1873, Zachary Pierce to Freeman

Pierce; 60 acres known as Holmes Hole

244. USFC-1880 North Stonington, under Pierce, Zachary; lists children. Zachary was living on the same property as his Brother William Pierce, as you can see from the numbers on the left of the Head of Household
245. USFC-1900 & 1910 Ledyard, see footnotes 228 and 229
246. LTH, TCO, Deaths, Volume page, dated April 6, 1915, Pierce, Zachary date of death
247. Eccleston Cemetery, #10 (hereinafter listed as EC#10), Route 2, Cossaduck Hill, North Stonington, Ct, Pierce, Freeman; date of birth
248. Griswold Town Hall (hereinafter listed as GrTH), School Street, Jewett City, Ct., TCO, Deaths, Brown, Elizabeth; from her death certificate, lists parents as Freeman Pierce and Eunice Babcock
249. West Plain Cemetery (hereinafter listed as WPC#11), West Main Street, Norwich, Ct, Pierce, Courtland, date of birth
250. Ibid, date of death
251. EC#10, Pierce, Elias F. date of birth
252. Ibid, date of death
253. Ibid, marriage to Lydia M. Maine
254. GrTH, TCO, Deaths, page 168, Brown, Elizabeth; date of birth from death certificate, lists parents as Freeman Pierce and Eunice Babcock
255. Ibid, date of death
256. "Genealogical and Biographical Record of New London County Connecticut containing Biographical Sketches of Prominent and Representative Citizens and Genealogical Records of Many of the Early Settled Families, Illustrated", J.H. Beers Co., Chicago, Ill: Copyright 1905; pages 929-931, under Russell M. Brown; Josiah Brown marriage to Elizabeth Pierce
257. NSTH, TCO, PO, Volume 3 page 347, dated March 22, 1892 Last Will and Testament of Freeman Pierce; daughter, Elizabeth Pierce, wife of Russell Brown
258. USFC-1850 North Stonington, under Pierce, Freeman, son William Pierce year of birth
259. GrTH, TCO, Deaths, page 173, Pierce, William, date of death, parents listed as Freeman and Eunice Pierce
260. USFC-1850 North Stonington, under Pierce, Freeman, son Joseph Pierce year of birth
261. Preston City Cemetery (hereinafter listed as PCC), Route 165, Preston, Ct., Pierce, Joseph date of death
262. USFC-1850 North Stonington, under Pierce, Freeman, son Samuel Pierce year of birth
263. GrTH, TCO, Book B page 146; dated March 11, 1863, marriage to Hattie Esther Pierce
264. USFC-1870, State of Connecticut, Windham County, Town of Scotland, M593-117, page 3; under Maine, Mary; date of birth for Ann S. Brown age 24
265. NSTH, TCO, PO, Volume 3 page 347, dated March 22, 1892 Last Will and Testament of Freeman Pierce; daughter, Ann S. Pierce, wife of George Brown
266. USFC-1860 North Stonington, under Pierce, Freeman, son George F. Pierce year of birth
267. NSTH, TCO, LR, Volume 6 page 565, dated January 13, 1849; Benjamin F. Billings

to Freeman Pierce, 100 acres for Cossaduck Hill property, bounded easterly by Billings Pond, westerly by the North Stonington/Griswold Town Line.

268. USFC-1850 North Stonington, under Pierce, Freeman, lists children and ages of the entire family
269. USFC-1860 North Stonington, under Pierce, Freeman, lists children,
270. USFC-1870 North Stonington, under Pierce, Freeman, lists children
271. USFC-1880 North Stonington, under Pierce, Freeman, lists people who are living with him
272. EC#10, Pierce, Freeman date of death
273. Ibid, Pierce, Eunice, date of death
274. USFC-1860 Preston, under Freeman Pierce, birth year from age on Census record
275. NSTH, TCO, Marriages, Book 1806-1851 page 155, dated September 13, 1835, Freeman Pierce marriage to Elizabeth Wheeler
276. GrTH, TCO, Book D page 24, deaths, dated December 26, 1891, states George W. Pierce was born in North Stonington and his parents were Freeman and Nancy Pierce, his age was 82 years. That is where is birth year came from.
277. Ibid, death date December 26, 1891
278. NCH, CCO, Vital Record Books, Book 2 page 786, marriage of George Pearce of North Stonington to Lydia Hurns of Norwich, Ct, dated July 12, 1835
279. USFC-1850, State of New York, County of Chenango, Town of Norwich, M432-487, under Samuel Pierce, year of his birth and family
280. USFC-1850 Montville, under Joseph Pierce, age for his birth year, also lists family
281. NCH, CCO, Vital Record Books, Book 2 page 919, marriage of Joseph C. Pierce of North Stonington to Lydia M. Stevens of Lisbon, Ct., dated March 17, 1845.
282. Preston City Cemetery, Preston, Ct., death date from gravestone
283. USFC-1850 Norwich, under Anthony Gallagher, William Wilcox and wife Nancy are living with Mr. Gallagher. The Census lists their ages as well as their children.
284. NCH, CCO, Vital Records Books, Book 2 page 817, marriage of Nancy Ann Pierce marriage William A. Wilcox, both of Norwich, Ct. dated November 4, 1838
285. USFC-1850 Montville, under Charles Rogers, Lucy E. Pierce year of birth
286. NCH, CCO, Vital Records Book, Book 2 page 884, dated January 19, 1843; marriage of Lucy E. Pierce of Norwich, to Edward Stevens of Chatham, NH
287. Ibid, Book 2 page 893, dated November 14, 1847; marriage of Lucy E. Stevens, of North Stonington, Ct. to Ch. L. Rogers of Montville, Ct
288. USFC-1880 North Stonington, under Betsey Rathbun, her birth year is taken from this record
289. NSTH, TCO, Book 1920-1950 page 8, dated March 19, 1930, Deaths, Betsey M. Rathbun, parents listed as Freeman Pierce born unknown and mother _______Cook, born unknown
290. USFC-1850 Griswold, under Asher D. Rathbone, Elizabeth M. Pierce marriage to Asher Rathbone
291. Sterling Town Hall, TCO, Deaths, page 121, dated November 14, 1898, Frances E. Babcock death record, lists her age as 64 years 9 months and she was born in Voluntown
292. Ibid, date of death from death certificate; Frances Babcock was the widow of Albert Babcock. The record does not list her parents.
293. Voluntown Town Hall (hereinafter listed as VTH), TCO, Marriages, dated July 4,

1849, marriage from Frances Pierce to Albert C. Babcock
294. PCC, year of birth from gravestone
295. Ibid, date of death from gravestone
296. USFC-1810 North Stonington, under Pierce, Freeman
297. USFC-1820 North Stonington, under Pierce, Freeman
298. USFC-1830, State of Connecticut, Windham County, Town of Voluntown, M10-11, under Pierce, Freeman
299. USFC-1840, State of Connecticut, Windham County, Town of Voluntown, M704-32, under Pierce, Freeman
300. USFC-1850, State of Connecticut, Windham County, Town of Voluntown, M432-51, under Freeman Pierce, lists family
301. USFC-1860 Preston, under Freeman Pierce
302. USFC-1870 Montville, under Freeman Pierce, shows he was living with his daughter Lucy and her family
303. Death date of Nancy Cook Pierce, she had to have died before 1835. Many of the children's death records show their mothers name was Nancy. Freeman Pierce was married at least twice. But Nancy Cook was the mother of all but one of his children.
304. Compiled by Authority of the General Assembly, "Record of Service of Connecticut Men in the II. War of 1812, III Mexican War", Hartford: 1889, page 102, Freeman Pierce, Private, Place of Service, Stonington, Commander, Daniel Carr, Period of Service, August 9, 1814 to Aug. 27, 1814.
305. North Stonington Historical Society, Abstract of Luther Palmer account book, for the years from 1816-1820
306. New London County Historical Society, Brown, Barbara W. and Rose, James M., "Black Roots in Southeastern Connecticut 1650-1900", IBSN: 0-9607744-5-9, Copyright 2001; page 367
307. PTH, TCO, LR, Volume 24 page 98, dated March 1, 1856; Elisha B. Fish of Preston to Elizabeth Pierce of Montville, Ct.
308. Ibid, Volume 29 page 553, dated November 3, 1871; James M. Pierce of Preston, Ct. to D. M. Dickerson of Norwich, Ct.
309. LTH, TCO, Book 1 page 53, Family Birth Records, under Avery W. Brown, Sarah E. Brown, date of birth
310. Ibid, Death, Sarah E. Main
311. BPMC, birth year for George P. Main, of 1847, from gravestone
312. Ibid, death year, 1929, from gravestone
313. PTH, TCO, Marriages, 1868, George P. Main and Sarah E. Brown
314. Written permission was given from Vivian Williams of North Stonington, Ct on December 19, 2003 for the pictures of George P. Main and wife Sarah E. Brown Main
315. BPMC, year of birth, 1868, Addie A. Main
316. Ibid, year of death 1884, Addie A. Main
317. BPMC, birth year of George E. Main, from gravestone, 1870
318. Ibid, death year of George E. Main, from gravestone, 1928
319. LCC, birth date from gravestone for Timothy B. Main, July 9, 1873
320. Ibid, death date from gravestone for Timothy B. Main, June 9, 1906
321. Ibid, wife of Timothy B. Main was Mary Corfey, from gravestone

322. BPMC, birth year from gravestone for Erastus John Main, 1874
323. Ibid, death year from gravestone for Erastus John Main, 1966
324. LCC, birth year from gravestone for Allyn T. Main, 1876
325. Ibid, death year from gravestone for Allyn T. Main, 1955
326. Ibid, wife of Allyn T. Main was Rosanna M. Rivers, from gravestone
327. Avery Stoddard Cemetery (hereinafter listed as ASC), Route 214, Ledyard, Ct., Avery W. Main birth year from gravestone 1880
328. Ibid, year of death for Avery W. Main from gravestone 1973
329. Ibid, wife of Avery W. Main was Grace A. Taylor, from gravestone
330. BPMC, birth year from gravestone of Elmer O. Main, 1882
331. Ibid, death year from gravestone for Elmer O. Main, 1930
332. USFC-1900 Ledyard, under George P. Main, son Amos G. Main, year of birth 1884
333. BPMC, birth year for Maria H. Main Pierce, from gravestone, 1885
334. Ibid, death year for Maria H. Main Pierce, 1964
335. Ibid, wife of Herbert B. Pierce was Maria H. Main Pierce, from gravestone
336. Ibid, birth year for Jennie S. Main Pierce from gravestone, 1888
337. Ibid, death year for Jennie S. Main from gravestone, 1923
338. Ibid, wife of Wallace Pierce was Jennie S. Main Pierce, from gravestone
339. Ibid, birth year for Daniel P. Main from gravestone 1890
340. Ibid, death year for Daniel P. Main from gravestone 1892
341. USFC-1900 Ledyard, under George P. Main, daughter, Annis B. Main, year of birth
342. USFC-1920 Ledyard, under Joseph P. Williams, Annis B. Main married Joseph Palmer Williams
343. The New London Day newspaper, dated October 10, 1939, under Old Mystic by Mrs. L.B. Norman, "Towns Oldest Resident Celebrates 93rd Birthday"
344. Noyes Greene, memories of his childhood, Location of the Flower Cottage
345. USFC-1880 Ledyard, under Main, George P.
346. USFC-1900 Ledyard, under Main, George P.
347. USFC-1910 Ledyard, under Main, George P.
348. USFC-1920 Ledyard, under Main, George P.
349. USFC-1930 Ledyard, under Main, Sarah E.
350. LTH, PO, Journal Book 2 page 515, dated September 19, 1889, to sell at public auction the real estate of Timothy Main, deceased
351. GTH, TCO, Volume 2 page 94, date December 17, 1810; birth for Timothy Main
352. Thomas Main Cemetery (hereinafter listed as TMC), Homestead Road, Ledyard, Ct.; date of death Timothy Main
353. Ibid, date of birth for Mary E. Gay Main, from gravestone
354. Ibid, date of death for Mary E. Main, from gravestone
355. BPMC, year of birth for Mary Ann Main Stillman, from gravestone
356. Ibid, date of death Mary Ann Stillman, from gravestone
357. Ibid, Mary Ann Main married Horatio Stillman, they are buried side by side
358. Brown, Cyrus H., "Genealogical Record of Nathaniel Babcock, Simeon Main, Isaac Miner, Ezekiel Main" (hereinafter listed as BMMM); The Everett Press, Boston, 1909; page 190; Thomas G. Main marriage Mary H. Maine
359. Ibid, date of birth for Abby A. Main, page 248
360. Ibid, date of death for Abby A. Main , page 248
361. Ibid, marriage of Abby A. Main to William D. Partelo, page 248

362. Ibid, date of birth for Timothy B. Main, page 248
363. Ibid, date of death for Timothy B. Main, page 248
364. Ibid, marriage from Timothy B. Main to Ann M. Crumb, page 248
365. Ibid, date of birth for Jedidiah R. Main, page 248
366. Ibid, date of death for Jedidiah R. Main, page 248
367. USFC-1860 Ledyard, under Timothy Main, son Dwight W. Main year of birth
368. USFC-1840 Ledyard, District #13, 3490; under Timothy Main, number of people in household and neighbors listed on the same page as Timothy Main,
369. USFC-1850 Ledyard, under Timothy Maine, listed wife and children with ages
370. USFC-1860 Ledyard, under Timothy Maine, listed family, plus which Town each person was born
371. USFC-1870 Ledyard, under Timothy Main
372. USFC-1880 Ledyard, under Timothy Main
373. NLCSCPSI, CSL, RG 3, Box 2, Mashantucket Pequot, 1758-1855; May 1836, Timothy Main
374. LHS, Abstract of the Town of Ledyard Tax List; 1866, under Timothy Main
375. GTH, LR, Volume 21 page 10, dated January 5, 1836; Thomas Main to Timothy M. Main, 55 acres of land
376. LTH, PO, Volume 3 page 591, dated March 7, 1887 Timothy Main
377. TMC, date of birth for Thomas Main, from gravestone
378. Ibid, date of death for Thomas Main, from gravestone
379. GTH, TCO, Marriages, Volume 2 page 94; dated April 20, 1806; marriage for Thomas Main of North Stonington to Louisa Brown
380. TMC, year of birth for Lois Brown Main, from gravestone
381. Ibid, death date for Lois Brown Main, from gravestone
382. GTH, TCO, Volume 2 page 94, dated February 13, 1807; Thomas B. Main birth
383. TMC, date of death for Thomas B. Main, from gravestone
384. GTH, TCO, Volume 1 page 53; dated November 15, 1835; marriage for Thomas B. Main and Lydia Hall
385. NLCSCPSI, CSL, RG 3 Box 1, Eastern Pequot, 1715-1855, January, 1850; Thos. B. Main
386. Ibid, June 1851, Thos. B. Main
387. Ibid, March 1853, Thomas Main
388. Ibid, April 1853, Thos. Main
389. GTH, TCO, Volume 2 page 94, dated May 14, 1808; birth for Aaron Main
390. BMMM, page 247, date of death for Aaron Main and where he died
391. GTH, TCO, Volume 1 page 31. Dated September 24, 1829; marriage of Aaron Main to Nancy Ashley
392. BMMM, page 247, children of Aaron Main
393. Ibid, description of Aaron Main's life
394. GTH, TCO, Volume 2 page 94, dated August 20, 1809; birth of John Main
395. TMC, date of death for John Main, from gravestone
396. GTH, TCO, Volume 1 page 49, dated February 1, 1835; marriage John Main to Nancy Barnes
397. BMMM, page 246, children of John Main
398. GTH, TCO, Volume 2 page 94; dated October 18, 1813; birth for Daniel Main
399. Ibid, Volume 1 page 60; dated October 8, 1838; marriage of Daniel Main to Delia A.

Roach
400. BMMM, page 246, 2nd and 3rd wives and children of Daniel Main and where they are buried.
401. GTH, TCO, Volume 2 page 94, dated February 10, 1815; birth of Louisa Main
402. TMC, date of death Louisa Main, from gravestone
403. GTH, TCO, Volume 1 page 49, dated September 28, 1834; marriage of Louisa Main to Corridon Maine
404. BMMM, page 246
405. GTH, TCO, Volume 2 page 94, dated July 8, 1817; birth of Zerviah Main
406. BMMM, page 249. Surviah B. Main death
407. Ibid, page 249. Surviah B. Main marriage to Albert Brown
408. Ibid, children of Albert Brown and Surviah Main
409. GTH, TCO, Volume 2 page 94, dated February 9, 1819; birth of Stanton Main
410. TMC, date of death for Stanton Main
411. BMMM, page 250. Stanton Main marriage to Susan Gray
412. Ibid, children of Stanton Main
413. Ibid, description of parents of Susan Gray and the Gray homestead
414. TMC, year of birth for Mary Esther Main, from gravestone
415. Ibid, date of death for Mary Esther Main Perkins, from gravestone
416. BMMM, page 251. Mary Esther Main marriage Miner A. Perkins
417. Ibid, children of Miner Perkins and Mary Esther Main
418. TMC, year of birth for Nathaniel B. Main
419. Ibid, date of death for Nathaniel B. Main
420. BMMM, page 251. Date of birth for Seth Main
421. Ibid, date of death for Seth Main
422. Ibid, Seth Main marriage to Maryanna Woodward
423. Ibid, children of Seth Main
424. Ibid, description of Seth Main's life
425. NLCSCPSI, CSL, RG 3 Box 2, Mashantucket Pequots, 1743-1887, 1866-1871, Seth Main was overseer for the tribe
426. Ibid, January 1, 1874, Seth Main paid for services as overseer
427. TMC, year of birth for Hannah Main, from gravestone
428. Ibid, date of death for Hannah Main Burrows
429. BMMM, page 247. Hannah Main marriage Paul Burrows
430. Ibid, children of Hannah Main and Paul Burrows
431. LTH, TCO, Book 1836-1855, page 20, dated April 30, 1845, marriage of Fannie E. Maine to George R. Parks
432. BMMM, page 247. Children of Fannie E. Main and George Parks
433. Ibid, page 252, date of birth for Amasa M. Main
434. Ibid, date of death for Amasa Main
435. Ibid, marriage of Amasa Main to Lucy O. Frink
436. Ibid, children of Amasa Main
437. Ibid, description of Amasa M. Main's life
438. Morgan Pond Cemetery (hereinafter listed as MPC), Sandy Hollow Road, Ledyard, Ct. date of birth for Deborah B. Main Morgan
439. LTH, TCO, 1836-1855, page 62, dated February 6, 1853, marriage of Deborah B. Main to Joseph Morgan

440. MPC, date of death for Deborah B. Main Morgan
441. BMMM, page 247, children of Deborah and Joseph Morgan
442. Ibid, page 246, description of Thomas Main's life
443. GTH, LR, Volume 14 page 38, dated December 22, 1801, Stanton Hewitt to Benajah Main and Samuel Main, 100 acres
444. Ibid, Volume 16 page 6, dated March 26, 1818, Samuel Main to Thomas Main, 72½ acres
445. Ibid, Volume 16 page 88, dated March 19, 1813, Stanton Hewitt to Thomas Main, one farm containing 40 acres
446. Ibid, Volume 16 page 144, dated April 1, 1815, Stanton Hewitt to Thomas Main, 35 acres
447. Ibid, Volume 18 page 195, dated January 9, 1828, Samuel and Abel Main to Thomas Main, 100 Acres
448. Ibid, Volume page, dated 1824, Rufus Williams to Thomas Main 32 acres
449. USFC-1810 Groton, under Thomas Main, also found neighbors
450. USFC-1820 Groton, under Thomas Main, also found neighbors
451. USFC-1830 Groton, under Thomas Main, also found neighbors
452. USFC-1840 Ledyard, under Thomas Main, also found neighbors
453. USFC-1850 Ledyard, under Thomas Main
454. USFC-1860 Ledyard, under Thomas Main
455. LTH, PO, Volume 2 page 170-172, dated March 22, 1864, Estate of Thomas Main, Inventory
456. Ibid, Estate of Thomas Main, deceased, Notes due, also in Inventory
457. Ibid, Volume 2 page 161-165 in the Probate Journal, dated January 30, 1858, Estate of Thomas Main, his Last Will and Testament
458. Permission was received from Corey Greene and Kimberly Pendleton to use the picture of their daughters Kayla and Kelsey standing in front of the Thomas Main Cemetery, off Homestead Road in Ledyard, Ct. Thomas Main built the stone wall that is behind them
459. GTH, TCO, Volume 2 page 94, dated July 4, 1812, birth date of William Leeds Main
460. BMMM, page 248, death date for William Leeds Main
461. Ibid, marriage of William Leeds Main to Sarah A. Frink
462. Ibid, date of birth for Sarah A. Frink
463. Ibid, date of death for Sarah Frink Main
464. William Leeds Main picture, was passed on to Shirley Holdridge Greene, from one of her Aunt Lois St. Pierre. This is an original photograph from the studio that took his picture.
465. BMMM, page 248, date of birth for Sarah Maria Main
466. Ibid, date of death for Sarah Maria Main Boss
467. Ibid, marriage of Sarah Maria Main to David Boss
468. Ibid, date of birth for John Latham Main
469. Ibid, marriage of John Latham Main to Phebe E. Frink
470. Ibid, page 249, date of birth for Leeds Main
471. Ibid, date of death for Leeds Main
472. Ibid, marriage of Leeds Main to Sarah Holdredge
473. Ibid, page 253-254, Leeds Main life

474. Ibid, page 249, date of birth for Phebe E. Main
475. Ibid, date of death for Phebe E. Main
476. Ibid, marriage of Phebe E. Main to John Finegan
477. Ibid, marriage of Phebe E. Main to William Harrington
478. Ibid, date of birth for Lurie H. Main
479. BPMC, date of death for Lurie H. Main, from gravestone
480. BMMM, Lurie H. Main life
481. BPMC, date of birth for Ira D. Main, from gravestone
482. Ibid, date of death for Ira D. Main, from gravestone
483. BMMM, page 257, date of birth for Alonzo Main
484. Ibid, marriage of Alonzo Main to Ethel Main
485. Ibid, Alonzo Main life
486. Ibid, page 258, date of birth for Melissa Main
487. LCC, date of death for Melissa Main
488. BMMM, page 258, marriage of Melissa Main to Joseph E. Holdridge
489. Ibid, page 256, date of birth for Frances A. Main
490. Ibid, marriage of Frances A. Main to William J. Richmond
491. Ibid, page 258, date of birth for Horace H. Main
492. Ibid, marriage of Horace H. Main to Phebe M. Partelo
493. Ibid, page 249, date of birth for Amos Main
494. Ibid, marriage of Amos Main to Lucy Mathewson
495. Ibid, page 248, William Leeds Main life
496. LHS, Abstract of the Town of Ledyard, Tax list, 1839, for William L. Main
497. Ibid 1851
498. Ibid 1860
499. Ibid 1865
500. Ibid 1866
501. Ibid 1869
502. Ibid 1871
503. USFC-1870 Ledyard, under William L. Main
504. USFC-1880 Ledyard, under William L. Main
505. LHS, Main school file, 1858
506. NLCSCPSI, CSL, RG 3 Box 2, Mashantucket Pequot, 1758-1855, dated 1846
507. Ibid Jan. 1855
508. Ibid Dec 1855
509. Ibid, RG 3 Box 2, Mashantucket Pequot, 1743-1887, March and April 1856
510. Ibid April 1864
511. Ibid, RG 3 Box 1, Eastern Pequot, 1822-1855; Jan. 1850, Wm. L. Main
512. Ibid, 1854
513. Ibid, RG 3 Box 1, Eastern Pequot, 1856-1877; August, 1856, Wm. L. Main
514. Ibid Feb.1861, William L. Main
515. Ibid Feb. 1861, William L. Main
516. Ibid Jan. 1871, Eunice Cottrel, Wm. L. Main
517. Ibid Jan 1871, Leonard Brown, Wm. L. Main
518. LTH, PO, Volume 3 page 653-664, dated September 22, 1890, Inventory of the Estate of William L. Main
519. Ibid, Volume 3 page 639, dated June 28, 1887, Under the Estate of William L. Main,

his Last Will and Testament
520. BMMM, page 258, children of Joseph and Melissa Holdridge
521. Joseph E. Holdridge and Melissa Main wedding picture was given to Shirley Holdridge Greene by Esther Clark Dubba in 1989.
522. BMMM, children of Horace and Phebe Main
523. Ibid, Horace Main life
524. USFC-1930 Ledyard, under Lurie Main and Jane Wheeler
525. LTH, TCO, Volume 1 page 53, Family Records of Avery Brown, birth date of Annis Holdridge Brown
526. BPMC, date of death for Annis Holdridge Brown, from gravestone
527. LTH, TCO, Volume 1 page 53, marriage of Avery W. Brown to Annis Holdridge
528. Ibid, date of birth for Avery W. Brown
529. BPMC, date of death for Avery W. Brown
530. LTH, TCO, Volume 1 page 53, all Avery W. Brown and Annis Holdridge children birth dates are listed on this page
531. Brown, Cyrus, "The Brown Genealogy" (hereinafter listed as BG), page 505 , died in infancy (Nathaniel Brown)
532. LTH, TCO, page 64, Marriages, marriage of Cynthia Brown to Elias Comstock
533. BG, page 505, died in infancy (Hannah F. Brown)
534. BPMC, date of death for Elias S. Brown from gravestone
535. BG, page 505, marriage of Elias S. Brown to Sarah Jane Norman
536. Ibid, Daniel H. Brown marriage to Mary
537. Ibid, Marriage of Nancy A. Brown to Isaac E. Norman
538. Ibid, Marriage of James A. Brown to Eliza Stanton
539. BPMC, Julia E. and Lucy A. White, the wives of William N. Brown, are buried here along with William N. Brown and his children by Lucy A. White Brown
540. BG, page 505, Marriage of Frances Brown to John H. Godfrey
541. Ibid, Mr. Godfrey was a blacksmith
542. BPMC, date of death for Lillie A. Brown from gravestone
543. "A Modern History of New London County Connecticut", Editor in Chief Benjamin Tinkham Marshall A.M.D.D., President of Connecticut College, New London, Connecticut, Lewis Historical Publishing Co., New York City, NY, 1922, Volume III, page 268, Albert Brown
544. LTH, TCO, Volume 1 page 53, Family Records of Avery W. Brown
545. LHS, Abstract of the Town of Ledyard Tax Levy 1866, under Avery W. Brown
546. Ibid, 1869, under Avery W. Brown
547. Ibid, Abstract of the 1st Baptist Church of Groton, page 9, Avery Brown
548. Ibid, page 38, Annis Holdridge
549. NLCSCRPSI, CSL, RG 3 Box 2, Mashantucket Pequot, 1758-1887, 1856, Avery W. Brown
550. Ibid 1855, Albert Brown
551. Ibid 1837, Albert Brown
552. USFC-1850 Ledyard, under Brown, Avery W.
553. USFC-1860 Ledyard, under Brown, Avery W.
554. USFC-1870 Ledyard, under Brown, Avery W.
555. USFC-1880 Ledyard, under Brown Avery W.
556. LTH, PO, Volume page, dated , Estate of Avery Wilbur Brown

557. Ibid, Will Book 4, page 455, dated March 24, 1902, Estate of Annis Brown
558. BG, page 504, under Nathaniel Brown
559. Holdridge Cemetery (hereinafter listed as HC), Indiantown Road, Ledyard, Ct., year of birth for Hannah Brown Holdridge, from gravestone
560. Ibid, date of death for Hannah Holdridge, from gravestone
561. LHS, Abstract of Amos Geer Marriage Records, dated February 14, 1799 in Groton, Ct.; marriage of Hannah Brown to Nathan Holdridge
562. GTH, TCO, Volume 2 page 11, dated July 10, 1760, date of birth for Nathan Holdridge
563. HC, date of death for Nathan Holdridge, from gravestone
564. Year of birth for Hannah Holdridge, I took from the date of the marriage of Nathan Holdridge and Hannah Brown which was 1799 and the date of birth for their second child Nathan Holdridge born about 1801. Hannah Pettis was listed first in the Distribution of the Estate of Nathan Holdridge, deceased. She had to be the eldest daughter. From these documents I put her date of birth about 1799.
565. STH, PO, Volume 4 page 145, dated March 29, 1821, Distribution of Estate of Nathan Holdridge, daughter Hannah Holdridge, wife of Benjamin Pettis
566. GTH, TCO, LR, Volume 20 page 142, dated April 1, 1833, Stephen and Hannah Comady to Randall Holdridge
567. USFC-1850 Preston, under Nathan Holdridge, year of his birth
568. GTH, TCO, Volume 1 page 32, dated October 18, 1829, marriage of Nathan Holdridge to Jane Wright
569. Judge Williams Cemetery (hereinafter listed as JWC), Shewville Road, Ledyard, Ct., date of birth for Mary Stanton, wife of James Stanton, from gravestone
570. Ibid, date of death for Mary Stanton, from gravestone
571. GTH, TCO, Volume 1 page 65, dated October 20, 1841, marriage of Mary Holdridge to James Stanton
572. STH, PO, Volume 4, page 145, dated March 29, 1821, Distribution of the Estate of Nathan Holdridge, daughter Betsey Holdridge
573. USFC-1850 North Stonington, Roll #M432_48, under Phinehas Holdridge, year of birth
574. Colonel Ledyard Cemetery (hereinafter listed as CLC, Meriden Street, Groton, Ct., date of birth for Stephen Holdridge, from gravestone
575. Ibid, date of death for Stephen Holdridge from gravestone
576. Ibid, Stephen Holdridge wife, Hannah Sterry, from gravestone
577. HC, year of birth of Eneas Holdridge, from gravestone
578. Ibid, date of death for Eneas Holdridge, from gravestone
579. Lisbon Town Hall, TCO, Book 1720-1899, page 72, Eneas Holdridge of Groton and Sarah Sullivan of Griswold marriage Sarah Sullivan
580. Spicer Cemetery (hereinafter listed as SC), Colonel Ledyard Highway, Ledyard, Ct., date of birth for Randall Holdridge, from gravestone
581. Ibid date of death for Randall Holdridge, from gravestone
582. GTH, TCO, Volume 1 page 39, dated March 25, 1832, marriage of Randall Holdridge to Emeline Reed
583. SC, year of birth for Emeline Reed Holdridge, from gravestone
584. Ibid, date of death for Emeline Reed Holdridge from gravestone
585. NCH, CCO, Volume 9 page 23, dated July 9, 1854, marriage of Randall Holdridge

to Nancy Main, they both were married previous. Nancy Barns married John Main (See Thomas Main section of the last chapter). He died and she remarried as her second husband, Randall Holdridge
586. LTH, TCO, Volume 1 page 51, dated May 11, 1817, date of birth for Nancy Barns, listed father as Nathan Barns
587. LCC, date of death for Nancy Holdridge, from gravestone
588. BPMC, year of birth for Almira Holdridge Peckham, from gravestone
589. Ibid, date of death for Almira Peckham, from gravestone
590. LTH, TCO, Volume 1836-1855, page 36, dated September 2, 1850, marriage of Rev. Stephen Peckham to Almyra Holdredge
591. BPMC, date of birth for Rev. Stephen Peckham, from gravestone
592. Ibid, date of death for Rev. Stephen Peckham, from gravestone
593. HTL,Avery, page 58, Rev. Stephen Peckham was the Pastor of 2nd Baptist Church
594. NLCSCPSI, CSL, RG 3 Box 3, Mashantucket Pequot 1758-1887, 1859 - May, under Stephen Peckham
595. Ibid, 1859 – September, Stephen Peckham
596. Ibid, 1860 – November, Stephen Peckham
597. Elm Grove Cemetery, (hereinafter listed as EGC), Greenmanville Avenue, Mystic, Ct., date of birth for Daniel Holdridge, from gravestone
598. Ibid, date of death for Daniel Holdridge from gravestone
599. LTH, TCO, Volume 1832-1855, page 22, dated September 11, 1845, marriage of Daniel Holdridge to Eliza Maine
600. Connecticut Historical Society, MS69156, Ebenezer Punderson, Account Books, Preston, 1762-1847; Volume 14; 1797 July – November; July 1797, under Nathaniel Holdridge/Nath'l Holdridge
601. USFC-1800 Groton, under Nathan Holdridge
602. USFC-1810 Groton, under Nathan Holdridge
603. USFC-1820 Groton, under Hannah Holdridge
604. USFC-1830 Groton, under Hannah Holdridge
605. USFC-1840 Ledyard, under Hannah Holdridge
606. STH, PO, Volume 11 page 145, dated March 29, 1821, Distribution of the Estate of Nathan Holdridge of Groton, Ct.
607. Ibid, Volume 12 page 281, dated March 12, 1825, Phinehas Holdridge choose as his guardian, Christopher Newton
608. LHS, Town Meetings, Randall Holdridge, surveyor
609. HTL,Avery, page 59, Randall Holdridge was a petitioner to form the 2nd Baptist Church
610. HC, year of birth for Phinehas Holdridge, from gravestone
611. GTH, TCO, Volume 2 page 36, dated January 1, 1815, date of death for Phinehas Holdridge
612. STH, TCO, Volume 3 page 34, dated December 16, 1746, date of birth for Mary Thompson, parents were James Thompson and Mary Dixon
613. GTH, TCO, Volume 2 page 36, dated November 9, 1814, date of death for Mary Holdridge
614. SC, date of birth for Nancy Holdridge Etheridge, from gravestone
615. Ibid, date of death for Nancy Etheridge
616. HC, year of birth for Phinehas Holdridge 2nd, from gravestone

617. Ibid, date of death, for Phinehas Holdridge 2nd, from gravestone
618. GrTH, TCO, 1815-1848, page 218, dated June 25, 1828, marriage of Phinehas Holdridge of Groton to Fanny Starr of Griswold
619. USFC-1850, State of New York, County of Ostego, Town of Plainfield, M432_580, dated July 11, 1850, year of birth for Thompson Holdridge
620. NSHS, Land Records notebooks, Thompson, Betsey, married Thompson Holdridge
621. USFC-1850 Ledyard, year of birth for Mary Holdridge Mason
622. STH, PO, Volume page, dated, Last Will and Testament of Phinehas Holdridge, daughter Mary Mason, Amos Mason
623. GTH, TCO, Volume 2 page 75, dated February 27, 1806, marriage of Phebe Holdridge to William Sisson
624. HC, year of birth for Cynthia Holdridge from gravestone
625. Ibid, date of death for Cynthia Holdridge from gravestone
626. USFC-1850 Bozrah, year of birth for Amos Holdridge
627. HC, year of birth for Sarah Holdridge, from gravestone
628. Ibid, date of death for Sarah Holdridge, from gravestone
629. STH, PO, Volume 7 page 622, dated October 25, 1801, Last Will and Testament for James Thompson
630. Ibid, Volume 8 page 40, dated April 19, 1809, distribution of property and personal items from the Estate of James Thompson
631. NSTH, TCO, LR, Volume 5 page 170, dated March 28, 1838, Gershom Eccleston to Phinehas Holdridge, 2 tracts of land, 1st tract was 10 acres bordered Alexander Thompson and the 2nd tract was 30 acres
632. GTH, LR, Volume 10 Page 5, dated January 19, 1771, Phinehas Holdridge to Benajah Packer, 15 acres of land
633. Ibid, Volume 7 page 169, dated November 12, 1771, Phinehas Holdridge from Samuel Newton, 60 acres of land
634. Ibid, Volume 11 page 24, dated December 25, 1786, Jedediah Leeds and Nathan Morgan to Phinehas Holdridge of Groton; 220 acres, with Mansion or dwelling house, and all other buildings thereon now standing
635. CHS, MS69156, Ebenezer Punderson, Account Books, Preston, 1762-1847; Volume 13; 1797 January – June, under Phinehas Holdridge and Daniel Toby
636. GTH, LR, Volume 19 page 140, dated December 16, 1830, Peter Williams of Groton to John Williams of Groton, 60 acres, in land description, one of the boundaries was called the Toby Orchard, this property also bordered the Pequot Tribe of Indians
637. NLCSCPSI, CSL, dated 1820, from the Town of Lebanon for care of Daniel Toby
638. STH, PO, Volume 9 page 373 377, dated January 11,13, 14, 1815, the Estate of Phinehas Holdridge, Inventory
639. Ibid, Volume 9 page 370, dated May, 12, 1814, Last Will and Testament of Phinehas Holdridge
640. Ibid, TCO, Volume 2 page 18, dated May 30, 1715, date of birth for Nathaniel Holdridge
641. CSL, Microfilm of Estate Papers to 1880: Norwich, Town of Preston, 1761, File # 5339 Nathaniel Holdridge
642. STH, TCO, Volume 3 page 78, dated October 9, 1735, marriage of Nathaniel Holdridge to Lydia Holdridge

643. Ibid, Volume 3 page 78, marriage of Nathaniel Holdridge to Prudence Parke
644. PTH, TCO, Volume 1 page 91, dated May, 13, 1729, marriage of Isaac Kimball to Prudence Parke
645. GTH, TCO, Volume 1 page 156, dated April 13, 1741, date of birth for Daniel Holdridge, son of Nathaniel and Elizabeth Holdridge
646. Ibid, dated March 25, 1743, date of birth for Zeborah Holdridge, daughter of Nathaniel and Elizabeth Holdridge
647. CHS, MS74254, Jonathan Wheeler Account Book, Stonington, 1735-1781; Manuscript
648. PTH, LR, Volume 5 page 560, dated December 12, 1754, Nathaniel and Prudence Holdridge to John Kimball, son, 1/3 of John Kimball father, Estate of Isaac Kimball, deceased
649. CSL, Microfilm of Estate Papers to 1880: Norwich, Town of Preston, 1761, File # 5339 Nathaniel Holdridge, Inventory, May 1761
650. Wightman Cemetery, Cold Spring Road, Groton, Ct., date of birth for Hannah, wife of Rufus Holdridge from gravestone
651. Ibid, death
652. Ibid, date of birth for Rufus Holdridge, from gravestone
653. USFC-1820 Groton, under Hannah Holdridge (she lived in South Groton)
654. GTH, LR, Volume 16 page 256, dated May 5, 1815, Lucy A. Fellows of Stonington to Hannah Holdridge of Groton, 21 acres
655. Ibid, Volume 16 page 179, dated February 3, 1821, Elisha Haley of Groton to Hannah Holdridge of Groton, 3 acres
656. Ibid, Volume 16 page 181, dated February 15, 1821, Jesse and Maria Starr of Stonington to Hannah Holdridge of Groton, 1 acre with dwelling house
657. BPMC, year of birth for Deborah Brown, from gravestone
658. Ibid, date of death for Deborah Morgan Brown, from gravestone
659. Ibid, year of birth for Nathaniel Brown, from gravestone
660. Ibid, date of death for Nathaniel Brown, from gravestone
661. HTL,Avery, page 287, year of birth for Temperance Brown, daughter of Nathaniel Brown
662. Ibid, date of death for Temperance Brown, daughter of Nathaniel Brown
663. BPMC, date of birth for Aaron Brown, from gravestone
664. Ibid, date of death for Aaron Brown, from gravestone
665. Ibid, year of birth for Mary Willcox Brown, from gravestone
666. Ibid, date of death for Mary Willcox Brown, from gravestone
667. Meech, Susan Spicer and Meech, Susan Billings, "History of the Descendants of Peter Spicer, Landholder in New London, Connecticut As early as 1666, And Others of the Name"; 1911, page 499; Children of Aaron Brown and Mary Willcox
668. Main Cemetery, North Stonington, Ct, year of birth for Matilda Brown, from gravestone
669. Ibid, date of death for Matilda Brown Main, from gravestone
670. GARWPF, page 185, Marriage of John Main to Matilda Brown
671. Ibid, Children of John and Matilda Main
672. HTL,Avery, page 304, year of birth for Sabrina Brown, daughter of Nathaniel Brown
673. Ibid, date of death for Sabrina Brown, daughter of Nathaniel Brown

674. BPMC, year of birth for Zerviah Brown, from gravestone
675. Ibid, date of death for Zerviah Brown, from gravestone
676. Packer Cemetery, Packersville, Canterbury, Ct, year of birth for Temperance Brown Lewis, from gravestone
677. Ibid, date of death for Temperance Lewis, from gravestone
678. Ibid, Temperance E. Lewis, daughter of Prentice and Temperance Lewis, from gravestone
679. USFC-1850, State of Connecticut, Windham County, Town of Canterbury, #M432_51, page 169, under Prentice Lewis, daughter Caroline living with her husband at her fathers home
680. Packer Cemetery, Packersville, Canterbury, Ct.; son Prentice Lewis is buried there
681. USFC-1850, Windham County, Town of Canterbury, #M432_51, page 169, under Prentice Lewis, daughter Priscilla Lewis
682. Ibid, son George W. Lewis
683. Ibid, son Richard Lewis
684. Ibid, daughter Hannah Lewis
685. USFC-1790, under Nathaniel Brown
686. USFC-1800 Groton, under Nathaniel Brown, also listed some of his neighbors
687. USFC-1810 Groton, under Nathaniel Brown, also listed some of his neighbors
688. USFC-1820 Groton, under Nathaniel Brown, also listed some of his neighbors
689. USFC-1830 Groton, under Deborah Brown, also listed some of her neighbors
690. "Historic Ledyard, Volume 1, Gales Ferry Village", reprinted 1997 by Ledyard Historical Society, page 89
691. STH, PO, Volume 11 page 133, dated March 14, 1820, Estate of Nathaniel Brown of Groton, Last Will and Testament
692. GTH, TCO, Volume 1 page 124, dated October 21, 1729, date of birth for Deborah Leeds
693. Packer Burrows Cemetery, Route 1, Mystic, Ct., date of death for Deborah Leeds, from gravestone
694. STH, PO, Volume 6 page 32-33, dated January 6, 1795, Estate of Timothy Morgan, Last Will and Testament of Timothy Morgan, lists his wife and children
695. Ibid, Estate of Timothy Morgan Last Will and Testament
696. Ibid, Volume 6 page 34, dated October 30 1795, Estate of Timothy Morgan, Inventory
697. Ibid, Volume 6 page 41, dated November 30, 1795, additional inventory with Notes due to the Estate of Timothy Morgan
698. GTH, TCO, Volume 1 page 124, dated April 17, 1717, marriage of Thomas Leeds to Mary Williams
699. Ibid, Volume 1 page 124, lists all the children of Mary Williams and Thomas Leeds
700. STH, PO, Volume 11 page 133, dated March 14, 1820, Estate of Nathaniel Brown of Groton, Last Will and Testament
701. LHS, Abstract of Amos Geer Marriage Records, dated February 14, 1799 in Groton, Ct.; marriage of Hannah Brown to Nathan Holdridge
702. Ibid, photocopy of William Williams Justice Records, dated March 28, 1773 for Hannah Alexander and Nathaniel Brown
703. BPMC, year of birth for Nathaniel Brown, from gravestone
704. Ibid, year of death for Nathaniel Brown, from gravestone

705. HTL,Avery, page 280, Mary Brown, wife of Nathaniel age 53
706. LHS, photocopy of William Williams Justice Records, dated March 28, 1773 for Hannah Alexander and Nathaniel Brown
707. Ibid, page 298, Hannah Brown, wife of Nathaniel (it gave no age for her)
708. LHS; The Historic Ledyard Center, Volume II, 1987, Ledyard Historical Society, page 136, Fanning Family
709. HTL,Avery, page 119, Fanning Family, James and Elizabeth Fanning
710. USFC-1790, New London County, under Nathaniel Brown, his neighbors are also listed
711. USFC-1800 Groton, under Nathaniel Brown, his neighbors are also listed
712. STH, PO, Volume 7 page 584, dated June 28, 1808, Estate of Nathan Brown, Administrators, Isreal Brown, William F. Brown and Samuel A. Brown
713. Ibid, Volume 7 page 566, dated 1808, citation, Prudence Partridge, late Brown, daughter of Nathan Brown
714. USFC-1790, State of Connecticut, Windham County, Town of Voluntown, under Alexander, James, John and Joseph
715. USFC-1790, New London County, under Elexander, James
716. Ibid, under Elezander, William
717. STH, PO, Volume page, dated March 12, 1825, Phinehas Holdridge choose as his guardian, Christopher Newton
718. Wheeler, Richard A. "History of the First Congregational Church, Stonington, Conn 1674-1874 with the report of Bi-centennial proceedings June 3, 1874 with Appendix containing Statistics of the Church", 1875, T.H. Davis and Company, Norwich, Ct; page 252, dated December 20, 1741, marriage of Stephen Mason to Joanna Newkuchuse
719. CHS, MS74254, Jonathan Wheeler Account Book, Stonington, 1735-1781; Manuscript, Stephen Mason worked for Jonathan Wheeler entry in 1740

SOURCES

TOWNS

Griswold Town Hall
 Historical Room
School Street
Jewett City, Ct 06351

Groton Town Hall
45 Fort Hill Road
Groton, Ct 06340

Ledyard Town Hall
741 Colonel Ledyard Highway
Ledyard, Ct 06339

Lisbon Town Hall
Corner of Route 138 & 169
Lisbon, Ct 06351

New London City Hall
181 State Street
New London, Ct 06332

North Stonington Town Hall
Main Street
North Stonington, Ct 06359

Norwich City Hall
100 Broadway
Norwich, Ct 06360

Preston Town Hall
389 Route 2
Preston, Ct 06365

Sterling Town Hall
Route 14a
Sterling, Ct 06373

Stonington Town Hall
Elm Street
Stonington, Ct 06378

LIBRARIES

Bill Library
Colonel Ledyard Highway
Ledyard, Ct 06339

Bill Memorial Library
240 Monument Street
Groton, Ct 06340

Connecticut State Library
231 Capitol Avenue
Hartford, Ct 06106

Westerly Library
Broad Street
Westerly, RI 02891

SOCIETIES

Connecticut Historical
 Society
Elizabeth Street
Hartford, Ct 06105

Ledyard Historical Society
Ledyard, Ct 06339

New London County
 Historical Society
11 Blinman Street
New London, Ct 06320

North Stonington Historical
 Society
1 Wyassup Road
North Stonington, Ct 06359

Rhode Island Historical
 Society Library
121 Hope Street
Providence, RI 02906

RESEARCH CENTERS

Indian & Colonial Research Center
PO Box 535
Old Mystic, Ct 06372

Mashantucket Pequot Museum and
Research Center
110 Pequot Trail
Mashantucket, Ct 06339
Website: www.Pequotmuseum.org

BOOKS

1. Black Roots of Southeastern Connecticut 1650-1900 by Barbara W. Brown and James M. Rose, published by New London County Historical Society
2. Brown Genealogy, by Cyrus Brown
3. Census of the Inhabitants of Rhode Island and Providence Plantations, 1774, by John R. Bartlett
4. Connecticut Militia, War of 1812
5. Genealogical Abstracts from Revolutionary War Pension Files, Volume III N-Z, by Virgil D. White
6. Genealogical and Biographical Records of New London County Connecticut, published by J.H. Beers
7. Genealogical Record of Nathaniel Babcock, Simeon Miner, Isaac Miner and Ezekiel Main, by Cyrus H. Brown
8. Historic Ledyard, Volume 1, Gales Ferry Village, by Ledyard Historical Society
9. Historic Ledyard Center, Volume II, by Ledyard Historical Society
10. History of the Descendants of Peter Spicer, Landholder in New London, Connecticut As early as 1666, And Others of the Name, by Susan Spicer Meech and Susan Billings Meech
11. History of the First Congregational Church, Stonington, Conn 1674-1874, by Richard A. Wheeler
12. History of New London County
13. History of the Town of Ledyard 1650-1900, by Rev. John Avery
14. History of Stonington, Conn., by Richard Anson Wheeler
15. Iroquois Culture & Commentary by Doug George-Kanentiio
16. Reminiscences of California Life, by Robert N. Wilcox

NEWSPAPERS
The New London Day
47 Eugene O'Neill Drive
New London, Ct 06320

DNA TESTING COMPANY

Oxford Ancestors, Ltd
PO Box 288
Kidlington
OX5 1WG
United Kingdom

Family Tree DNA
1919 North Loop West
Houston, Tx 77008

Census Records
1790 State of Connecticut, New London County
1790 State of Connecticut, Windham County, Town of Voluntown
1800 State of Connecticut, New London County, Town of Groton
1810 State of Connecticut, New London County, Towns of Groton, North Stonington
1820 State of Connecticut, New London County, Towns of Groton, North Stonington
1830 State of Connecticut, New London County, Towns of Groton, North Stonington
1830 State of Connecticut, Windham County, Town of Voluntown
1840 State of Connecticut, New London County, Towns of Ledyard, North Stonington
1840 State of Connecticut, Windham County, Town of Voluntown
1850 State of Connecticut, New London County, Towns of Ledyard, North Stonington, Griswold, Bozrah, Montville, Norwich, Preston
1850 State of Connecticut, Windham County, Town of Canterbury
1850 State of Connecticut, Windham County, Town of Voluntown
1850 State of New York, Chenango County, Town of Norwich
1850 State of New York, Ostego County, Town of Plainfield
1860 State of Connecticut, New London County, Towns of Ledyard, North Stonington, Groton, Preston
1870 State of Connecticut, New London County, Towns of Ledyard, North Stonington, Montville
1870 State of Connecticut, Windham County, Town of Scotland
1880 State of Connecticut, New London County, Towns of Ledyard, North Stonington
1900 State of Connecticut, New London County, Town of Ledyard
1910 State of Connecticut, New London County, Town of Ledyard
1920 State of Connecticut, New London County, Town of Ledyard
1930 State of Connecticut, New London County, Town of Ledyard

Written Permission was given from the following people to use their names in the book:

Corey A. Greene
Sadie Louise Greene Lewis
Kimberly Greene Pendleton
Goldie Ada Willcox Collins Robbins
James L. Williams
Vivian Williams

Interview:
Noyes P. Greene

CEMETERIES

Avery Stoddard Cemetery
Route 214
Ledyard, Ct

Brown Peckham Main Cemetery
Iron Street
Ledyard, Ct

Colonel Ledyard Cemetery
Monument Street
Groton, Ct

Eccleston Cemetery
Route 201
North Stonington, Ct

Elm Grove Cemetery
Greenmanville Avenue
Mystic, Ct

Holdridge Cemetery
Indiantown Road
Ledyard, Ct

Ledyard Center Cemetery
Center Groton Road
Ledyard, Ct

Jewett City Cemetery
Anthony Street
Jewett City, Ct

Morgan Pond Cemetery
Sandy Hollow Road
Ledyard, Ct

Packer Burrows Cemetery
Route 1
Mystic, Ct

Preston City Cemetery
Route 165
Preston, Ct

Rixtown Cemetery
North Stonington Road
Griswold, Ct

Robbins Cemetery
Route 165
Voluntown, Ct

Spicer Cemetery
Colonel Ledyard Highway
Ledyard, Ct

Thomas Main Cemetery
Homestead Road
Ledyard, Ct

Union Cemetery
Route 49
North Stonington, Ct

West Plains Cemetery
West Main Street
Norwich, Ct

Wightman Cemetery
Cold Spring Road
Groton, Ct

Yantic Cemetery
Lafayette Street
Norwich, Ct

Packer Cemetery
Packersville
Canterbury, Ct

INDEXES

Native American Tribes Index:

Tribe, Page

World Clans Index:

Clan, Page

Name Index:

Place/Company/Books Index:

ABOUT THE AUTHOR

I, Shirley Greene, was raised in Stonington, Ct. I went to Stonington High School and I took the business course that was offered to us. When I was a senior in high school, I was accepted in what was called the "Core Group". The business students that were the top of the class were accepted into this group. From the training I received here, I qualified for a job at the Stonington Town Hall in the Town Clerks office. I started to work there before I graduated from high school on a part time basis. Once I graduated I started full time employment with them. I received an Assistant Town Clerk certificate from Storrs College. While working there, I learned how to read deeds and because we had to record birth, marriages and deaths, they were a part of my daily routine. We also dealt with many people who were looking for their ancestors. Even at that young age, those people who came in or wrote to us to find a birth, death or marriage certificate, fascinated me. Stonington Town Hall was great to work in because in the Town Clerks office, the records went back to the late 1600's. This learning experience helped me greatly when I started doing our research. I knew then, that those older records were very valuable, but I did not realize how valuable they would be to me someday.

Years later, after my children had grown, I worked at the Ledyard Town Hall in the Tax Collectors office. I met many of my relatives from Ledyard, while I worked there. I also learned that a local historian had copied all the tax records from the beginning of the Town of Ledyard, which was 1836 to1870. This information became valuable to me, when I was doing my research. Those records helped bring some of our Ancestors back to life.

My mother in law, Sadie A. Greene, was really into genealogy. She was always searching out new information on her family history. She knew who was related to whom and how they were related, where they lived, as well as a few stories to tell about that person or family.

For the last seven or eight years, I have had the opportunity to really do some serious researching, both on Noyes's line and my own. I have met many interesting people, who were also doing either their family history or genealogy. I have been told you can not do one without the other. Family history and genealogy go hand in hand. That was very valuable advice. You can learn so much more on your ancestors, when you look at doing research from this perspective.

I am a member of the Connecticut Genealogy Society and the Rhode Island Genealogy Society. I am also a member of the Connecticut Historical Society, Indian Colonial Research Center, North Stonington Historical Society, Ledyard Historical Society, New London County Historical Society and the Mashantucket Pequot Museum and Research Center. I was a member of the New England Genealogy Society, Killingly Historical Society and the Mystic Seaport Museum.